John Owen.
10 Mai 2011.

Desire Lines

By Ian Rowlands

This play was produced by Sherman Cymru and first performed at Chapter, Cardiff on Friday 8 April, 2011.

Cover image: ©istockphoto.com/runamock
Design: Rhys Huws
Typeset in Wales by Eira Fenn Gaunt, Cardiff
Printed in Wales by Cambrian Printers, Aberystwyth.
This book is published with the financial support of the Welsh Books Council.

ISBN: 978-1-907707-04-9

CAST

Man	Ifan Huw Dafydd
Middle-Aged Man	Huw Garmon
Young Man	Joshua McCord
Older Woman	Sue Roderick
Younger Woman	Alys Thomas

PRODUCTION TEAM

Director	Irina Brown
Designer	Chloe Lamford
Lighting Designer	Tim Mascall
Video Designer	Ian William Galloway
Composer	Matthew Scott
Sound Designer	Mike Beer
Assistant Director	Sarah Bickerton
Company Stage Manager	Brenda Knight
Deputy Stage Manager	Ben Tyreman
Technical Stage Manager	Gareth Gordon
Set Construction	Mathew Thomas
Scenic Artist	Charlotte Neville

THANKS

Arriva Trains Wales; Associated British Ports.

SHERMAN CYMRU

We aim to make and present great theatre that is ambitious, inventive and memorable for our audiences, and to create strong, responsive and enriching relationships with our communities. We produce work in both English and Welsh, and tour widely within Wales and the UK.

For more information about Sherman Cymru events visit - **www.shermancymru.co.uk**

Sherman Cymru Redevelopment

The Sherman Cymru building is at a crucial point in its transformation. The demolition work has nearly finished, the exciting construction stages are about to begin and we will soon be able to see the theatre taking its new shape. Sherman Cymru's new building will be home to creative opportunities including performances, writer and artist development projects and participatory engagement for all members of the community.

Fundraising Campaign

We are now halfway to reaching the £1.36 million fundraising target for the redevelopment. We greatly appreciate the support that we have received from many donors and funders over the past 18 months but we still have a long way to go and with only 10 months left of the campaign, we need your help...

Sit With Us – Adopt a Seat

For as little as £10 a month (over 24 months) why not adopt a seat in the new Sherman Cymru? You will receive a named plaque on your seat for 10 years, priority booking and an exclusive tour of the new building.

Diamond Appeal

Reflecting the new look building, the Diamond Appeal gives you the opportunity to support the campaign with a £30 donation – you'll receive a certificate and an invitation to be one of the first people in the new Sherman Cymru building.

Attend a Fundraising Event

Watch out for news about forthcoming events in 2011.

For further information about the appeals and the campaign please contact:
Suzanne Carter, Appeals Manager
029 2064 6970 | suzanne@shermancymru.co.uk | www.shermancymru.co.uk/capital

SHERMAN CYMRU STAFF

Director
Chris Ricketts
General Manager
Margaret Jones
Associate Directors
Arwel Gruffydd & Amy Hodge
Artistic Associate
Elen Bowman
Artistic Coordinator
Kate Perridge
Literary Manager
Siân Summers
Move Champion & Facilities Manager
Marina Newth
Administrator
Elin Partridge

CREATIVE LEARNING

Acting Head of Creative Learning
Phillip Mackenzie
Creative Learning Associates
Jason Camilleri & Llinos Mai
Creative Learning Assistant
Heather Jones

DEVELOPMENT

Head of Development
Emma Goad
Appeals Manager
Suzanne Carter

FINANCE

Head of Finance
Philippa McGrath
Finance Assistant
Marion Price

MARKETING & CUSTOMER RELATIONS

Head of Marketing & Customer Relations
Haleh Tozer
PR & Campaigns Manager
Alice Baynham
Marketing Officer
Bethan Way
Web & Marketing Officer
Kenon Man

PRODUCTION & OPERATIONS

Head of Production & Operations
Nick Allsop
Chief Electrician
Rachel Mortimer
Deputy Chief Electrician
Katy Stephenson
Production Electrician
Gareth Evans
Wardrobe Manager
Deryn Tudor

Ifan Huw Dafydd
Man

Theatre
Credits include: *Blackthorn, Arden of Faversham, Festen, Memory, Under Milk Wood, A Christmas Carol, Afore Night Come, Rape Of The Fair Country* (Clwyd Theatr Cymru); *Rosencrantz & Guildenstern are Dead* (UK Tour); *An Enemy For the People* (Ruth is Stranger than Richard/Sgript Cymru).

Television
Credits include: *Gavin and Stacey* (Baby Cow); *Midsomer Murders* (Bentley Productions); *Foyle's War* (Greenlit Productions); *Hearts of Gold, Care, Heartburn Hotel, Drover's Gold, The Silent Twins, The Indian Doctor, Holby City* (BBC Television); *Queen & Country* (Valentine Productions); *Alys, Con Passionate* (S4C); *The Last Detective* (ITV).

Film
Martha, Jac a Sianco (BAFTA Cymru Best Actor 2009 – Apollo); *Abraham's Point*; *Daddy's Girl* (Boda); *Season of Mists* (Zaleski Enterprises); *Gadael Lenin* (Gaucho Films).

Huw Garmon
Middle-Aged Man

Huw trained at East 15 Acting School.

Theatre
Credits include: *Maes Terfyn* (Sherman Cymru); *Cariad Mr Bustl* (Theatr Genedlaethol Cymru); *Mae Gynnon ni Hawl ar y Sêr* (Llwyfan Gogledd Cymru); *Pwyll Pia'i, Hela'r Twrch Trwyth, Breuddwyd Branwen* (Cwmni Mega); *Amdani* (Sgript Cymru).

Television
Arwyr, Mandel, Treflan (S4C); *Pobol y Cwm, Y Tŵr* (BBC Wales); *Cadfael* (Central Television).

Film
Bride Of War (Lluniau Lliw/TVP Poland); *Left Luggage* (Shooting Star Film Company); *August* (Granada Television); *Hedd Wyn* (Pendefig); *Patagonia* (Boomerang Films); *Killer Elite* (Atlas Entertainment); *A Mind To Kill* (Lluniau Lliw).

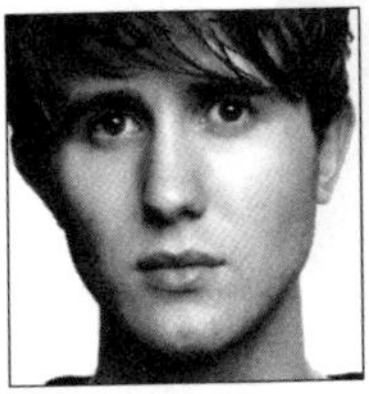

Joshua McCord
Young Man

Joshua trained at the Royal Welsh College of Music and Drama.

Theatre
Credits include: *The Spies in Room 502* (Old Vic New Voices); *Carrie's War* (National Tour); *To Kill A Mockingbird, Flora's War* (Clwyd Theatr Cymru); *The Secret of Belonging* (Antic Theatre); *The Truth Will Out* (Old Vic – US/UK Exchange); *The Druid's Rest* (Finborough Theatre); *I Can't Even Look In Your Eyes Without Shaking* (Old Vic 24 Hour Plays); *Chatroom* (Two Metre Gap in association with National Theatre Studio); *The Government Inspector* (Gravel); *Miss Brown To You* (Hijinx Theatre); *Lush* (Egin:SpringBoard Festival, Sherman Cymru); *Shift. Delete. Erase* (Graduate Theatre Company).

Television & Film
Rob Brydon's Annually Retentive (BBC Television); *Owl Creek Bridge* - BAFTA Cymru Best Short Film 2008 - *The Trek* (It's My Shout/ ITV).

Radio
Wales Observed (BBC Radio Wales).

Sue Roderick
Older Woman

Theatre
Credits include: *Servant of Two Masters* (Wales Theatre Company); *3 Minute Hamlet* (Looking Glass Theatre); *Granny Annie, Sleeping with Mickey* (Grass Roots); *Blood Wedding* (Almeida Theatre).

Television
Credits include: *Ista'nbwl, Caerdydd, Pobol Y Cwm, Licyris Olsorts, Dinas* (S4C); *Streets of Gold, Mortimer's Law, Satellite City, Trip Trap, Oliver's Travel, The Lifeboat, Selected Exits, The Life of Eliza, Casualty, The Max Boyce Show, A Penny For Your Dreams* (BBC Television); *A Mind To Kill, The Committee, To Each His Own* (HTV); *The Bill, Coronation Street, End of Season, Shelley* (ITV); *The Angry Earth* (Channel 4).

Film
Credits include: *Patagonia, Twin Town, Morphine & Dolly Mixtures, Rebecca's Daughter, Hedd Wyn.*

merch Dyfed Thomas

Alys Thomas
Younger Woman

Alys trained at the Royal Welsh College of Music and Drama.

Theatre
Credits include: *Dancing at Lughnasa, Toy Epic, Arcadia, The Way It Was, Stone City Blue, Flora's War* (Clwyd Theatr Cymru); *Cityscape* (Sherman Cymru); *Uncle Vanya* (Shakespeare at the Tobacco Factory/Bristol Old Vic); *Paradwys Waed* (Bara Caws).

Television & Film
Crash, Mistresses, Dr Who Interactive, Not Getting Any, Score (BBC Television); *Caerdydd, Teledu Eddie, Xtra* (S4C); *Ali Meek Gets A Result* (Channel 4); *Patagonia* (Malacara); *The Big I Am* (Cinematic Productions); *Arthur's Dyke* (Quirky Productions).

Radio
Shadow of the Sickle, Colin and Cumberland (BBC Radio).

Ian Rowlands
Writer

Ian was born in the Rhondda Valley. Originally trained as an actor, he has been the Artsitic Director of four theatre companies: Theatr y Byd (during which time *Marriage of Convenience* ran and *Blue Heron in the Womb* premiered at The Tron, Glasgow), Bara Caws (national community touring company), Cwmni Theatr Gwynedd (building-based Welsh language Rep.) and Llwyfan Gogledd Cymru (the north Walian company dedicated to multi-lingual work).

Credits as a director include: *Lludw'r Garreg* (trans. *Cendres des Cailloux*), *Sundance*, *Deinameit!*, *Ta-ra Teresa*, *Our Lady of Sligo* (First Irish tour), *Branwen* and *Frongoch* (both collaborations with Project, Dublin).

Credits as a writer include: Television - *A Light in The Valley* (BBC, Dir. Michael Bogdanov - Royal Television award). Radio - various radio plays for Radio 4, Radio Wales and Radio Cymru (including *Blinc* – his own radio adaptation of *Blink*). Theatre - includes *Love in Plastic, Glissando on an Empty Harp, Marriage of Convenience, Blue Heron in the Womb, New South Wales, Pacific, Butterfly*, and *Blink* (which ran at 59E59, New York as part of the Brits Off Broadway Festival 2008).

He is currently developing a two play project, *Troy Story* and *On Script /Off Broadway* (Dir. Daniella Topol) under the umbrella of The Lark Theatre, New York.

Irina Brown
Director

Born and educated in St Petersburg, Irina has been living and working in Britain for over twenty years. From 1996 to 1999 she was Artistic Director of Tron, Glasgow. She is Joint Artistic Director of Natural Perspective Theatre Company, London.

Theatre work includes: *The Importance of Being Earnest* (Open Air Theatre, Regent's Park); *Jenufa* (Natural Perspective/Arcola); *Three Tall Women* (Oxford Playhouse); *The Vagina Monologues* (West End & National Tour); *The Cosmonaut's Last Message to the Woman He Once Loved in the Former Soviet Union* (Tron, Glasgow); *Further than the Furthest Thing* (National Theatre, Tron, Edinburgh Festival, Tricycle & British Council Tour of South Africa); *A Midsummer Night's Dream* (Southern Shakespeare Festival, Florida). Opera includes: *War and Peace* (Scottish Opera/ RSAMD at Theatre Royal, Glasgow/ Edinburgh Festival Theatre); *The Letter* (world première, Scottish Opera); Dominique Le Gendre's *Bird of Night* (world première, Royal Opera House); *Boris Godunov* (Royal Opera House, L'Opéra de Monte Carlo & St Petersburg's Mariinsky Theatre).

Future work includes: *War & Peace at the Circus* (writer/director - Giffords Circus, 2011 Tour); *Britannicus* (Natural Perspective/Wilton's Music Hall); *Hoffmanniana* (adaptor/director – National Theatre Studio); *Consuelo* (opera libretto, music by Elena Firsova).

Chloe Lamford
Designer

Chloe trained in Theatre Design at Wimbledon School of Art. She won Best Design at the 2007 TMA awards for her design for *Small Miracle* by Neil D'Souza.

Chloe's designs for theatre include: *The Country* (Salisbury Playhouse); *Ghost Story* (Sky Arts Live Drama season); *My Romantic History* (Sheffield Crucible & The Bush Theatre); *Joseph K.*, *The Kreutzer Sonata* (Gate Theatre); *Songs From A Hotel Bedroom* (Linbury Studio, Royal Opera House & Tour); *Sus* (Young Vic); *It Felt Empty...* (Clean Break, installation at Arcola's Studio K); *Everything Must Go!* (Soho Theatre); *This Wide Night* (Soho Theatre & Tour); *The Mother Ship, How To Tell The Monsters From The Misfits* (Birmingham Rep); *Romeo & Juliet* (Pilot Theatre); *Blithe Spirit* (Watermill Theatre); *The Snow Queen* (Sherman Cymru); *Antigone at Hell's Mouth* (Kneehigh Theatre & National Youth Theatre); *Silence* (National Youth Theatre); *Lola* (Trestle Theatre Company); *Small Miracle* (Tricycle Theatre & Mercury Theatre, Colchester); *The Shy Gas Man* (Southwark Playhouse)

Her designs for opera include: *The Magic Flute* (English Touring Opera); *War and Peace* (Scottish Opera & Royal Scottish Academy of Music and Drama), *The Cunning Little Vixen, Orpheus in the Underworld* (Royal College of Music); *La Calisto* (Early Opera Company).

Chloe has also designed various music videos and promos, as well as *The Full Monteverdi*, an opera feature film by Polyphonic Films.

Tim Mascall
Lighting Designer

West End credits include: *Why the Whales Came* (Comedy Theatre); *The Vagina Monologues* (Wyndams Theatre); *Lies Have Been Told: An Evening with Robert Maxwell* (Trafalgar Studios); *Well* (Apollo Theatre); *Evening of Wonder* (Garrick Theatre); *Something Wicked This Way Comes* (Old Vic); *Enigma* (Adelphi Theatre). Other London productions include: *How to Disappear Completely And Never Be Found* (Southwark Playhouse); *Breakfast with Jonny Wilkinson, Ruby Wax: Losing It* (Menier Chocolate Factory); *Jenufa* (Arcola); *Cotton Wool* (Theatre 503); *Marilyn and Ella* (Theatre Royal, Stratford East); *The Importance of Being Earnest* (Open Air Theatre, Regent's Park); *Vote Dizzy* (Soho Theatre); *The Lady of Burma* (Riverside Studios); *Professor Bernhardi, Rose Bernd* (Oxford Stage Company at the Arcola); *The Gamblers* (London Philharmonic at The Royal Festival Hall).

Other credits include: *A Small Family Business* (Watford Palace); *Nora* (Mercury Theatre, Colchester); *A Doll's House* (Exeter Northcott Theatre); *Pete and Dud: Come Again, Trainspotting, Stones In His Pocket, The Importance of Being Earnest* (New Wolsey Theatre & Touring); *Bad Jazz, Gizmo Love* (ATC).

Ian William Galloway
Video Designer

Ian is a designer, director and filmmaker working with all forms of video for live performance.

Credits include: *Beautiful Burnout* (Frantic Assembly & National Theatre of Scotland); *Flashdance* (West End); *A Midsummer Night's Dream, Medea/Medea* (Headlong Theatre); *The Kreutzer Sonata, Nocturnal* (The Gate Theatre); *Bunny* (Nabokov Theatre); *The Gods Weep* (Royal Shakespeare Company); *The Lion's Face, Seven Angels* (The Opera Group); *Proper Clever* (Liverpool Playhouse); *The Spanish Tragedy* (Arcola); *Blood* (The Royal Court); *A Minute Too Late* (Complicite); *Hitchcock Blonde* (South Coast Repertory, LA & The Alley Theatre, Houston); *Hotel de Pekin* (Nationale Reisopera Netherlands).

He has toured the UK, Europe and Japan as a musician, designed and directed projections for concerts (Leona Lewis, Interpol, RizMC) and has directed and produced music videos and shorts. He works as part of Mesmer, a collaboration of video and projection designers working in the fields of theatre, opera, music, art and fashion.

Matthew Scott
Composer

Matthew trained at the Guildhall School and City University London followed by studies at the Berlin Hochshule fur Musik and in New York where he worked as Music Assistant to Lotte Lenya. He is an Associate of Birmingham Rep and Chichester Festival Theatre, Head of Music at the National Theatre, London and Honorary Vice President of the Chichester City Band.

Recent theatre credits include: *The Merry Wives of Windsor, Eurydice, The Schoolmistress, Entertaining Angels, In Praise of Love, The Life and Adventures of Nicholas Nickleby Parts I & II, Pravda, Twelfth Night and Hobson's Choice* (Chichester Festival Theatre); *The Critic/The Real Inspector Hound, The Master Builder, Taking Sides, Collaboration, In Praise of Love, Office Suite* (Minerva Theatre, Chichester); *The Habit of Art* (National Theatre); *The Importance of Being Earnest* (Regent's Park); *The Silver Darlings* (His Majesty's Theatre, Aberdeen); *The Tempest* (Liverpool Everyman); *The Hypochondriac* (Almeida); *The Duchess of Malfi* (Wyndham's Theatre); *Mother Clap's Molly House* (National Theatre & Aldwych). His recent work for children includes *Horrible Histories, George's Marvellous Medicine* and *Horrible Science*.

Mike Beer
Sound Designer

Mike started his career at the Sherman Theatre, Cardiff in 1986. Since then he has toured theatre and corporate events worldwide with companies including DV8 Physical Theatre, Diversions Dance, Theatre Royal Bath, West Yorkshire Playhouse, Birmingham Stage, National Theatre Wales, Imagination, Orbital, Clwyd Theatr Cymru, Act Productions, Fiery Angel, Theatr Gwynedd, Vodafone, Sony, Ford Motor Car Company and Motorola.

Theatre designs include: *Deffro'r Gwanwyn* (Theatr Genedlaethol Cymru); *Love Steals Us From Loneliness* (National Theatre Wales/ Sherman Cymru); *The Persians, A Good Night Out In The Valleys* (National Theatre Wales); *BFG* (Fiery Angel); *Great Expectations* (Aberystwyth Arts Centre); *The Stories of Hans Christian Andersen, The Borrowers, Merlin and the Cave of Dreams* (Sherman Theatre Company); *The Firework Maker's Daughter, Danny the Champion of the World* (Birmingham Stage Company); *Single Spies, Legal Fictions, The Importance of Being Earnest* (Theatre Royal Bath); *Don Quixote* (West Yorkshire Playhouse).

Mike now works closely with Stage Sound Services as sound designer and production consultant.

Sarah Bickerton
Assistant Director

Sarah trained with Living Pictures and Sherman Cymru participating in a year-long theatre directing programme.

Directing credits include: *Unprotected, Never, Fear, Love* (Velvet Ensemble & Wales Millennium Centre); *Kindling* (Mess up the Mess Theatre Company); *Alaw* (Theatr Iolo); *A Place With The Pigs* (Sherman Cymru & Living Pictures); *ScriptSlam* (Sherman Cymru).

Assistant Director credits include: *Cinders, Yr Argae, The Watching, Amgen:Broken, A Christmas Carol* (Sherman Cymru); *Miss Julie* (Living Pictures); *Outdoors* (Emerging Director for National Theatre Wales & Rimini Protokoll).

DESIRE LINES – AN INTRODUCTION

If you regularly eat in one of the two Wagamama restaurants in Cardiff, an exchange in Ian Rowlands' *New South Wales*, first performed at the Edinburgh Fringe in 1999, makes comically uncomfortable reading:

CABBY:
. . . I dropped her off outside Wagamama's noodle joint, you know it? Japanese sa-o-nara shit.

MAN:
I know the sort of place

CABBY:
Got one in Cardiff?

MAN:
Not yet

CABBY:
No?

MAN:
No. Cardiff's a 'not yet' sort of city

CABBY:
You'll get one don't worry. Then, all the arseholes in creation will split their chopsticks to eat in it. It's like the chicken and egg thing, isn't it . . . what came first, the noodle bar or the git, you know what I mean?

Rowlands' *New South Wales* was one of the first dramatic engagements with the prospect of a devolved Wales and what such a place might feel like to live in. The coming of multi-national restaurant chains was one of the less desirable anticipated consequences of a capital city energised by devolution. It doesn't stop there. The same joke extends to the coming of Waitrose (not actually seen in Cardiff until 2008, though they got one before that in Barry!) and provides a note neglected in many accounts of Rowlands' writing, namely an acute sense of humour coupled with an awareness of the nuances of popular culture, particularly those that relate to the condition of Wales.

Such jokes of course are actually part of a high seriousness coupled with both a powerfully emotional response to questions of nationhood and the way that national identity intertwines with a fundamental, never-ending search for the self. In 1999, for Rowlands' leading character ('Man'), racing home to Wales in time for the result of the 1997 referendum, Wales remained a '. . . fuck knows sort of country' defined only by being 'Not English . . .' and 'a nation in denial'. Despite this he makes his journey back via a two hundred pound taxi ride instead of boarding a plane to Australia. For him the real New South Wales lies in his home in Splott: 'a territory of the heart'.

The 'Man' of *New South Wales* is a self-confessed 'dreamer' who sustains his epic encounter with the 'Cabby' who drives him from London to Cardiff by telling him a fantasy story about his recent life. Over a decade later Rowlands' latest 'Man' (the leading character in *Desire Lines*) is a much more complex creation who undertakes a number of multi-layered 'journeys'.

First and perhaps foremost it is a journey around Wales. A journey that is frequently uncomfortable on all kinds of levels. Rowlands' information, in a note at the start of *Desire Lines*, that he is a non-driver who has 'become overly familiar with public transport in this country', helpfully explains one of the heartfelt sources of what becomes a rich and densely worked metaphor.

This is a journey of a kind that is all too familiar to many who have tried to understand Wales as a unified nation. Two train rides and two bus rides seem almost modest for a trip that makes a mammoth circular tour of Wales from Bangor (Tabernacle in the play – there is a helpful glossary) via Bluerinse Bay (Colwyn Bay), Chavton (Rhyl) and all stops to Our City (Cardiff) and then back on the route through Dullage (a risky offence to Bridgend residents!), Ugly (Llanelli) and Gogsham (Dolgellau).

The baroque-sounding place names are just a small indication of the free linguistic rein that Rowlands has allowed himself. As he says in his note on performance, 'Thoughts tumble – they are not considered' and later on 'The overall effect should be one of atmosphere, almost musical in its composition . . .'. There are unmistakeable echoes here of Samuel Beckett:

MAN:

Fiat Lux!
Fear begins with light;
A slapped arse,
Unwelcome pain.
Then the thought,
'Let me back in!

Closer to home, there is Dylan Thomas and the way that the English language takes on new possibilities in this bilingual nation. Also shared with Thomas are the highly conflicted feelings one might have for the place of one's birth. Anyone even slightly familiar with Ian Rowlands' work cannot imagine that he doesn't care passionately about Wales, but his isn't a mawkish, sentimental passion (as the invented place names themselves suggest).

Between writing *New South Wales* and *Desire Lines* Ian Rowlands has had spells where writing has had to take second place to the painful business of Welsh institutional politics, not to mention the sheer logistical challenge of running theatre companies. In *Desire Lines* he appears to find freedom again, revelling in dense allusive layers of language and a narrative structure as demanding as anything he has written.

As many will perhaps know, 'desire lines' are paths that defy routes that are laid out in any official way – they are those taken instinctively and worn by successive waves of those that have followed the muddy 'unofficial' route across an area of country, rather than the marked way. More attractively, they have been described as paths that 'indicate yearning'. Rowlands' play is very much about different kinds of yearning and, over a decade into the life of a devolved Wales, this includes a sense of yearning for what this nation can be. However, it is a feeling that is entwined in a complex exploration of the journey of all of us through the stages of our lives, the decisions and turnings that we make and how the consequences of those remain with us in ways that are not always obvious.

Desire Lines is receiving its Welsh premiere shortly after another milestone in the Welsh political journey. At the time of writing, the outcome of the latest referendum on the extent of powers granted to the Welsh Assembly Government is unknown, but the Wales that we glimpse on the journeys and in the imaginations of the characters in *Desire Lines* is, on the whole, a nation trying to look outward and forward. A couple argue about moving back to Wales from London:

YOUNGER WOMAN:

> I just want our child to grow up
> Not believing that he has to get out
> To be big;
> As you tried to be.
> I don't want our child to believe the shit
> you swallowed

And a little later in the same exchange:

YOUNGER WOMAN:

It's time to go home, Adam.
Time to go home because I want our child to believe
In himself,
In his country,
In his own language.
Not to feel the constant need to ask for permission to 'be' in their tongue
To be constantly sorry, sorry, sorry!
It stops with me!
With us . . .
With him

To suggest that *Desire Lines* is a play primarily about a changing Wales would be manifestly wrong and, to say the least, highly reductive. However, the play's tantalisingly allusive journey around a mythologized version of the country resonates powerfully in an age that seems all about changing global certainties. As Rowlands' 'Woman' reminds us – 'Small Country doesn't mean small . . . Big Country doesn't mean big . . .'

For all this though, many will experience *Desire Lines* more as a moving journey through the stages of ageing that we must all go through. As the circular trip draws to a close, an elderly couple prepare to be parted by the one journey that, Rowlands reminds us, must be taken alone. The 'Man' is fearful and regrets his choices, the 'Woman' (the most frequent talker of good sense in *Desire Lines*) sees that life itself is sharpened by struggle and difficulty:

OLDER WOMAN:

If you could live it all again.
What would you change?

MAN:

I don't know

OLDER WOMAN:
Would you change me?

MAN:
No

Beat

MAN:
I'd change myself;
Think less . . .
Pain less . . .

OLDER WOMAN:
Without pain, there's nothing, Adam.
You never understood that.

Desire Lines confirms Ian Rowlands as a brave writer, delighting in the power of language, but also one who offers endless possibility as well as complexity for the directors of his work. The latter might be because he has often asserted the right to be the first to direct his work himself and therefore understands more than most what this means.

Desire Lines, written 'in exile' (in New York), offers us an important perspective on a country still at the beginning of a journey. That, however, is only part of its story and in the end this feels both like a very personal play and a play that reaches out for the universal. I suspect that it will divide opinion, as always, but there is little doubt that this is a work of great intelligence, wit and human understanding that deserves to be seen and read and re-interpreted by companies long after the immediacy of this historical moment has past.

Steve Blandford
March 1st 2011

DESIRE LINES

by **Ian Rowlands**

For the Prince of New York
And a little girl born in silence
Who, thankfully, never stops talking

'This is the life of men on earth.
Out of darkness we come at birth
into a lamplit room, and then –
go forwards into dark again'

Lost in the Stars Kurt Weill
Lyrics: Maxwell Anderson (after The Venerable Bede)

'Buy the ticket, take the ride'

Hunter S Thompson

'By measuring the distance, we come home'

Border Country Raymond Williams

A NOTE ON PERFORMANCE

Thoughts tumble – they are not considered. They have yet to pass through the filter that checks the spoken word. They are the subtext – a wild ride upon a runaway train! Ride each word.

The thoughts are also, at times, simultaneous – layered dialogue. Also note, the 'real time' dialogue spoken on the journey is minimal, and that which is said is, in the main, mundane.

The overall effect should be one of an atmosphere almost musical in its composition and minutely choreographed / conducted to the last movement / note.

On casting – Man plays himself in all the scenes where thought 'shifts'. Older Woman does not double.

THE JOURNEY

As I don't drive, I have become overly familiar with public transport in my country. People say, 'It must be great, you can work on trains'. Let me say 'No, you can't'. After the umpteenth journey, the novelty wears thin. By now, any journey is interminable; stunning views are passed by without a glance, other passengers, barely tolerated. I have wasted years on the line, this play is an attempt to reconcile a life lived *in transit*.

The first three drafts of *Desire Lines* were written during the summer of 2008 in an apartment on West 72nd Street. It was liberating to write of the Old World whilst in the New. Both *Marriage of Convenience* and *New South Wales* were also plays written in exile – distance offering a perspective of sorts. Over the next year, *Desire Lines* was read in its several forms in NY, Cardiff and London – growing from reading to reading, interpretation to interpretation.

May I thank the many actors who gave of their time and vision (in particular, John Doman and Christian Conn), the directors (Sturgis Warner, Stephen Fried, Irina Brown, Leigh and *The Collective*) who helped forge a coherent text, John, Michael, Amanda and Suzy at *The Lark Theatre*, NY and Chris, Amy and Siân at *Sherman Cymru* – the theatres that kept faith with the play's development – and the funding bodies who facilitated the process (Wales Arts International and Arts Council Wales – Creative Wales Award)

Most of all, may I thank my beautiful wife who rarely travels with me but shares the journey.

CHARACTERS

MAN
MIDDLE-AGED MAN
YOUNG MAN

OLDER WOMAN
YOUNGER WOMAN

FIRST TRAIN

A train travels through the tunnel immediately after Tabernacle Station. The lights have failed in the carriage. In the darkness we hear the rhythmic sound of wheels traversing the track. Over this, a man speaks. There is fear in the darkness!

MAN:

In the darkness,
Cow-gut darkness,
I wonder what a foetus dreams . . .
As it crouches there,
Wrapped up like a fist in a fuck?
Does it have nightmares;
Little unformed nightmares,
Irrational fears?
No . . .
How can it!
It doesn't know what day is.
It can only know night;
One, long, wet night.
You've got to know day to fear the dark.
You've got to know loss before you cherish hope.
No nightmares . . .
Not yet!
Not yet, little baby, not yet . . .
Lightmares maybe.
Fear of the no-dark . . .
Fear . . .
Of the dry, no dark something or other.
An eye-blinding fear;
Fluorescence, cracking open the black . . .

The train horn sounds. The train emerges from darkness into light.

We see a train carriage. Seated, are Man and two women – the Younger Woman and the Older Woman. The Older Woman sings a lullaby. We also see a Guard (the Middle-aged Man).

MAN:

Fiat Lux!
Fear begins with light;
A slapped arse,
Unwelcome pain.
Then the thought,
'Let me back in!
Let me crawl back into the black.
Please, it scares me.
Don't like this light thing!'
Fear, a seed,
A cuckoo chick growing;
Slowly at first, growing until a whole life is eaten by it.
Born to be eaten,
Born to fear . . .
To know the pain of loss . . .
Of light . . .
Of hope . . .

Beat

MAN:

My eyes! My eyes!
That kid shouted,
The one dressed as Dracula in that kid's party . . .
Wait . . . (*stops himself*)
It was your party, wasn't it? (*Uncertain*)
Was it?

Beat

MAN:

'My eyes' you screamed.
And you wouldn't open them,
You wouldn't open your eyes whilst your vampire cape
was on,
Just in case . . .
. . . in case the light'd blind you;
Dissolve to dust.
Remember?
Remember, my little Champion?
Oh, my son . . .
My little son . . .

Older Woman stops singing

GUARD:

(*Over the loudspeaker*)
Welcome aboard this 'first light' train
From Ferryton to Bastion
If you've just joined us at Tabernacle,
We will be stopping at
The Junction
Bluerinse Bay
Chavton
Poverton
And arrive at Bastion, our final destination,
In good time for whatever you have to do.
First stop, the Junction,
We'll be there in a bit now . . .

Beat

MAN:

There in a bit now, bit, bit, bit
In a bit now, bit, bit, bit . . .

There in a bit now, bit, bit, bit
In a bit now, bit, bit, bit . . .

(*The beat of passages such as the above are to be spoken to the rhythm of a train traversing track*).
Train horn blows. The Older Woman glances at the Man. He looks away.

MAN:
Would pain die with us on this train today?
If, for some reason –
Some Andromeda strain –
Everybody died in the world,
Just died, whilst we were riding this train around this small country.
If a virus wiped out everyone,
Apart from us,
And we were the only ones left on this earth;
A seven out of Africa,
Out of here –
One Adam and the common Eves of future mankind.
Would fear live on with us?
Would mankind survive . . .
Perpetuate?

He glances at the Older Woman again

YOUNGER WOMAN:
First love . . .

MAN:
No

YOUNGER WOMAN:
First time!

MAN:

Not today . . .

(*Then Younger Woman, under Man's lines*)

YOUNGER WOMAN:

. . . bastardbastardbastardbastardbastard . . .

MAN:

. . . the Eves on this train
Are more eve than break of day:
Too old . . .
Too late!

YOUNGER WOMAN:

. . . bastard only time!

MAN:

Too damned late.

YOUNGER WOMAN:

The first time Dad'd done anything for us . . .

MAN:

Thank God

YOUNGER WOMAN:

. . . apart from cut me out of the will because of you.
The first time he'd done anything;
Given in,
Softened,
Given us something . . .
And you threw it back in his face.
Deliberately,
Spitefully, you shit.

She draws the Man's attention. Her youth scares him

YOUNGER WOMAN:
Ok, there was a cockroach in the sofa, but it was dead!

MAN:
(*With trepidation*) Oh, no . . .

YOUNGER WOMAN:
Dry dead.
We'd shaken it out.
We sprayed the death out of that thing

MAN:
A beautiful Dawn . . .

(*Then under Younger Woman's line*)

. . . beautifulbeautifulbeautiful . . .

YOUNGER WOMAN:
Still you wouldn't sit on it

MAN:
. . . an Eve in Eden!

A Guard approaches

GUARD:
Tickets ready for inspection!
Please!

Man catches himself

MAN:

Fuck it!
No, no, no, no . . .
No more pain.
Fear dies with us on this train . . .

GUARD:

Ticket, sir?

Man looks at the Guard

MAN:

Mmm?

GUARD:

Ticket please?

MAN:

Yeah, of course, sure . . .
Sorry, it's here somewhere . . .
I um . . .

Man searches for his ticket. Guard is lost in thought

GUARD:

I'd brought you coffee, for God's sake!
Thought it was strange; all those cards,
Couldn't work it out.
What's the occasion? I said,
The occasion is my birthday!
Your birthday!
Oh, shit . . .
You've forgotten it again, haven't you?
Again, you said

And then 'Again!' for effect.
Again, again, again . . .

Man takes a long time; empties pockets

MAN:
Sorry about this . . .

GUARD:
Take your time, sir.
What's a birthday anyway?
Just one year less to live.
Who cares?
I care, you said
Shit, I care as well.
You don't care
I do care
You don't care
I do care
You don't care . . .
Crying out loud!

MAN:
I thought I'd put it in my bag . . .
Ah, here it is . . .

Man hands the Guard his ticket

GUARD:
Small Country pass . . .

MAN:
Yeah . . .

GUARD:

Where you going, sir?

Guard inspects the pass. The inspection creates unfounded guilt in the Man

MAN:

Just travelling . . .

Guard hands ticket back to Man

GUARD:

Nice.
Never find the time to travel, myself

MAN:

No . . .

GUARD:

Too busy getting there and back

MAN:

Mmm . . .

GUARD:

Any request stops?

MAN:

No

GUARD:

Have a good journey.
(*He hands back the ticket*)

Thank you.
And uh,
Sorry about the lights in this carriage.
They're working in the next one.
If you want to move along . . .

MAN:
No. I'm fine

GUARD:
Not many tunnels on this line

MAN:
Thanks

GUARD:
No problem . . .

The Guard moves on to the Younger Woman

GUARD:
Ticket, love?
Ticket?

YOUNGER WOMAN:
Yeah

GUARD:
No rush . . .
I could waste my whole life standing over you;
Right over you.
Bend down to your bag
That's it, darling . . .
Oh my God . . .

Down, boy,
Bad boy,
Dirty boy.
Think of the maintenance,
Think of the kids

YOUNGER WOMAN:
I've got it somewhere

GUARD:
Oh, you have . . .
(*Sings his next line – from* Bananarama)
. . . Baby you've got it
I'm your Venus
I'm your fire . . .

Man sees Younger Woman clearly for the first time

MAN:
She must've joined the train at Ferryton, before I got on

YOUNGER WOMAN:
I think I left my ticket in the case

GUARD:
No rush

She gets up to look in her bag which is on the rack

YOUNGER WOMAN:
It's in here somewhere.
Sorry

GUARD:
Take your time

MAN:
I fear . . .

GUARD:
. . . All the time in the world . . .

MAN:
. . . I fear pain would live on with us . . .

GUARD:
One deposit in the Wank Bank . . .

MAN:
Bastard! I know his look

GUARD:
On credit . . .

YOUNGER WOMAN:
Look at him staring

GUARD:
. . . for future withdrawal:
Kerching!

The next two lines overlap with the word 'guilty'

MAN:
Making her feel guilty . . .

YOUNGER WOMAN:
. . . guilty for doing nothing

GUARD:

I am your Willie Wonka

MAN:

Making me guilty!

GUARD:

(*Sings under the next paragraph or so to the tune of* 'I've got a golden ticket' *from Willie Wonka and the Chocolate Factory*)
You've got a golden ticket
Show me your golden ticket . . .

MAN:

Look at him look at her!
I bet he'd try and beat me to her;
Beat me off with his ticket puncher.
It's my train! My bloody train!
And you're not playing!
'Make tracks!' he'd probably say.
Make tracks.
Get on down the line!
Damn him!
He looks stronger . . .
Younger, maybe?
Is he? (*Uncertain – always uncertain about his own age*)
Fuck him!
If he wants to play Adam, let him.
If he wants the pain,
I'll take the pleasure . . .
In time,
In good time.
I'll wait in a cave at the foot of a mountain . . .
I'll wait . . .
Then I'll get her.

One day, when he's out hunting, I'll take her:
Caressing and listening.
Because she'd be bored to death with him by then;
With his ticket-punching hands,
His football conversation!

YOUNGER WOMAN:
I knew I had it somewhere

GUARD:
Thanks

Guard to Younger Woman

GUARD:
Change at the Junction

YOUNGER WOMAN:
The Junction?

GUARD:
Yeah . . .

MAN:
No!

GUARD:
. . . The Junction.

MAN:
You can't leave me at the Junction.

GUARD:
You won't wait long for a connection

MAN:
We are the future

YOUNGER WOMAN:
Thanks

MAN:
Eve and Adam

GUARD:
Thank you

MAN:
You can't leave at The Junction!

GUARD:
Any more tickets please!

Man is mortified

MAN:
Always The Junction!

Guard passes on

YOUNGER WOMAN:
Careful, Sweetie . . .

MAN:
A left turn at the gate in the morning

YOUNGER WOMAN:
The police have had a quiet word.

MAN:

And you miss someone . . .

YOUNGER WOMAN:

Apparently he's under surveillance
Look, if you want,
I know someone who can teach him a lesson . . .

MAN:

Bloody Junction . . .

YOUNGER WOMAN:

Nothing serious, just enough to scare . . .
Leave him, Dad, please.
I'll sort it out myself,
Just don't interfere.
Ok, Dad?
Ok, Sweetie.
Look, I know I've been hard on you, but . . .
It's not easy, for a father . . .
For me . . .
Since your mother . . .
I know, Dad . . .
I know . . .

Older Woman sings

YOUNGER WOMAN:

Is he treating you well?
Who?
Him.
Yes, Dad.
Are you sure?
Yes, Dad
Got everything you need?

Yes, Dad
There's the old sofa in the garage,
You're welcome to it, if you want it.
Thanks, Dad, thanks.
I thought you'd be pleased with my father's gift,
I thought that's what you wanted.
You moaned enough about being banned from his pub after we got together,
But that's all you cared about were the lost pints with your friends.
I was stupid . . .
Totally blind!
I lost my family because of you,
I didn't see my father for a year
Because of you; because of him . . .
Stubborn as each other!
Then six months working,
Worming my way back to him;
Our way into him.
Trying to convince my Dad you weren't a bastard
When all along . . .

The Guard is on a mobile between the carriages. During the next speech, the Younger Woman gets up and goes towards the toilet. Younger Woman's line under the Guard's – diminuendo.

YOUNGER WOMAN:
. . . bastardbastardbastardbastardbastard . . .

GUARD:
. . . I'm really sorry, love.
Look, I'll be back by seven.
Yeah . . .
What if you dump the kids with your mother,
We'll go down to the Chinese buffet.

You like it there . . . it's cheap.
(*Realises his mistake*)
Not that I want to stint on your birthday, but . . .
What with the new boiler and everything.
What do you say?

Beat

GUARD:
I know, and I'm really sorry.
Look, I would've taken the day off if I'd known.
I know I should've remembered but . . .
That's why I said you should always remind me.
You know what I'm like: head like a sieve.
If you'd told me, love, I would've . . .
Love?

She has obviously hung up

GUARD:
Shit!

He dials again – it's answered

GUARD:
Hello, can you give me a number for a florist, please?

Guard is standing in front of the toilet door

YOUNGER WOMAN:
Can I? (*as in, use the lavatory*)

GUARD:
Sorry, love, this one's out of order.
Try the other end . . .

Not you, love. (*Into mobile*) Yes. Where?
In Ferryton . . . that's it, Ferryton.
Yeah, put me through please . . .

Younger Woman walks, past the Man, through the train to the back of the carriage

MAN:
We could be Genesis . . .

GUARD:
Is that Daff-o-Dilys? (*Daf-oh-dil-lis*)

MAN:
(*Inaudible. To himself*)
Hello . . .
(*He smiles. She smiles, uncertain*)

YOUNGER WOMAN:
Why did I stay?
Why did I begin?
Barely legal; totally stupid

MAN:
You remind me of someone,
Someone I'd punch that guard's lights out for.
Just say the word,
I'd have a go.
And from us, a new civilization will be born,
A better one!
Well, maybe just another one.
For you, my love, I'd endure . . .
Perpetuate.
We could be the world

In the toilet

YOUNGER WOMAN:

Then on my eighteenth birthday
You came home late
Again!
Home late: deliberately
To argue with me,
Again!
To make <u>me</u> the bastard
Again!
So you'd feel less guilty.
It was all 'my fault'
I never cared, apparently
I didn't understand . . .
And my lack pushed you . . .
<u>I</u> pushed <u>you</u> –
That's rich –
Without knowing,
To go with other women.
All the nights when I was working,
Earning your beer money,
Nine little bitches . . .
Sniffing your arse,
Lapping it up.
And bitch number ten . . . waiting;
Waiting in the car outside for you to leave me.
Leave the little girl, who wasn't woman enough
To understand what a real man is . . .
Needs . . .
Wants . . .
A little girl who left everything
For you,
For nothing.
All my fault, you said!

That's why you were leaving.
What had I ever done?
What had I ever done!
Why did you make an excuse of me, then walk out?
You just walked out, and the bitch drove you away to her kennel
To do it doggy fucking doggy!
Bitchbitchfuckingbitch!
And you just left me sitting on a sofa no-one wanted;
Horrible sofa, never liked it.
Thought my father'd thrown it out before he offered it to us.
Never want to see it again
Never want to see you.
I'm going to go far away.
Far, far away;
To the other side maybe.
Live on a boat, no sofas on a boat . . .
Well some, but not a trawler
I'll trawl a reef, a great big reef . . . catch fish.
Sail far far away
As far away from this 'Small Country' as I can get

She sings under Guard's lines. Her song is ethereal – a world beyond the tracks. Once established, her singing underscores the next speech.

YOUNGER WOMAN:
. . . far far far away
. . . from here
. . . far far far away
. . . from here
. . . far far far away
. . . from here
. . . far far away

GUARD:

Red roses, the biggest ones you've got, yeah . . .
No!
Hold on . . .
A dozen pink ones with one big red one in the middle . . .
A special onc;
She is the one, sort of one.
Before us, there were just 'nothing much' sort of women.
But she is The Red Rose Woman.
Yeah!
So how much is that?
(*Taken aback*) Shit!

Rethink

GUARD:

How about carnations?
What?
(*Corrects himself*)
No, you're right, it's got to be roses;
Red roses,
Bite the bullet . . .
No . . . no message, I hate messages.
Just – Carlon.
No, not kay like Klingon . . .
Just put cuh . . . cuh, yeah . . . cuh
. . . and a kiss

YOUNGER WOMAN:

(*She cries as she sings*)
. . .far far far away
. . . from here
. . . far far far away
. . . from here
. . . far far far away

. . . from here
. . . far far away . . .

MAN:
My Village!

GUARD:
. . . next stop,
The Village;
The Village,
Next stop

Younger Woman stops singing now

MAN:
(*He suddenly sees through the train window*)
Oh, my God, it's me!
Freewheeling on my bike from Kirin Villa down the mountain road.
Past the Village Idiot pub,
Under the railway bridge.
There I go.
Lookatme! Lookatme!
Seaside kid, brown and easy.
What am I? Eight? Nine?
Look at me speed
Past the bowling green,
The beach café.
Onto the pebbles
And there, in front of me . . .
Clicketty clack, down the track
Clicketty clack down the track,
There and back,
Clickety clack . . .
I hate this line;

Thin vein between sea and mountain . . .
Full of memory . . .

The train stops. The Young Man boards it. He is listening to his iPod. He is oblivious to the world. However, periodically, he will hum along to his personal soundtrack – it underscores moments adding to the crescendos of sound during the following action. The Younger Woman leaves the toilet and passes the Young Man on her way back to her seat.

YOUNGER WOMAN:
(*Rises out of her tears*)
. . . thank you! Fuck you! Good night!
My father'll be pleased
Glad I've ditched you.
He's got friends who could teach you a lesson.
You're dead . . .

There is a moment of eye contact between the Young Man and the Younger Woman

YOUNGER WOMAN:
. . . I'm fishing!

She smiles flirtatiously

MAN:
Is there a trolley on this train?

The Older Woman drinks tea from a flask and hums a tune

MAN:
I should've brought a flask,
The one you bought for me.

Looks like hers,
Exactly like hers,
Exactly . . .
I know that song . . .

The Older Woman turns to him and smiles. He looks away sheepishly, not wishing to connect with her gaze. The Younger Woman talks on her mobile phone, Man cranes to see her

YOUNGER WOMAN:
Dad, I'm coming home,
Leaving him . . .
Yeah, I'm glad too . . .
I know, you said.
Cockroach . . .

MAN:
Yes!

YOUNGER WOMAN:
Da-ad . . .

MAN:
Now I know who you are!
(*The memories tumble over each other*)

YOUNGER WOMAN:
Can you lend me a few thousand?

MAN:
You're my ex-girlfriend's friend!

YOUNGER WOMAN:
I'm going away . . .

MAN:

We were both 'exes', remember?
We met to console each other
In that bar, that night;
Days, I hadn't washed.
Why wash if you don't expect?
And I didn't,
But I was caught out.
We fell into each other,
Fell back to your flat.
I stank
And you politely said good night.
Regrets eh!
Had a few . . .
. . . there again,
You're the girl who followed me to that shop,
Challenged me with my own name and I took it up.
We got on,
We got off.
Two . . . three in the morning;
You wouldn't let me in,
You got out.
You left for a taxi,
I stayed in bed.
You could've been mugged!

Train horn sounds

MAN:

No, no, no, got it!
You're that girl from Montpellier.
I'd just had a fight
You sat next to me
On a Georgian Step
Before a Georgian House.

That's it . . .
You were so beautiful;
So quintessentially Big Country.
I was really small that night.
Drunk and small . . .
Yeah . . .
You were patient, then lost it and left.
I never knew your name . . .
Charlotte, Beatrice?
No, I know,
You're Christianne in the Alsace
Je t'aime, I shouted as you crossed that bridge.
No, no.
You're that Spanish girl on the Arctic train!
The poem . . .
Remember the poem?
It's you, isn't it . . .
Isn't it?

GUARD:
Next stop the Junction

MAN:
Who the hell are you?

The lights change. The thoughts of a New Year's Eve party in a bar in Tabernacle. It is many years earlier. (The Younger Woman plays the wife. The Older Woman bears witness)

YOUNGER WOMAN:
It is you, isn't it?

MAN:
Is it?

Beat

YOUNGER WOMAN:
I'm sure it's you.

MAN:
Well, if you're sure . . .

YOUNGER WOMAN:
(*Affirming*) I knew it was you

MAN:
It must be me then.
(*Jokingly*)
Who am I?

YOUNGER WOMAN:
Adam.

MAN:
. . . Dawn

YOUNGER WOMAN:
I saw you and I thought . . . it's him!

MAN:
Here I am

They smile

YOUNGER WOMAN:
So what are you doing here?

MAN:
Can't I be here?

YOUNGER WOMAN:
'Course you can

MAN:
Good.

YOUNGER WOMAN:
But how come?

MAN:
Oh, I was in the Village Idiot with a friend,
And he said let's go to Tabernacle;
Let's hit town for midnight,
And here I am . . .

YOUNGER WOMAN:
Great

MAN:
Haven't been in this bar for years

YOUNGER WOMAN:
Still bad

MAN:
Still home

Beat

YOUNGER WOMAN:
Someone said you were working in The Big City.
You went there for university, didn't you?

MAN:
Yeah, but I always come back for New Year's.

YOUNGER WOMAN:
Welcome home.

MAN:
Thanks

Beat

YOUNGER WOMAN:
So . . .
Big City.

MAN:
Yeah

YOUNGER WOMAN:
I'd love to go there

MAN:
You've never been?

YOUNGER WOMAN:
Not yet.
Want to go though

MAN:
If you're ever there . . .

YOUNGER WOMAN:
Too busy . . .

MAN:
. . . but if you ever are . . .

YOUNGER WOMAN:
Sure . . .

Beat

YOUNGER WOMAN:
What's it like living in Big Country then?

MAN:
It's not small

YOUNGER WOMAN:
No

MAN:
It's . . . (*lost for words*)

YOUNGER WOMAN:
Big?

MAN:
Yeah

They smile

YOUNGER WOMAN:
So what do you <u>do</u>?

MAN:
How do you mean?

YOUNGER WOMAN:
For work . . .

MAN:
Ah, it's boring . . .
You know.
And you?

YOUNGER WOMAN:
I own a shop

MAN:
At twenty-three!

YOUNGER WOMAN:
A small shop

MAN:
Great

YOUNGER WOMAN:
Just beads and stuff . . .

MAN:
I'd be useless in a shop

YOUNGER WOMAN:
Really?

MAN:
No business sense

YOUNGER WOMAN:
No?

MAN:
I'd probably give stuff away

YOUNGER WOMAN:
It's been bred into me;
My grandmother,
My mother,
We've always had stalls . . .

MAN:
Yeah, I remember

YOUNGER WOMAN:
Do you?

MAN:
Yeah, down the market . . .
I saw you . . .

YOUNGER WOMAN:
Did you?

MAN:
Once . . .
A few times . . .

Beat

YOUNGER WOMAN:
So what <u>do</u> you do?

MAN:
You really want to know?

YOUNGER WOMAN:
Yeah

MAN:
I proof read

YOUNGER WOMAN:
What's that?

MAN:
I told you, it's boring;
Just words and stuff

YOUNGER WOMAN:
Ok

MAN:
It's a living, just about

Beat

MAN:
Good to see you though

YOUNGER WOMAN:
Yes . . .
Good to see you too

Beat

MAN:
I still remember that Valentine's card you sent me; fourth year

YOUNGER WOMAN:
Please . . .

MAN:
Roses are red
Violets are blue . . .

YOUNGER WOMAN:
. . . Don't . . .

MAN:
. . . You'll never guess
Who sent this to you

YOUNGER WOMAN:
. . . so embarrassed.

MAN:
But I did.
I can picture your writing;
Swirls, round . . .

YOUNGER WOMAN:
I've got kids writing

MAN:
. . . the hearts, the Xs . . .

YOUNGER WOMAN:
Really embarrassing

Beat

MAN:
Sorry, I never sent you one

YOUNGER WOMAN:
You were someone else's.

MAN:
Yes . . .
Guess I still owe you a kiss.

The bells of midnight strike New Year. They dance and sing Auld Lang Syne. *At the end, they cannot quite bring themselves to kiss*

YOUNGER WOMAN:
Is there someone . . .?

MAN:
. . . no, not at the moment.
And you?

YOUNGER WOMAN:
No

MAN:
Right . . .

YOUNGER WOMAN:
Right

MAN:
No

YOUNGER WOMAN:
Right

Beat

YOUNGER WOMAN:
So where are you staying tonight?

MAN:
Well, I'm going to walk home to my parents

YOUNGER WOMAN:
Back to The Village!

MAN:
I'll never get a taxi . . .

YOUNGER WOMAN:
. . . not tonight

MAN:
No . . .
So I'll walk, I guess

YOUNGER WOMAN:
It's far . . .

MAN:
I'll be ok

Beat

YOUNGER WOMAN:
Look, um . . .
Don't think I'm coming on to you, but . . .
You could crash at my place if you want.

MAN:
No, no . . .

YOUNGER WOMAN:
No, I live close.
Got my own house

MAN:
You have a shop <u>and</u> your own house!

YOUNGER WOMAN:
Small house

MAN:
More than I've got

YOUNGER WOMAN:
Well you're welcome to stay . . .
If you want, that is . . .

MAN:
I wouldn't want to . . . (*take advantage*)

YOUNGER WOMAN:
. . . you wouldn't

Beat

MAN:
. . . well, if it's . . .

YOUNGER WOMAN:
. . . it's ok

MAN:
Ok, then . . .
Great . . .
Thanks

She touches him tentatively. Gradually, they embrace

MAN:
You took me

YOUNGER WOMAN:
. . . took my chance

MAN:
. . . my beauty

YOUNGER WOMAN:
. . . not that I'd waited . . .

MAN:
. . . mounted me

YOUNGER WOMAN:
. . . just hoped

MAN:
. . . married me

YOUNGER WOMAN:
. . . just wished . . .

MAN:
. . . 'til death

YOUNGER WOMAN:
. . . wished all along you'd walk back into my life

MAN:
. . . we flew away to Big City

YOUNGER WOMAN:
. . . walk up to me

MAN:
. . . your house

YOUNGER WOMAN:
. . . hold me

MAN:
. . . a deposit

YOUNGER WOMAN:
. . . sealed with a loving kiss

MAN:
. . . on our new home

BOTH:
. . . a life together

Beat (*as they drift apart*)

MAN:
. . . now you're gone

Back on the train. Younger Woman is embarrassed as she passes

MAN:
Bye

The Young Man smiles at the Younger Woman as they pass each other – a love lost before it has begun!

MAN:

Damned youth!

As the Younger Woman leaves the train, Man sneaks a look at the Older Woman. She looks accusingly at him. He avoids her gaze. He is embarrassed by it

MAN:

(*Under his breath*)
Mankind definitely dies with us
(*as in, the Older Woman and him*)

He looks away. She looks his way. There is a sadness in her gaze.

GUARD:

(*On the loudspeaker*)
We are now at The Junction.
Make sure you have all your possessions before you leave the train.
And please, mind the gap as you disembark.
Next stop Bluerinse Bay . . .

The Older Woman sings. The miles pass

MAN:

Bluerinse Bay
Chavton
Poverton
Then somewhere a border;
Invisible line,
Between
A small country and a bigger one.
No custom control,
No paranoia;

No America / Canada here.
Just a line on a map,
Through history . . .
Through lives:
A life . . .

Beat

Older Woman keeps on singing

MAN:
Tired,
And I've barely begun . . .

GUARD:
(*On the loudspeaker*)
Next stop, Bastion

MAN:
Bastion,
A station between us and them.
First stop across the border;
A border within me . . .
Sorry.
Naughty, naughty Small Country,
Big Country knows best!
And stop gurgling on about identity
In your infantile tongue –
Bloody spitting over everyone!
Sorry
(*'Sorry' said as an apology rather than as a request for clarification*)
What?
Sorry
Bloody should be!

Sorry was us, sorry was me;
Sorry damn nation,
Always the apology . . .
But my son
My Champion,
He is!
No sorries
(*He laughs*)
We'll gurgle on about identity, he'd say,
(without a hair on his tongue),
We'll gurgle on, until you realise
Your Empire's gone,
You are not Great,
We are not United,
You are just a country
And we are, another one;
Smaller, but another!
Oh, my Champion . . .

Guard walks through the train

GUARD:
Bastion, next stop.
Change here
For all stations south.

Man gazes at Young Man who is humming. He recognises himself in the youth

MAN:
Eighteen . . .
I was eighteen
Eighteen?
I was you (*the Young Man*)
Eighteen . . .

Am I still?
No.
Was eighteen,
Must be.
At eighteen,
I crossed the border . . .
Rode the line
Past Bastion
To The Big City.
Capital, Big Country.
'Beware!
They eat dragons there!'
People warned;
Small people; people who'd only ever travelled on TV!
'Stay at home,
Forget learning,
Learning only gives you airs.
What good are airs, Son?
And don't start me on graces!
Listen to reason,
Small is heaven enough for any man!
Understand?
Seek within and you shall find . . .
Seek without and you sin!
Ah, fuck off then!
Just don't come back crying
When you're eaten!'

Beat

MAN:

Looked within,
Looked without . . .
A small country looks very big from the inside, I saw.
I saw, but looking is a matter of seeing.

Perspective . . .
I wanted to judge size.
To see.
How small is small?
How big is big?
Measure my own country on a foreign scale.
Is that your journey? (*The Young Man*)
To see with borrowed eyes . . .
Can you borrow eyes?
You can borrow a tongue:
But eyes?
Ears?
Lend me your ears . . .
Did they actually lend them?
Sensation.
To touch yourself with someone else's hand!
You can't!
You just can't!
That is our failing,
Our utter isolation.
So alone . . .

GUARD:
. . . next stop, Bastion!

MAN:
But at eighteen . . .
So much ambition . . .
Desire,
To journey to the centre;
Glimpse a fleeting grace,
Hear
Smell
Taste
Touch

Then penetrate.
To see, to grow . . .
Small Country men to a man.
Our mayfly ambitions . . .
Our hopes . . .
Our day in the sun;
To make big in Big,
(The true measure of a Small man),
Then travel home first class and say
Look at me, look at me!
I didn't get eaten.
In the Big City, I ate!
Headline in the local press
Small town prodigal eats penny and the bun!
At eighteen,
I had ambition,
An appetite to 'go large';
Frieswiththat? Coke?

Guard walks past

GUARD:

I wonder if she's had the flowers yet?
What do florists do when they want to say sorry?
What do florists do . . .

MAN:

Eighteen
Twenty-eight
Thirty-eight
Forty-eight
Fifty-eight
Sixty-eight . . .

(*The above can dovetail under below – to end around 'beetroot'*)

GUARD:

I'd like to see her face when she gets them.
Be a pretty sight;
Like a beetroot, I bet, like a beetroot!
I can hear all her friends now
See he does love you, love!
Because she's probably gone on and on
About what a horrible man I am;
On and on,
All bloody morning,
On and on . . .
He might as well be Jehovah's Witness.
He celebrates nothing!
No love, I forget.
They make a deliberate choice to ignore;
To mess up their kids,
Piss off their wives.
Things just slip my mind.
Don't mean to . . . they just do
Anyway, better late than never, I say!
Always too late . . .

Below underscores Guard's speech. Young Man hums along to music. Older Woman sings. The soundscape builds

MAN:

Clicketty Clack, down the track
Clicketty Clack down the track, there and back
Clicketty Clack, down the track
Clicketty Clack down the track, there and back

GUARD:

She'll find something to moan about in heaven

Always moaning;
On and on,
Same round tune,
Day in, day out.
On and on and on . . .
Is this it!
Is this just it?
Is this love?
Just forgetting and moaning?
Moaning,
Forgetting.
Year in, year out?
Same old tune
Repeating . . .
. . . 'til the end?
God's sake get me off this bloody train!

The train blows its horn. Older Woman, Young Man and Man stop. A silence of sorts. The Guard's mobile rings. Suddenly he changes

GUARD:

Yeah?
Ah, you got them!
Yeah, I know, like a sieve . . . like a sieve.
Sorry . . .
Happy birthday, love . . .
And many of them . . .
Happy Birthday . . .
Warn me next time.
Got to go.
Chinese?
Great

Beat

GUARD:
Bastion, next stop,
Where this train will terminate

MAN:
Excuse me, so do I change here for Our City?

GUARD:
Uh, yes, sir,
You can either go direct via Shireton,
Or change via Allpoints East

MAN:
I hate Allpoints East

GUARD:
It's not a pretty station

MAN:
No.
So, on which platform will the Shireton train be?

GUARD:
See the Guard and he'll see you right.
Next stop Bastion!
All change.
All change.

The Man, Older Woman, Guard and Young Man prepare to disembark. They head for different exits. They leave the train and enter again through each other's exit doors. They take their seats; different ones this time.

SECOND TRAIN

Older Woman sings. We hear the voice of a guard on the loudspeaker. Young Man sits quietly reading throughout the journey. He reads the first section of the chapter 'Section the Second. The Vision of Sudden Death' English Mail-Coach *by Thomas de Quincey. Younger Woman is now a Trolley Woman*

GUARD:
(*OOV*)
Welcome to the Seacastle train
If you've only just joined us at Shireton, we'll be stopping at:
Grayling
Lionchurch
Mappaton
Five Ways
Newtown
Newbridge
Our City
Dullage
Foxton
Nest
Whitorse
Ugly
The Dock
Final stop, Seacastle, where this train will terminate.
First stop Grayling. We'll be there in a bit now.

The next speech underscores the Guard's announcement.

MAN:
There in a bit now, bit, bit, bit,
In a bit now, bit, bit, bit.

There in a bit now, bit, bit, bit,
In a bit now, bit, bit, bit . . .

GUARD:
(*OOV*)
And we are sorry for the delayed departure of this service.
This was due to a fatality on the line.
Unfortunately, he is no longer with us.
We thank you for your patience

YOUNG MAN:
(*Reading from book*)
Section the Second

MAN:
Fear . . .

MIDDLE-AGED MAN:
(*speaking a word which pierces him*)
Silence . . .

TROLLEY WOMAN:
Shame . . .

YOUNG MAN:
The vision of sudden death

MAN:
Would fear die with us,
Today,
On this train?

Trolley Woman wheels her trolley down the train

MAN:

If, for some reason –
Some Andromeda strain –
We were the only ones left on this earth,
Would fear live on with us?
Perpetuate . . .

MIDDLE-AGED MAN:

Pain . . .

Man sees Trolley Woman

TROLLEY WOMAN: *(Almost sings)*

Tea,
Coffee . . .

MAN:

She?
Maybe, she . . .
Maybe baby . . .
She is May in Quebec,
Season's end;
The sap already risen on the maple tree.
Sweet syrup,
Late bottled,
Poured liberally.
Would she sweeten the pain?

MIDDLE-AGED MAN:

Pain but not silence!
It shouldn't have been there . . .
Shouldn't have been there . . .
There should've been sound;
Laughing . . .

TROLLEY WOMAN:
Anything from my trolley, love?

MIDDLE-AGED MAN:
. . . crying

TROLLEY WOMAN:
Tea?

MIDDLE-AGED MAN:
. . . not silence

TROLLEY WOMAN:
Coffee?

MIDDLE-AGED MAN:
. . . not fucking silence!

TROLLEY WOMAN:
Me?

His attention is drawn. Older Woman sings

MIDDLE-AGED MAN:
Um . . .
I'll have a tea . . .

TROLLEY WOMAN:
Milk?

MIDDLE-AGED MAN:
No thanks
It shouldn't have been there . . .

TROLLEY WOMAN:
Sugar?

MIDDLE-AGED MAN:
Please
Anything but silence.
Shit, shit, shit!

MAN:
How old are you? (*the Trolley Woman*)
Am I as old as you?
Am I?
Older?
Younger?
Difficult to tell.

MIDDLE-AGED MAN:
It was that bloody nurse's fault.
She kept you too long in the anteroom.
She should've taken you . . .
Sooner,
Much sooner to the theatre.
You needed a doctor . . .
You needed . . .

MAN:
Never look in mirrors . . .
Never look down . . .
Hate reflection

TROLLEY WOMAN:
Here you are, love.

MAN:
Hate . . .

TROLLEY WOMAN:
Napkin?

MIDDLE-AGED MAN:
Thanks

TROLLEY WOMAN:
And a stick for the bag . . .

MIDDLE-AGED MAN:
You didn't need silence,
You didn't need that.
Even the pain was silent;
Numb,
Beyond feeling . . .

Trolley Woman having served, moves on

MAN:
If we pinched the skin on the back of our hands
Whose skin would smooth first?
Yours?
Mine?
Do you have children?

Trolley Woman approaches Man

TROLLEY WOMAN:
Tea?

MAN:
Scars?

TROLLEY WOMAN:
Coffee?

MAN:

Stretch marks?

TROLLEY WOMAN:

Snacks?

She smiles at an old man.

MAN:

Um . . .
Tea, please

TROLLEY WOMAN:

Milk? Sugar?

MAN:

No thanks.

Trolley Woman pours tea

MIDDLE-AGED MAN:

Out she came,
Little thing.
Cord wrapped once,
Wrapped twice.
Nothing unusual in that, but . . .
Slapping her
Flicking
Trying to pain life into being!
But nothing . . .
You looked straight ahead . . . avoiding.
I looked across you;
Across you at our baby on that life support machine.
You daren't look at that
You looked dead ahead

Our gaze; a cross.
And she . . . our little thing
In that incubator;
Oxygen,
Injections,
More flicking.
One . . .
Two . . .
Three . . .
More minutes.
Nothing.
No explanation.
Then they took her away
And we were left alone . . .
In silence.
No noise!
A child should be born with noise.
Yeah,
Noise is life.
Silence . . .
Kills

Trolley Woman puts tea down on a table in front of the Man

TROLLEY WOMAN:
Here we go . . .

MAN:
Thank you . . .

TROLLEY WOMAN:
And a stick for the bag . . .
That's one fifty

Man pays her

MAN:

One twenty . . .
Forty . . .

TROLLEY WOMAN:

Shame about the boy, eh?

MAN:

Boy?

TROLLEY WOMAN:

On the line . . .

MAN:

Fifty

TROLLEY WOMAN:

Suicide.

MAN:

(*Non committal*) Mmm . . .
Thank you

TROLLEY WOMAN:

Totally inconsiderate

Trolley Woman moves on and intones

TROLLEY WOMAN:

Tea,
Coffee . . .

The Trolley Woman walks towards the Young Man who is still reading from de Quincey. He wrestles with the complexity of the text.

YOUNG MAN:
Caesar, the dictator,
At his last dinner party . . .
(On) being asked what death,
In his judgement,
Might be pronounced the most eligible,
Replied . . .

TROLLEY WOMAN: (*With an affected voice*)
Celia is modelling the latest in lingerie . . .

YOUNG MAN:
'That which should be most sudden.'

TROLLEY WOMAN:
Anything from my trolley, love?

YOUNG MAN: (*He ponders*)
Most sudden?

TROLLEY WOMAN:
Tea?
Coffee?

He dismisses her.

Look at me!
I could've been a model,
I could've turned heads.
I could've . . .

She passes on

MIDDLE-AGED MAN:
Eight long minutes!

Eight minutes dead.
There she lay,
Little thing,
In the incubator:
Barely living,
But alive,
Alive . . .
Eight minutes dead, they said.
(*He fights the crying*)

TROLLEY WOMAN:
You have the bone structure,
The body for it, he said

MIDDLE-AGED MAN:
. . . Shit!
Lots of babies swallow,
The nurse said.
But she breathed in.
Her first breath,
Almost her last,
Filled her lungs with it.
Not with life,
But her own shit!
Welcome to the world
This is it!
The pain of it.
Never forget!

TROLLEY WOMAN:
Here's my card.
Give me a ring, he said.
Never did . . .
Thought about it, didn't I . . .
Thought a lot;

Turned the card over and over.
Catwalk, aisle?
Aisle, catwalk?
But I was afraid, wasn't I . . .
So I chose the bloody aisle . . .
Did the expected . . .
All my beauty, wasted!

YOUNG MAN:
Sudden death . . .

Middle-aged Man gets up and goes toward the inter-carriage corridor. The following passages overlap.

MAN:
Clicketty clack, down the track
Clicketty clack down the track, there and back,
Clickety clack down the track
Clicketty clack down the track, there and back . . .

Under above, Young Man reads from de Quincey

YOUNG MAN:
'. . . Sudden death
(by Christians),
Is ranked among the last of curses.
And yet, by the noblest of Romans,
It was ranked . . .
The first of blessings . . .'

By now, the Middle-aged Man is on his phone in between carriages. Trolley Woman takes out a dog-eared business card and studies it

MIDDLE-AGED MAN:
How's she doing?

It's not normal to fit . . .
Is it?
Are the drugs working?
Have they said anything?
Time . . .

MAN:
Want to go home, you said,
Three months pregnant.

MIDDLE-AGED MAN:
. . . Shit!

MAN:
We belong somewhere else, Adam . . .
We belong at home
And I long, so much.
God, Dawn!
If longing was an Olympic event,
Small Country'd take the bloody gold for 'Longing',
We're champions of it!

Adam and his wife, thoughts of a time before they left Big City for Our City

YOUNGER WOMAN:
Sometimes you can be a real shit, Adam!

MAN:
Look, Dawn . . .

YOUNGER WOMAN:
No, you look.
I gave up everything for you

MAN:
Did you . . .

YOUNGER WOMAN:
I sold everything
And came here,
To this City,
For you . . .
For us

MAN:
So, why throw it back in my face?

YOUNGER WOMAN:
I'm not throwing it back in your face

MAN:
You are!

YOUNGER WOMAN:
I'm not

MAN:
You are.
For God's sake, I've just had promotion.
You know how long I've been waiting for that

YOUNGER WOMAN:
I know and I'm pleased for you,
But I want something more

MAN:
And you've got it.
And I'm thrilled for you,
For both of us.

It's great. . .
A baby's bad timing, but . . .

YOUNGER WOMAN:
Adam!

MAN:
What?

YOUNGER WOMAN:
Don't . . .

Beat

MAN:
But, let's put things into perspective, eh?

YOUNGER WOMAN:
Perspective!

MAN:
There's no rush.
I wasn't aware there was a time limit;
After ten years
I'd be a bloody pumpkin!
We didn't say,
Ten years from now whatever happens, we're going home

YOUNGER WOMAN:
No, but . . .

MAN:
This is home for me,
I'm happy here

YOUNGER WOMAN:
You should've married a girl from here then!

MAN:
But, I didn't . . .

YOUNGER WOMAN:
. . . maybe you should've

MAN:
Maybe I should've . . .

YOUNGER WOMAN:
Oh, that makes me feel really good

MAN:
But I didn't!
I married you.
I love you.
For God's sake!

YOUNGER WOMAN:
Do you?

MAN:
I do . . .
Even though you can be difficult . . .

YOUNGER WOMAN:
Me!

MAN:
I still love you . . .

YOUNGER WOMAN:
Oh great

MAN:
(*Sincere*) Oh, come on . . .
And now you're having our child,
That's fantastic.
It's what you wanted;
What we wanted.
That's not the problem.
The problem is,
I just don't understand your problem with this city

Beat

YOUNGER WOMAN:
I just don't like it here;
Never have,
You know that.
But I stayed,
For you . . .
For us . . .
But 'us' is now us three.
And you always said . . .

MAN:
. . . yeah, yeah . . .

YOUNGER WOMAN:
. . . you always said,
We'd go home, if we had a baby . . .

MAN:
God's sake, Dawn . . .
I'm only thirty-three

YOUNGER WOMAN:
Jesus!

MAN:
I still have ambition

YOUNGER WOMAN:
And?

Beat

MAN:
What would there be . . .
Back home . . .
For me . . .
Now?
Nothing.
I don't like it here, but

Beat

YOUNGER WOMAN:
Nobody else cares about you here, apart from me . . .

MAN:
I know

YOUNGER WOMAN:
You don't have to prove anything to me

MAN:
I know, I just . . .

YOUNGER WOMAN:
What?

Beat

YOUNGER WOMAN:
What!

MAN:
Oh, I don't know . . .
I know, but . . .

YOUNGER WOMAN:
No you don't.
You think you know,
You think,
But you don't . . .
Not in there (*his heart*)
Small Country doesn't mean small, Adam
Big Country doesn't mean big . . .

Beat

MAN:
Sorry?

YOUNGER WOMAN:
It's 'what', not 'sorry', Adam!
Little words;
That make the world of difference between
Us and them.

MAN:
What then?

YOUNGER WOMAN:
I just want our child to grow up
Not believing that he has to get out
To be big;
As you tried to be.
I don't want our child to believe the shit you swallowed

MAN:
Oh, thanks

YOUNGER WOMAN:
You know what I mean!
You're not still eighteen, Adam!
Times have changed,
Our Country's not the same country you left all those years ago

MAN:
I know . . .

Beat

YOUNGER WOMAN:
It's time to go home, Adam.
Time to go home because I want our child to believe
In himself,
In his country,
In his own language.
Not to feel the constant need to ask for permission to 'be' in their tongue
To be constantly sorry, sorry, sorry!
It stops with me!
With us . . .
With him

Beat

Things are changing back home
Nothing will change here.
Nothing
They'll cling on,
It's what they do best.
They accuse us of being
Small minded and backward looking . . .
When we just want to move on.
They refuse the future, not us.
They won't move in that direction,
So it's up to us to move towards it despite them

Beat

YOUNGER WOMAN:
Look, I'm not saying, let's move tomorrow,
Next week or next year.
I'm just asking . . .
Can we just think about it?
Can we put a few things into 'perspective'. . .
Get a sense of proportion . . .
Can we?
Please . . .
For our baby?

Beat

MAN:
I love you . . .

YOUNGER WOMAN:
I love you too

Beat

MAN:
If that's what you want . . .

YOUNGER WOMAN:
What do <u>you</u> want?

We are back on the train. Sound of horn.

GUARD: (*OOV*)
Next stop, Our City

MAN:
What <u>did</u> I want?
What did I want from life?
What did I desire?

MIDDLE-AGED MAN:
So helpless.
So useless.
So fucking far away . . .
Even when I'm there!
Fucking shit!
Leave it, John,
Leave it . . .
Leave it

He reaches for his mobile and dials. Trolley Woman studies the business card again . . .

YOUNG MAN:
'. . . the difference is,
That the Roman,

By the word "sudden",
Means "unlingering"'

MIDDLE-AGED MAN:
God!

MAN:
Dignity
Just . . . dignity
Isn't that what we all want?

YOUNG MAN:
'Whereas the Christian . . .,
By "sudden death",
Means death *without warning* . . .'

Beat

MAN:
. . . fear

Older Woman underscores the following with song

MIDDLE-AGED MAN:
I want to corner that nurse and kill her.
I want to fucking kill her!
She played God with our baby's life,
She played God with you both.
I want to play God with her.
If our child . . .
If she . . .
Ah! Shit!
Stop it, stop it, John!
Stop it!

GUARD: (*OOV*)
If you're leaving the train at Our City,
Please make sure you take all your possessions with you.
Next stop, Our City!

Older Woman sings

MAN:
Our City
Her City
His City
My City?
Our City
Your City
Easy City
Inter City . . .

Young Man reads from de Quincey

YOUNG MAN:
'Sudden death . . .'

TROLLEY WOMAN:
Fucking divorce . . .

YOUNG MAN:
'. . . where death,
In some shape is inevitable,
Proposes a question of choice which,
Equally in the Roman and Christian sense,
Will be variously answered
According to each man's variety of temperament . . .'

TROLLEY WOMAN:
You could be a model, that man said.

You could walk down the catwalk,
Not the bloody aisle.
You don't want to marry yet, babe
Your beauty will be wasted
On kids and shit.
You'll be wasted
When you were born to kill . . .
Here's my card, babe, take it . . .
Celia is wearing a little number called 'Regret' . . .

GUARD: (*OOV*)
Our City, folks.
If you're leaving this train,
Make sure you have all your possessions.
If not, stay on, for all stations West.
Have your tickets ready, new guard. Full ticket inspection.
Our City, next stop . . .

Then Trolley Woman, Middle-aged Man and Young Man prepare to leave the train. Older Woman continues to sing

MAN:
You were right, Dawn.
We had a good life here, didn't we?
Twenty years we lived in this city
Before moving on;
Moving further West;
West is best,
East is least –
Ours was a different country;
The same, but different,
You were right, my love . . .
Right all along.

Beat

MAN:

Always right
It's what was right about you.
And I . . .

Beat

MAN:

I wasn't wrong, just . . .
Forgive me . . .

By now, a new guard (the Younger Woman) has embarked on the train (we never see her). She announces with efficiency, then fires her thoughts off quickly.

GUARD: (*OOV*)

If you've just joined us at Our City,
This is the Seacastle train.
It's a full train,
So would you kindly take your bags off seats
And have all tickets ready for inspection.
Thank you.

Almost machine-gun like

GUARD: (*OOV*)

If I pick Jake up from Club by six,
I can dash over to the supermarket,
They can have pizza, it'll be quick.
Then if John comes home at seven,
If he doesn't I'll be livid,
I can get back to the school by quarter past
For that bloody parents meeting;

Waste of time, always is,
As if I haven't got better things to do with my life . . .

A Young Man enters the carriage. It appears as if all seats are taken, he motions to Man 'May I sit by you?' Man motions for him to sit. Throughout, the Young Man is glued to his mobile phone. The young woman knits throughout the next section. The Middle-aged Man reads a newspaper – both killing time!

YOUNG MAN:

. . .yeah, I know,
Heard about it on the news.
Bet his mother had a fit;
I was like 'What'!

In the beat, knitting needles click

YOUNG MAN:

God, I know . . .
Eighteen!
Exactly . . .
'Cause of his mincing gait, they said
What?
Me?
A screaming flower?
Queen of Sheba when you walk in!
Poor kid,
Can't imagine it?
Don't want to imagine it,
His life'll be hell . . .

MAN:

. . . hell for us all,
If we have to listen to this shit

YOUNG MAN:

Well, I phoned up Graham when I heard.
And he said, I knew something was going to happen.
Well that's easy to say after the event, isn't it, Graham,
I said!

MAN:

What happened to privacy?

YOUNG MAN:

Listen,
He said he knew something was going to happen,
Because he'd been talking to Andrew . . .
Who?
God, not her.
Blonde Andrew,
That's him;
Fabulous glasses,
Yeah, works in the bank.
Well he knows Liam.
They went to school together . . .
Who?
Graham?
No, Andrew!
Graham knows Andrew,
Andrew knows Liam,
Listen!

MAN:

. . . we're all listening!

YOUNG MAN:

. . . Graham!

MAN:

. . . the whole carriage is listening;

YOUNG MAN:

. . . he was talking to Andrew

MAN:

. . . forced to listen.

YOUNG MAN:

. . . exactly!

MAN:

. . . tortured

YOUNG MAN:

. . . Graham's got nothing to do with it, right!

MAN:

. . . Michael Caine . . .

YOUNG MAN:

. . . listen, will you!

MAN:

. . . *The Odessa File.*

YOUNG MAN:

. . . listen!

MAN:

. . . the pain!

YOUNG MAN:

Graham was talking to Andrew,

And Andrew said,
He knew something was going to happen,
Because he'd been talking to Liam.
What?

Suddenly the Man grabs the Young Man's phone from his grasp

MAN:

Graham was talking to Andrew,
Andrew was talking to Liam!
What don't you understand?
It's clear as day here.
We're all listening to this shit;
Your lives,
Invading ours
With your asinine rhetoric!
I'm not prejudiced,
I just champion the private.
Leave us alone.
Leave us out of your world.
Our own worlds are complicated enough!
We don't want to know.
We don't care who did what
To whom and what happened.
Is there no peace any more?
No peace for the wicked!
These things are a fucking curse!

He flings the mobile phone. Suddenly, the Young Man changes into the Son. We are in a dingy bedsit on the shadier side of the tracks

SON:

Why, Dad?

Why did you leave?
Without explanation.
I don't understand.
Mam is lost

MAN:
Oh, Son . . .

The following is thought. Throughout, the Son waits for an answer

MAN:
What do you want from me?
The truth?
A father should never saddle his son with the 'truth';
Kill him before he lives,
Clip before he's flown.
Would a son ever listen anyway?
Do you really want to know why, my little Champion?

Beat

MAN:
Do you want to know
How your grandmother died,
Seeing Jesus in everything;
Cancer in the brain,
Leaving your grandfather alone.
My father,
Your gramps.
The pain he felt . . . the loss . . .
Do you?
You don't want to know that.
The smell of whisky and piss on a man
Who always prided himself on self-control;

The stench of fear and loss.
How that disturbed something in me;
A balance easily tipped,
Too easy.
You don't want to know how weak your father is;
How weak I've become . . .

SON:
Dad?
Answer me

MAN:
Just tell me what your mother wants . . . needs, and I'll say it.
Would it be easier if it was another woman?
Would it?
Does your mother need to know that,
To make sense of the loss?
Something is easier than nothing, I guess.
I'll lie, if you want,
If she wants . . .
But there was no one . . .
There is no one.
Just a pissed-up grandfather,
And I saw me in him,
And you in me,
And it scared the hell out of me,
That the pain could go on and on . . .
Perpetuate.
Not sin, Son,
Just . . .
This living.
You were still a baby at the time.
Your mother wanted another one . . .
Oh, God . . .

(*Exhales*)
How could I create pain again?
And one night,
Carrying my father to his bed,
(his trousers wet;
Pissy, shitty pants)
The indignity, he said.
The indignity!
And I thought, I would rather die alone,
Than die like that.
The inhumanity of it . . .
Die alone . . .
Because I never want you to have to carry me up the stairs like that.
Never . . .
I never want you to feel how I felt with my father in my arms . . .
The smell of his piss on my skin for days after. . .

Beat

MAN:

And it played on my mind,
Played with me in the silences,
Invading thought;
Eating, like a virus.
And I wanted to stop it.
How could I stop things, break the line?
So I thought,
If I was alive,
I could never cope with losing your mother.
I'd piss my pants for sure
And I'd be carried . . .
By you.
So I thought,

Never knowing,
If she was dead or not,
Means she could always be living . . .
Somewhere . . .
In there (*taps his head*)
And I'll die in ignorance . . .
Alone,
Without causing pain . . . to you;
Die alone with a certain dignity
And you'll be saved the shame.
But, you were still small.
So, for your sake, I stayed,
I waited the years . . . years
Then one day,
(you'd long gone)
I looked at your mother and I thought,
Get out, now, before it's too late.
Get out before the whisky and the piss,
Just run . . .

Beat

MAN:
It's pathetic really, my Champion . . .
This living.
But you don't want to know that . . .
Not yet

A dialogue resumes

SON:
I'm waiting, Dad

MAN:
Oh, Son . . .

Beat

MAN:

Oh, I don't know

Beat

MAN:

Remember you talked about 'the wall', remember?
The wall you hit running that marathon.
I couldn't run to the end of the road,
But you are my Champion . . .

SON:

Dad, please . . .

MAN:

Sorry . . .
It's just . . .
I've just hit a wall as well
And I'm too tired to run through it.
I want to . . .
I just need time,
To sort things out;
Strengthen.
Then, hopefully . . .
Tell your mother I'm sorry.
Tell her that please.
. . . just time

SON:

No-one else?

MAN:

Would it be easier?

SON:
God, no.

MAN:
No

Beat

SON:
Have you seen a doctor?

MAN:
Yes

SON:
What did he say?

MAN:
Time . . .
Heals everything, he said

SON:
Did he give you something?

MAN:
He offered,
But I didn't want to take.
I think I need to work this out myself . . .
It'll be better in the end

Beat

SON:
There's no shame, Dad

MAN:

Doctor said.
'There's no stigma . . .'
You're my Champion, Son

SON:

Please, Dad . . .

MAN:

You'd keep running,
I know you would.
You're my inspiration . . .
My life . . .

SON:

Dad, please . . .

MAN:

. . . and I am trying

SON:

Good.

Beat

SON:

God, this room is . . .

MAN:

Yeah

SON:

It's the wallpaper

MAN:

I know . . .
I thought I'd seen the last of it,
Thirty-five years ago
When I left to be with your mother;
Different city,
Same room though . . .
Same wallpaper.

SON:

You don't want to be here, Dad

MAN:

I know, Son

Beat

MAN:

Hey, tell me.
How's work?

SON:

I don't want to talk about work now, Dad!

MAN:

Ok

SON:

Sorry

MAN:

No, no,
I only asked
Because I want you to know . . .

Whatever you do in your life, Son,
You'll never disappoint me.
Whatever you do . . .

SON:
Dad . . .

MAN:
No, please . . .
Whatever you want to be . . .
Whatever you are . . .
Just . . .
Just don't be like me.

SON:
Fuck's sake, Dad

MAN:
Don't swear, Son, you weren't brought up like that

SON:
Dad, please

MAN:
You have nothing to live up to;
No shoes to fill
Understand?
You are already better than I could ever have been

SON:
Dad, please!
I don't want to listen to this

Beat

SON:

Just come back home, ok
Come back to us

MAN:

I will

SON:

Soon.
Mam needs you

MAN:

I just need time

SON:

No rush,
Just . . . come back . . .

MAN:

In time . . .

Older Woman sings. A look between father and son. We come back onto the train. The Young Man has a second, identical mobile phone. He continues talking as if the above has not happened

YOUNG MAN:

I said,
Graham was talking to Andrew,
And Andrew said,
He knew something was going to happen,
Because he'd been talking to Liam
And Liam said he was getting shit from the boys . . .
I don't know what boys;
Local boys, bad boys, yes.

And he was upset about it
And you know what he's like.
Liam's very sensitive
And he'd been taunted . . .
Why do you think?
Exactly . . .
We've all been there, girl!
So Liam said to Andrew,
I'm going to have to do something about it.
Andrew said he could sort them out if he wanted.
But Liam didn't want to do it that way
Because he'd have to live there after that
And there's more than one way to skin a cat!
Yes, a cat
What?
A cat!
Keep your voice down!
I'm on a bloody train!
Andrew said,
Liam said
There's more than one way to skin a cat
Yes!

MAN:
Please

YOUNG MAN:
And he was going to deal with it his way.
I'm not sure. . .
They'd called him names;
Said he wasn't a real man,
Whatever that is?
And proud of it, bitch!
Don't you start, listen . . .
Will you listen!

So, they said to Liam, if he was a man,
He'd do something to prove it.
And Liam said, to show them, he would . . .

Beat

YOUNG MAN:

I know . . .
Knifed . . .
Twice, in the chest.
The old man died there and then.
Hardly any money;
A few hundred . . .
Not worth a life!

Beat

YOUNG MAN:

They caught them running away on CCTV
They recognised Liam
Because, and I quote,
Because of his 'mincing gait'.
Mincing bloody gait, my arse!
He'll get years,
His life'll be hell.
I'd rather die,
I'd kill myself

Beat

YOUNG MAN:

Eighteen . . .
And dead, because . . .

Beat

YOUNG MAN:

I thought we were over things like that.
Even if Liam killed that man,
Who's guilty, eh?
Still so much hate . . .
So much bloody hate in this world . . .

Man looks at the Young Man

MAN:

My God . . .

Young Man looks at Man and realises that he has been listening

YOUNG MAN:

It's terrible, isn't it

Man nods.

YOUNG MAN:

Tragedy
(*Into phone*)
No, this man, next to me
(*To Man*)
Life is sick . . .
Really sick, you know.
They say it's murder but . . .
There's a reason for everything, isn't there?
A reason for everything.
Oh god, I just feel for him . . .
Poor kid . . .
Excuse me . . .

An empathetic beat. Then back to his phone

YOUNG MAN:

Anyway, are you going out tonight?
No, I don't really feel like it either, but . . .
I just feel I need something . . .
Yeah . . .
A stiff one!
Please!
See you in the club at ten.
Yeah, bye, girl

He hangs up. Silence, bar the rhythm of the train. Man wants to say something, but he is unsure how to begin

YOUNG MAN:

Sorry,
I just . . .
It's just, so tragic;
For the old man . . .
For the boy

MAN:

Yes

YOUNG MAN:

A waste . . .

MAN:

Mmm. . .

YOUNG MAN:

It's a shitty life;
Nothing 'fabulous' about it, is there?
Nothing!

MAN:
No

GUARD: (*OOV*)
Seacastle, next stop.
Change here for the Far West and for buses north.
This train terminates at Seacastle . . .

YOUNG MAN:
Sorry (*motions the phone*)
Bye

MAN:
Hope your friend . . .

YOUNG MAN:
Yeah

GUARD: (*OOV*)
Please make sure you have all your possessions with you when you leave the train.
Mind the gap as you disembark.
If my mother can pick up Jake from school, before Club;
If she can do that.
Then if John picks him up from her house when he finishes work
(Because I won't be back before half seven . . .)
Tomorrow'll be sorted.
Next week will be hell . . .
Thank you for travelling with us today.
Have a safe onward journey.

They all disembark. The Man and the Older Woman now wait for the Seacastle to Rivermouth bus.

MAN:

Waiting for a bus now, bus, bus, bus
For a bus, now, bus, bus, bus
Waiting for a bus now, bus, bus, bus
For a bus, now, bus, bus, bus

Beat

It's cold. He speaks to keep warm – quickfire / maybe more of a smouldering ember

MAN:

To be old . . .
To wait;
Wait for the kids to ring,
Wait for excuses,
Wait for explanations.
Wait for parcels from Amazon;
(their parcels).
Wait for their gas man,
Their builder,
Their electrician . . .
Wait on your children's children.
Waiting . . .
In waiting rooms,
For prescriptions.
Wait for doctors to write them.
Wait for the surgeon.
Always waiting, but mostly,
For dying . . .
And buses in the cold!

Beat

MAN:

Trains are for the young.
They make tracks!
Kids wave at them.
No one waves at buses,
Apart from those who just miss them!
Buses are for the invisible.
They carry the inept and the decrepit
Up and down the west coast of this small country:
The dying coast, next stop Avalon!
We'll retire there, shall we?
You said. Go back home?
It'll be quiet there . . .
You'll get better.

The Man exhales.

MAN:

Better!
Better be a bus now bus, bus, bus
Be a bus, now, bus, bus, bus

Still waits

MAN:

Dear Prime Minister of Small Country,
National Assembly,
Our City. First things first,
Congratulations for eventually wrestling some kind of freedom
From Big Country.
You got my vote
Freedom!
My wife's wildest dream.
And now, her son will live it!

But after my lifetime, I guess . . .
I guess I'll miss <u>that</u> bus!

Beat

Which brings me to my second point:
Buses . . . and bus passes . . .
Your government's decision to grant free bus travel to the
  old is sadistic.
To be frank and,
In the spirit of open government you champion,
Inhuman!
Buses are for the old and the mad.
They are Charon's craft across the Styx!
A bus pass is hardly a badge to be waved with pride
At a bus driver who then prints a wasted ticket.
(and on that point,
Why print a ticket when you have a pass?
The pass is the ticket!
What about the planet?
The future?
Again, my son?
What good is freedom
If you lose the world through waste!)
But anyway . . .
To receive a bus pass is a reminder, from the state,
As if you need reminding,
That you're just a bus ride away from death?
Is it perhaps your devious plan to drive your older
  subjects mad
With their own sense of mortality?
Mad enough to commit
Mass suicide on the Seacastle – Rivermouth bus?
In future, will you supply a blade with each pass?

Beat

MAN:
Yours, looking a gift horse in the mouth . . .

A bus approaches

MAN:
. . . at last, a bus!

Man, Middle-aged Man, Young Man and Older Woman catch the bus. It is driven by the Younger Woman.

FIRST BUS

Older Woman boards the bus and slips into her seat unnoticed. The Man boards the bus

MAN:
Rivermouth, please

DRIVER:
Are you a pass?

MAN:
(*With irony*) Pass . . .

She prints a 'wasted ticket' for the Man. He takes it, we see his disgust, the driver does not register it.

DRIVER:
Where the hell am I meant to find a thousand?
Even with overtime!

A thousand'll take weeks . . .
I slave to the bone, as it is.
I'm so annoyed;
So angry with that school of his!
Why don't they tour somewhere closer to home?
Just because the Catholic school's going to The Great
Wall. . .

To the Middle-aged Man who appears preoccupied

DRIVER:
Where to, love?

MIDDLE-AGED MAN:
Rivermouth, please

DRIVER:
Single?

MIDDLE-AGED MAN:
Um. . .

DRIVER:
You coming back tonight?

MIDDLE-AGED MAN:
No . . .
Well, hopefully . . .

DRIVER:
So it's a single

MIDDLE-AGED MAN:
Well, possibly . . .

DRIVER:
You don't want to pay double, do you?

MIDDLE-AGED MAN:
No, you're right.

DRIVER:
A return then

MIDDLE-AGED MAN:
Return, yeah,
Just in case . . .

DRIVER:
That'll be five fifty then . . .

MIDDLE-AGED MAN:
Sure,
Sorry . . .

Over the next speech, money is exchanged, ticket printed

DRIVER:
Always money . . .
Always something . . .
Now this.
And I can't say no;
Make him hate me more than he does already
For being the 'No' parent;
They knew what they were doing,

MIDDLE-AGED MAN:
(*Takes ticket*)
Thanks . . .

DRIVER:

They knew. . .
Letting him bring that letter home;
Knowing he'd hand it to me,
With his father's eyes.
As if I could refuse him?

Young Man boards the bus

YOUNG MAN:

Rivermouth

DRIVER:

Return?

YOUNG MAN:

One way . . .
Out of here

DRIVER:

And he was looking at me . . .
Looking . . .
Daring me to say no;
Daring me to make a martyr of him . . .
She never lets me!
She never lets me!
He's always moaned;
Moaned from the moment he was born.
No need to slap him,
He just came out moaning!

MAN:

I know this road well
Too well . . .
. . . feels like the back of my hand

DRIVER:

A thousand deposit –

MAN:

(*Follows the veins on the back of his hand*)
Back of my hand,
A thin vein flowing West . . .
(*Points at an intersection*)
There – I retired
Every morning
You'd travel to work
But I'd have nowhere to go,
So I'd catch a bus –

DRIVER:

A thousand!

MAN:

A bus to nowhere in particular . . .
Just to anywhere . . .

DRIVER:

I can't afford that –

MAN:

Trying to retrace the journey I'd made in my life
Up to that point when I lost it . . .

DRIVER:

And there'll be spending money!

MAN:

. . . was lost to it;
When I walked amongst people,

But I didn't walk with them;
A ghost amongst men

MIDDLE-AGED MAN:
Too late . . .

YOUNG MAN:
If we were the only ones left on this earth
If there was this big fuck-off virus
And everybody died apart from us . . .
We'd be the shag end of creation!

DRIVER:
Dad would want me to go, he said
He probably would,
But Dad's not here to pay, is he, love!
Yeah, well, that's your fault!
Here we go . . .
Not tonight, love,
Oh, just forget it then, Mam!
Just forget it . . .
Love . . .
Love!
I try my bloody best for you . . .
It's all I can do . . .

YOUNG MAN:
How did you get your inspiration for the film?
I thought you'd ask this question

MIDDLE-AGED MAN:
To have been someone

YOUNG MAN:

To be honest,
It's inspired by myself.

MIDDLE-AGED MAN:

To have inspired . . .

YOUNG MAN:

You inspired yourself?
Yes.
I travel a lot . . .
Do you?

MIDDLE-AGED MAN:

To have moved

YOUNG MAN:

Always moving;
Here and there, up and down . . .
And I got thinking one day,
When I was on this bus,
What if this crazy virus
Killed everybody in the world apart from us?
Would mankind survive?
How do you mean?
Well, was there someone . . .
You know, that I could . . .
Would we . . .
You know?
Can I say . . .

MIDDLE-AGED MAN:

Fuck!

YOUNG MAN:

. . . and if there was,
What would happen?
Or would it be Mankind rest in peace.
Simple as that really,
Hence the title –
R.I.P.
Rip

MIDDLE-AGED MAN:

Dead loss

YOUNG MAN:

That's genius
No, just . . .

MIDDLE-AGED MAN:

Oh, I don't fucking know . . . (*in exasperation*)

YOUNG MAN:

Thanks
Yeah, it is . . .

MIDDLE-AGED MAN:

Too fucking late

YOUNG MAN:

But, you know, on the shoulders of giants, eh?

DRIVER:

I just thought . . .
I just thought
It was just another cry for help.
You'd done it before,

You'd probably do it again . . .
To get close . . .
As you'd say,
To feel . . .

MAN:
. . . like the back of my hand;

DRIVER:
Anyone for Dragon's Boast?

MIDDLE-AGED MAN:
Always too late

MAN:
The times I've travelled this road;
Villages like beads threading a line . . .

DRIVER:
'. . . strung up again!' she said, on the phone,
'He's strung up again, you'd better come.'
(What was she doing there?)
To hang within an inch of your death;
To feel the flatline before coming down.
How many times?
How many times had you hung?
How many times had I come home
To the hanged man?
I'd had enough!
Do it then!
Hang yourself!
Don't fuck about,
Stop fucking with me,
Think of your son!
Spare him or do it for real!

Go on . . .
Stop playing at it!
Just do it!
Hang yourself then!
Do something in your life more than jacking up and being a Jack shit!
So when she phoned that day, I thought
Sod him!
I finished work; in my time;
Drove home; didn't rush.
How was I to know the knot had tightened on your vein?
Dad would still be alive, if you'd been there for him!
If you'd rushed home, straight!
How can I tell him?
How can I tell him how his father died and lived!
Odd Sins Inn anyone?

YOUNG MAN:
How can I explain . . .
They just drive and drive looking for other survivors . . .
City to city,
Country to country . . .
Not that city and country mean anything in the New World!
They just drive, looking.
But they can't find anybody; no sign of life

MIDDLE-AGED MAN:
You just keep going

YOUNG MAN:
They don't give up;
Travelling

MIDDLE-AGED MAN:
On and on

YOUNG MAN:
Because that's what life's about, isn't it?
Just moving on

MIDDLE-AGED MAN:
Blow by fucking blow . . .

YOUNG MAN:
That's profound

MIDDLE-AGED MAN:
All shit

YOUNG MAN:
No, not really . . .
You called me genius,
But I'm just this guy who likes buses.
And for your next song?

Older Woman, Middle-aged Man and Young Man sing different songs

MAN:
Dragon's Boast
Odd Sins Inn
Butcher's Block
Oxbridge;
Small towns . . . long ribbon.
The Spot
Small Mill
Little Urs
Fordham

Ten miles on,
Rivermouth.
You'll get better there, you said.
We'll live in Rivermouth and everything will be fine,
You'll see.
I never really thought . . .

DRIVER:
I should've been there, should I?
Should've saved him, should I?
So that you could've grown up
With a pin cushion for a father;
Tracks all over,
Is that the sort of father you'd have wanted me to save?
Is it?

YOUNG MAN:
You should've been there really

MIDDLE-AGED MAN:
Never got anywhere . . .

YOUNG MAN:
It was fucking awesome
Shit, I can't say that on TV!
Can I?

DRIVER:
When you dream of him,
Do you dream of a smacked-up father who fucked around?
Do you?
No . . .
I know what you dream,
You dream of a king . . .
A father,

Dripping gold,
Giving permission!
And that's good.
And I want you to dream that;
Let you hate me,
Blame me for everything.
Just keep dreaming.
Because I don't want the truth to hurt you.
Not yet;
Enough time for that,
Life's hard enough as it is.
I'll find the money
I'll find the money, Son
Somehow . . .
Get off the fucking road!

MAN:

I never thought you'd die before me,
Not really.
If I had,
I'd never have come home,
Moved to Rivermouth with you.
I would've stayed in that room in the city,
Shut out the world,
And hid;
Alone until the end.
But I came back thinking,
Ah, men ordinarily die before women,
I'll die first,
It won't be a problem.
You'll be alright,
You'll make new friends.
I pictured you dancing slow tangos at eighty.
And I'd be happy for you;
Knowing you could live without me.

But, without you . . .
Without you
There's just longing,
That Small Country word again,
Longing . . .
I can't move further west!
There's only the sea!
I long for Avalon,
But however far I'd sail
I'd never arrive,
So I keep travelling . . .
Making the circle round
I keep searching.
Because if I stop . . .

DRIVER:
Anyone for Butcher's Block?

During the next the lighting changes to denote a room in the family house

MAN:
. . . if I stop moving
I'll think . . .
I'll remember . . .
I don't want to remember
That day you mounted and married me.
I should've let myself be taken, then fled;
Wiped clean on the curtain and left!
Why did I stay for the chat?
Why did we say 'I do' for decency's sake!
(*Passionately with loss*)
Lovers should die together!
They shouldn't be separated one inch;
Less than that,

An impossible distance.
I long for a country not on this earth,
I cannot arrive there,
But I keep travelling . . .
Travelling . . .
If I stop moving
I'll think . . .
I'll remember . . .

A shift in thought. (Son is played by Middle-aged Man). After his wife's funeral

SON:
Dad?

MAN:
Oh hello, Son

SON:
Are you alright?

MAN:
Mmm . . .
Has everybody gone?

SON:
Yes

MAN:
Thanks for dealing with them.
I just couldn't face your mother's family

SON:
Sure . . .
Ok?

Beat

MAN:
No, but . . .
Leave me, Son, I'll be alright

SON:
I'll tidy up first

MAN:
Not tonight, just leave it . . .

SON:
No, I'll do it

MAN:
Leave it, Son

SON:
Two minutes . . .

MAN:
(*With frustration*)
Leave it . . . please!

Beat

MAN:
Sorry

Beat

SON:
It's ok

MAN:

No,
I shouldn't have . . .
It'll give me something to do

SON:

Sure.
I don't want to leave you alone tonight, Dad

MAN:

I'll be all right alone, Son . . .
A few whiskies . . .
Knock me out and . . .
I'll be all right

Pause

SON:

Do you remember New Amstel, Dad?

MAN:

Mmm?

SON:

Do you remember New Amstel?
We went there on holiday with Mam.
We never went on holiday.
Why did we go there?

MAN:

A college friend was getting married

SON:

Mam loved it

MAN:
Yeah, she did

SON:
When we arrived at the hotel,
That porter took us to our room,
And he tousled my hair,
My curly blonde hair I used to hate;
I would love to hate it now!
Everybody tousled it;
And he called me the Prince of New Amstel.
And that's why Mam always called me her Prince.
Remember, Dad

MAN:
My Champion . . .

Beat

SON:
I wish we could be there again . . .
With Mam

MAN:
Yeah . . .

SON:
Shame . . .

MAN:
I shamed myself.

SON:
Dad?

The next is thought

MAN:

I was ashamed of you,
Because you didn't wear the clothes
I thought you should.
You had beautiful clothes at home.
But whenever you travelled,
You always travelled heavy but light;
A case full of coordinates;
Cheap thin things,
Lots of them!
I wanted you to wear the heavy things
You'd left at home;
The dresses, boots and coats that ennobled you,
Crowned by your smile.
In the most expensive city on this earth
(a Medici city of walking jewels screaming wealth),
You decided to whisper poverty.
And to my shame . . .
I was ashamed of you. . .
As if I was a pretty picture!
I am an ugly man, my love,
I could never find beauty in anyone,
I only ever saw the flaw.
I married the most beautiful woman in the world
Who never once commented upon the clothes I wore,
Only how heavy I was on them,
When you repaired them.
I am ashamed of myself more than anyone!
Yeah, I want to go back to New Amstel.
Walk down Wideway
With our little Prince swinging between us . . .
Happy . . .

SON:

I fear memory tonight, Dad.

MAN:

. . . regal,
Proud.

SON:

I fear it's waiting for me . . .

MAN:

I'm sorry, my love, I'm sorry

SON:

. . . on the edges of the day

MAN:

One second more, that's all a sorry would take, please!

SON:

I fear . . .

MAN:

One moment more in New Amstel
Enough to say sorry, my love . . .

The next two sections are spoken simultaneously.

MAN:

Sorry, sorry, sorry, sorry . . .
Sorry, sorry, sorry, sorry . . .
Sorry, sorry, sorry, sorry . . .

SON:

I fear the waking memory, Dad;

A torturer from the Heart of Darkness.
He opens a first aid box
To reveal a pair of pliers and a screwdriver.
Which one do you want?
He spits . . .
Acid fucking wit!
Pliers or screwdriver?
Does it fucking matter?
Torture is torture . . .

Pause

MAN:
Son?

SON:
Just thinking

MAN:
Yeah . . .
It was a good holiday

SON:
Mam was happy . . .
So happy

MAN:
Yes

Beat

SON:
I've taken the week off work, Dad.
If you need anything?

MAN:
You shouldn't have

SON:
Just in case

MAN:
You're a Prince . . .

SON:
Look, Dad . . .

MAN:
What?

Beat

SON:
I don't want to . . . (*Impose*)
But, can I stay tonight, here with you?
Please

Beat

MAN:
Of course.
Your Mam would like that . . .
I'd like it

Back on the bus

DRIVER:
Next stop, Rivermouth station.
If you're heading north,

The bus to Tabernacle will be waiting on the stand in front of ours.

YOUNG MAN:
. . . picking up the award was great . . .

MIDDLE-AGED MAN:
I should've been something

YOUNG MAN:
. . . And everyone was on their feet

MIDDLE-AGED MAN:
. . . someone

YOUNG MAN:
. . . and me, just a small boy from Small Country . . .
Awesome.

MIDDLE-AGED MAN:
And, as I would've . . .
Should've said in a speech
For an award I should've won . . .
For something . . .
Anything;
This is for my mum . . .

YOUNG MAN:
. . . the important thing is the going
It doesn't matter where . . .

MIDDLE-AGED MAN:
We know our cradles

YOUNG MAN:

. . . 'cause that's what life's about, isn't it?
The travelling

MIDDLE-AGED MAN:

We never guess our graves

YOUNG MAN:

. . . you are a genius.
Yeah
And for your final song?

Older Woman sings as they disembark and board another bus – the final bus from Rivermouth to Tabernacle.

SECOND BUS

The Middle-aged Man is the Driver on this bus. The Younger Woman – a passenger. The Man hangs back until he's the last to climb aboard

DRIVER:

(*In an ugly accent*)
Can you move along the bus, please!
Move along.
Make room!
Ok, sir,
Where you going?

MAN:

Home

DRIVER:
Don't forget your ticket

MAN:
Thanks . . .

Man takes his 'wasted' ticket. The bus is full. The Younger Woman and Older Woman are sitting next to each other. Young Man lounges over a few seats, he sleeps, hood over his head. The Man has to stand. After a while the Younger Woman gets up. She offers her seat to the Man. Man and Older Woman sit next to each other for the first time

MAN:
No, I'm all right

YOUNGER WOMAN:
Please, I've been sitting down all day at work

MAN:
Well . . .
Thank you

YOUNGER WOMAN:
That's ok

Younger Woman stands by the Driver

DRIVER:
All right, darling?
No seats back there?

YOUNGER WOMAN:
No

DRIVER:
Keep me company then.
Where you going again?

YOUNGER WOMAN:
Henlys

DRIVER:
Ah, I used to live in Henlys . . .
Not a bad little place

YOUNGER WOMAN:
Boring

DRIVER:
You're right . . .
Arse end.
Live in Gogsham now.
It's ok,
Locals can be a bit funny, you know,
But it's their country, I . . .

An awkward look between them. The Younger Woman is obviously Small Country.

DRIVER:
I think it looks like rain . . .

Suddenly the Older Woman talks to Man

OLDER WOMAN:
You've been ignoring me

MAN:
What?

OLDER WOMAN:
'What', not 'sorry'! (*With irony*)

MAN:
Sorry . . .

OLDER WOMAN:
You've ignored me all journey

MAN:
I know

OLDER WOMAN:
You haven't said anything

MAN:
Mmm. . .

Beat

OLDER WOMAN:
You've hurt me

Beat

OLDER WOMAN:
You can't even look at me . . .

MAN:
Who are you?
Are you that woman at the top of an escalator
In that New Amstel toy shop?
And, as I passed with my Champion,
I didn't know whether to look or not
As the sun shone through your transparent skirt.

Are you?
No, I know who you are,
You're that woman in the Irish pub.
You were small,
Beneath my gaze,
And you stood in front of me for an age,
Willing me to look down at you,
But I didn't dare look,
And in the end, you got annoyed,
Called me a Godsake and left . . .
I never saw your face,
I wondered what you looked like.
Is that you?
No, no I know who you are . . .
You're all the left turns I didn't take at the gate

OLDER WOMAN:
Don't be a fool, Adam!
You know damned well who I am . . .
I'm the right turn you made

MAN:
Keep your voice down

OLDER WOMAN:
Only you can hear me . . .

MAN:
What?

Beat

OLDER WOMAN:
Do you miss me?

MAN:
Yes

OLDER WOMAN:
Would you still walk in front of me,
Down the Wideway, in New Amstel?
Would you?

Man looks at her

OLDER WOMAN:
Still ashamed of me?

MAN:
I was never ashamed of you

OLDER WOMAN:
Oh, you were . . .

MAN:
I . . .

OLDER WOMAN:
I what?

MAN:
I just thought
You just didn't make the most of yourself . . .
On that particular occasion

OLDER WOMAN:
I was happy being me;
Being us was enough for me.
I didn't care what you wore walking down the street

MAN:
Sorry

Beat

OLDER WOMAN:
Doesn't matter . . .
Do you like my coordinates?
Travel things,
Just for you!
Would you prefer me nude?

She begins to undress, Man rises to stop her

MAN:
Dawn, please

OLDER WOMAN:
I told you, no one can see me.
They can see you though

DRIVER:
Are you all right back there, sir?

MAN:
Yes, thank you

OLDER WOMAN:
Sit down before you make a fool of yourself

DRIVER:
Better sit down, sir

Man sits down

DRIVER:
Do you know Peter?
Drinks at the Arms Tavern in Henlys?

YOUNGER WOMAN:
No

DRIVER:
No?
(*To himself / She looks at the Man*)
What do you know?
Do you know how beautiful you are?
Do you know how good you make me feel . . .
Standing beside me
As I drive the twisting roads;
Drive the years back . . .
(*She turns to him*)
Perhaps your dad knows him?

YOUNGER WOMAN:
Maybe . . .

Beat

OLDER WOMAN:
How's my little Prince?

MAN:
Still my Champion

OLDER WOMAN:
We didn't deserve such beauty, did we?

MAN:
You did.

But how he came from me,
God only knows!

OLDER WOMAN:
You can't be that ugly!
I married you,
And I have taste.
Maybe not abroad, but . . .

MAN:
I said I'm sorry . . .
I was wrong

OLDER WOMAN:
I was happy;
Cool, in the way I wanted to be.
Whilst you sweated in your leather shoes!

MAN:
I needed them

OLDER WOMAN:
I knew you did.
I knew everything about you . . .
Yet, I still loved you!

Beat

OLDER WOMAN:
So tell me . . .
What was it like to kiss me dead?

MAN:
What?

OLDER WOMAN:
How did you feel . . .
To kiss my cold lips?

MAN:
Angry;
I was really angry with you.
You always drove too fast on the country lanes.
I kept telling you,
Drive slower

OLDER WOMAN:
(*With sarcasm*)
Sorry, Daddy. . .

A look between them

OLDER WOMAN:
(*With sincerity*) Sorry.
What was it like to kiss death?

Beat

MAN:
I wished death was kissing me instead

OLDER WOMAN:
Oh, Adam . . .

Pause

MAN:
I'm tired, Dawn

OLDER WOMAN:
I know

Beat

OLDER WOMAN:
Do you know what went through my mind
As my head shattered against the windscreen?
Oh, you were lucky,
You saw me much later!
Before that, I was . . . in pieces!
Do you know what I thought, in that moment?
So many things I could've thought about:
Reeled through my life,
Prayed to God,
But I didn't.
I just thought,
Damn!
I've forgotten to darn his favourite socks.
In the moment it took to leave this world,
I panicked, because I'd promised to darn your socks.
Is life that pathetic . . .

MAN:
Is it?

Beat

OLDER WOMAN:
Take your shoes off

MAN:
What?

OLDER WOMAN:
Take off your shoes
Go on,
Let me see!

MAN:
See what?

OLDER WOMAN:
Your socks!

MAN:
I can't take my shoes off in public

OLDER WOMAN:
You're an old man,
You can do anything!

MAN:
God

OLDER WOMAN:
Show me!

Man takes off his shoes

YOUNGER WOMAN:
He's taking his shoes off

DRIVER:
Who is?

YOUNGER WOMAN:
The old man

DRIVER:
He's just old

OLDER WOMAN:
As I thought!
Useless without me!
Here . . .

MAN:
What!

OLDER WOMAN:
Give them to me . . .

MAN:
I can't

OLDER WOMAN:
Give them!

YOUNGER WOMAN:
He's taking his socks off

DRIVER:
If he smells,
He's off;
Old or not

Beat

OLDER WOMAN:
Oh, Adam . . .

She looks at him through a hole in his sock

OLDER WOMAN:
What would you have done without me, eh?

MAN:
I don't know

OLDER WOMAN:
What would I have done without you?

Beat

OLDER WOMAN:
I could've fixed these . . .
Too late, now, sorry

She hands back the socks (a chance to exchange them)

OLDER WOMAN:
Sometimes you were hard to love, Adam

MAN:
I know

OLDER WOMAN:
But I still loved you; always loved you,
Loved you even before you knew my name,
Loved you with words on a card, sealed with a loving kiss,
For better or for worse.
I still love you
And I'm sorry . . .
Sorry it was you who owed me the kiss . . .

The Younger Woman looks at the Man. She turns to the Driver

YOUNGER WOMAN:
The old man's crying

DRIVER:
On a bus!

She goes up to the Man

YOUNGER WOMAN:
You all right?

MAN:
Yes

YOUNGER WOMAN:
Are you sure?

MAN:
I'll be ok

YOUNGER WOMAN:
Here . . .

She hands him a tissue

YOUNGER WOMAN:
The whole bus is looking

MAN:
I don't care who's looking!

OLDER WOMAN:
Adam!

MAN:

What?

YOUNGER WOMAN:

I'm only trying to help

OLDER WOMAN:

She's only trying to help

MAN:

I know . . .
But I'll be all right,
Please . . .
No fuss . . .
I just . . .
I'll be all right

DRIVER:

Is he all right back there?

MAN:

I'm all right

DRIVER:

What did he say?
Didn't understand.
Is he speaking the lingo?

YOUNGER WOMAN:

He says he's all right

DRIVER:

I don't want you dying on me, old man

YOUNGER WOMAN:
He'll be all right

Young Woman's attention split between Driver and recovering Man

DRIVER:
Had this guy last week –
Had a fit . . .
In front of everyone!
Worst was, when he came round, he said,
I always have a second . . . and it's worse.
And he started fitting again . . .
Screaming . . .
Really screaming.
Horrible to know something like that is coming, and you can't stop it;

YOUNGER WOMAN:
You ok?

MAN:
Yes, thanks

DRIVER:
Horrible

MAN:
If we were the only ones left on this planet,
Would fear live . . .

Younger Woman doesn't understand his look

YOUNGER WOMAN:
Got to go, sorry.

My stop.
You ok?

MAN:
Mmm

DRIVER:
Do you want to get off here?

YOUNGER WOMAN:
Please

Bus stops.

MAN:
Bye

DRIVER:
Bye, love

She leaves the bus

OLDER WOMAN:
You're a sad man, Adam

Young Man wakes from his slumber

YOUNG MAN:
Shit!
Drive!
Wait!

Young Man disembarks

YOUNG MAN:
Thanks, mate

DRIVER:
(*Unheard by Young Man*)
I'm not your fucking mate, mate . . .

As the bus drives off

OLDER WOMAN:
'Manners maketh the man'.
Do you know my one regret . . .

MAN:
Not now, please

OLDER WOMAN:
My one regret . . .
We didn't have a daughter.
I would've liked to have had a little girl, Adam

MAN:
I know

OLDER WOMAN:
Why didn't you want another child, Adam?

Beat

OLDER WOMAN:
Didn't you love me, Adam?

MAN:
Dawn . . .

OLDER WOMAN:
Didn't you?

MAN:
I did, you know I did

OLDER WOMAN:
Then why wouldn't you give me a girl?

Beat

OLDER WOMAN:
Why?
If you loved me so much, Adam,
Why didn't you given me that?

MAN:
Because . . .

She cuts him off

OLDER WOMAN:
. . . I know.
I know your fear, Adam

MAN:
I'm sorry

OLDER WOMAN:
That's ok . . .

The journey continues. Older Woman sings the towns by. She strokes his hair as she sings

OLDER WOMAN:

Henlys
Gogsham
Crossmount
The Port
Castleton;
Our country.
As beautiful as it ever was,
As heaven ever will be

MAN:

I'm tired

OLDER WOMAN:

Nearly there

DRIVER:

Tabernacle station!

MAN:

So soon.
Seems only this morning I left

OLDER WOMAN:

So much can happen in a day . . .
Moment leading to moment,
And before you known it,
There's a life!

MAN:

Is this it?
Do we get off?

OLDER WOMAN:

Yes.

Come on,
You've got a train to catch

She helps him up

MAN:
Thank you

DRIVER:
Feeling better?

MAN:
Yes

DRIVER:
You nearly died on me

MAN:
I've got a train to catch . . .

DRIVER:
Bye, old man

MAN:
Not that old . . .
I hope . . .

OLDER WOMAN:
C'mon

They disembark. They walk arm in arm to the station

OLDER WOMAN:
If you could live it all again.
What would you change?

MAN:
I don't know

OLDER WOMAN:
Would you change me?

MAN:
No

Beat

MAN:
I'd change myself;
Think less . . .
Pain less . . .

OLDER WOMAN:
Without pain, there's nothing, Adam.
You never understood that.
Without pain,
Our little Prince,
Your Champion,
Would never have reigned for a day over New Amstel!
His reign was worth the world:
All the pain of being.

MAN:
We'll go back there . . .
To New Amstel,
One day . . .

OLDER WOMAN:
We can't,
We're here.
Come on . . .

Let's cross to the station.
Your train will be here soon

They walk to Tabernacle Station

MAN:
Late again

OLDER WOMAN:
You were three days late, your mother said.
You didn't want to come out,
Screaming to get back in!

The train's horn sounds in the distance

OLDER WOMAN:
Here it comes

MAN:
Come with me
Please
I won't ignore you this time.
This time we'll have a daughter

OLDER WOMAN:
I can't

MAN:
Come on, it'll be a lovely ride along the coast.
We'll stop off at the beach;
Build sandcastles,
Eat ice cream

OLDER WOMAN:
We can't, Adam

MAN:
But I don't want to travel alone,
It's lonely

OLDER WOMAN:
I know

MAN:
I hate travelling

OLDER WOMAN:
That's your problem . . .
Front or back?

MAN:
Mmm?

OLDER WOMAN:
Plenty of seats

The train arrives

MAN:
I'm scared

OLDER WOMAN:
Think of socks . . .

MAN:
Socks!

OLDER WOMAN:
You've got to think of something . . .

Beat

MAN:
Why can't we take this train together?

OLDER WOMAN:
We take it alone

MAN:
Oh, Dawn.

They embrace

OLDER WOMAN:
Be brave, Adam

Beat

OLDER WOMAN:
Hey, do you remember when we used to come and wave you off at the station?
And our little Prince would race the train
Along the platform?

MAN:
Yes

OLDER WOMAN:
I'll race you to the tunnel!
I bet I'll get there before you,

Beat

MAN:
I love you

OLDER WOMAN:
I know.
I knew,
Even before you knew me

They kiss a final time

OLDER WOMAN:
Roses are red,
Violets are blue . . .

MAN:
. . . I don't want to live without you

OLDER WOMAN:
You don't have to . . .
Go

They embrace. Man boards the train. She motions for him to take off his shoe and look at his sock

MAN:
What?

She mouths 'look at your sock'. He takes of his shoes. His sock is darned

MAN:
How did you do that?

She mouths

OLDER WOMAN:
I love you

The train pulls off. Man journeys alone into darkness again.

GUARD:(*OOV***)**

Welcome aboard this 'first light' train
From Ferryton to Bastion.
If you've just joined us at Tabernacle,
We will be stopping at:
The Junction
Bluerinse Bay
Chavton,
Poverton,
And arrive at our final destination,
In good time for whatever you have to do.
First stop, the Junction,
We'll be there in a bit now . . .

Pause

MAN:

There in a bit now, bit, bit, bit
In a bit now, bit, bit, bit . . .
There in a bit now, bit, bit, bit
In a bit now, bit, bit, bit . . .

The train enters the tunnel as it leaves Tabernacle Station. Man begins to panic

MAN:

In the darkness,
Cow-gut . . . darkness,
I wonder what a foetus dreams. . .
As it lies. . .
Crouching . . .
A fist in a fuck?

In darkness. . .
Nightmares?
Little . . .
Fears . . .
Fears, no
How can it?
Doesn't . . .
Doesn't know . . .
Only knows . . .
You've got to know . . .
To know . . .
You've got to know loss . . .
In the darkness.
Know . . .
No!
Lightmares then. . .
Fear of the no-dark
Eye-blinding fear . . .
Cracking open the black . . .

Beat

Fiat Lux
Let there be . . .
Please
Let . . .
Let there . . .
In the darkness
Let there be . . .

The train horn blasts. This time, the train does not emerge from the tunnel into light. There is just darkness.

For geographic reference
(rounding the country clockwise)

First Train

Tabernacle	Bangor. The Tabernacle church in Bangor (a cathedral city) was converted into a home for the proto-National Welsh Language Theatre Company (*Cwmni Theatr Cymru*) in the 1970s. *Tabernak*! is also a powerful expletive in Quebecois.
The Village	Llanfairfechan.
The Junction	Llandudno Junction.
Bluerinse Bay	Colwyn Bay. A retirement town full of ageing incomers.
Chavton	Rhyl. Rhyl has two of the poorest council wards in Wales.
Poverton	Prestatyn. The poorer relation of Rhyl!
Bastion	Chester. Welsh name, *Caer*. Trans. castle / bastion.

Second Train

Shireton	Shrewsbury. The shire town of Shropshire.
Grayling	Ludlow. In Welsh, *Llwydlo* – grey calf (my translation).
Lionchurch	Leominster.
Mappaton	Hereford. The *Mappa Mundi* (Map of the World, *c.*1300) is kept in Hereford Cathedral
Five Ways	Abergavenny. Five ways is a village near Abergavenny. It is also the title of a painting by Sarah Snazell and the possession of that painting is the subject of the play, *Butterfly*.

Newtown Cwmbran. Cwmbran is a new town.

Newbridge Newport. *Casnewydd* in Welsh. Trans. New Bridge.

Our City Cardiff. Made a city in 1905. Capital of Wales since 1955.

Dullage Bridgend. An excruciatingly dull place – to be avoided more than Llanelli (see below).

Foxton Port Talbot. Port Talbot was a port developed by the landowning Talbot family (of Margam Abbey) in the 19th century.

Nest Neath . *Nyth* (pronounced neath in Welsh). Trans. a nest.

Whitorse Swansea. After the White Horse Tavern, NY one of Dylan Thomas' haunts – Swansesa being his birthplace.

Ugly Llanelli. In an 18th century guide book it stated '(Llanelli) has no redeeming features whatsoever, avoid at all costs'.

The Dock Pembrey and Bury Port. There, on the 17th of June 1928, the American aviator, Amelia Earhart, landed following her solo trans-atlantic flight.

Seacastle Carmarthen. In Latin *Maredunum*. Trans. Seafort.

First Bus

Dragon's Boast Pencader. According to Girlaldus Cambrensis (Gerallt Gymro / Gerald of Wales), in his *Descriptio Cambria*, the Old Man of Pencader prophesied (to Henry II in 1163) 'Nor do I think that any other nation than this of Wales, nor any other language, whatever may hereafter come to pass, shall on the day of examination before the Supreme Judge answer for this corner of Wales'.

Odd Sins Inn Synod Inn.

Butcher's Block Llanybydder. This village has a massive abattoir. Its miasmic stench often hangs over the village like a death sentence .

Oxbridge Lampeter. Apart from Oxford and Cambridge, the University of Lampeter (*Llanbedr Pont Steffan*) is the oldest university in England and Wales to award degrees. Its charter was granted in 1828.

The Spot Cribyn. Cribyn lies in an area known as *Y Smotyn Du* (trans. The Black Spot) the heartland of Unitarianism in Wales.

Small Mill Felinfach. Literal trans. from the Welsh.

Little Urs Aberarth. Literal trans. the estuary of the Arth river, but *arth* also means bear in Welsh / *urs* in Latin.

Fordham Llanrhystyd. There is a beautiful ford in this village.

Rivermouth Aberystwyth. Trans. the estuary of the Ystwyth river.

Second Bus

Henlys Machynlleth (*Henlys* – Literal trans. Old Court) This was the capital of free Wales under Owain Glyndŵr's reign at the beginning of the 15th century. He held his Parliament here.

Gogsham Dolgellau. The Welsh for north is *Gogledd*. The inhabitants of the north are affectionately called *Gogs* by the *Hwntws* (their southern neighbours).

Crossmount	Trawsfynydd. Literal trans. – *traws* / across, *mynydd* (mutated to *fynydd*) / mountain.
The Port	Porthmadog. Madog's port. In 1170, Tywysog Madog, Prince Madoc (son of Owain Gwynedd) is reported to have sailed to America from this port – two centuries after the Vikings, but three centuries before Columbus!
Castleton	Caernarfon. In 1969 Prince Charles was 'invested' in Caernarfon Castle. The castle, a symbol of historic oppression, is hated by the Welsh in this, the most Welsh-speaking town in Wales.

Others

Ferryton	Holyhead. The Dublin ferry port on Anglesey, *Ynys Môn.*
Big City	is obviously London.
The Wideway	Broadway
New Amstel	New York (New Amsterdam).
Allpoints East	Crewe. A soulless station in a soulless town.
Montpellier	Cheltenham.

Dalier Sylw Publications

Y Cinio (Geraint Lewis)
Hunllef yng Nghymru Fydd (Gareth Miles)
Epa yn y Parlwr Cefn (Siôn Eirian)
Wyneb yn Wyneb (Meic Povey)
"i" (Jim Cartwright – Welsh trans. John Owen)
Fel Anifail (Meic Povey)
Croeso Nôl (Tony Marchant – Welsh trans. John Owen)
Bonansa! (Meic Povey)
Tair (Meic Povey)

Sgript Cymru Publications

Diwedd y Byd / Yr Hen Blant (Meic Povey)
Art and Guff (Catherine Treganna)
Crazy Gary's Mobile Disco (Gary Owen)
Ysbryd Beca (Geraint Lewis)
Franco's Bastard (Dic Edwards)
Dosbarth (Geraint Lewis)
past away (Tracy Harris)
Indian Country (Meic Povey)
Diwrnod Dwynwen (Fflur Dafydd, Angharad Devonald, Angharad Elen, Meleri Wyn James, Dafydd Llywelyn, Nia Wyn Roberts)
Ghost City (Gary Owen)
AMDANI! (Bethan Gwanas)
Community Writer 2001-2004 Robert Evans, Michael Waters and others)
Drws Arall i'r Coed (Gwyneth Glyn, Eurgain Haf, Dyfrig Jones, Caryl Lewis, Manon Wyn)
Crossings (Clare Duffy)
Life of Ryan... and Ronnie (Meic Povey)
Cymru Fach (Wiliam Owen Roberts)
Orange (Alan Harris)
Hen Bobl Mewn Ceir (Meic Povey)
Aqua Nero (Meredydd Barker)
Buzz (Meredydd Barker)

Sherman Cymru Publications

Maes Terfyn (Gwyneth Glyn)
The Almond and The Seahorse (Kaite O'Reilly)
Yr Argae (Conor McPherson –Welsh trans. Wil Sam Jones)
Amgen:Broken (Gary Owen)
Ceisio'i Bywyd Hi (Martin Crimp - Welsh trans. Owen Martell)
Cardboard Dad (Alan Harris)
Llwyth (Dafydd James)
Cityscape (Emily Steel, Tracy Harris, Bethan Marlow, Kit Lambert)
Gadael yr Ugeinfed Ganrif (Gareth Potter)
Cinders & Plum (...and me, Will!) (Louise Osborn)

Available from -

Sherman Cymru, Senghennydd Rd, Cardiff, CF24 4YE.
029 2064 6900

A selection of playtexts are also available from – www.amazon.co.uk/shops/sherman_cymru

Embedded!

FIRST EDITION

Embedded!

FIRST EDITION

Go Embedded!

FIRST EDITION

by

Asang Dani
Yashavant Kanetkar

BPB PUBLICATIONS
B-14, CONNAUGHT PLACE, NEW DELHI - 110 001

FIRST EDITION 2008

ISBN 10 : 81-8333-253-6
ISBN 13 : 978-81-8333-253-8

Distributors:

COMPUTER BOOK CENTRE
12, Shrungar Shopping Centre, M.G. Road, BANGALORE-560001 Ph: 25587923, 25584641

MICRO BOOKS
Shanti Niketan Building, 8, Camac Street, KOLKATA-700017 Ph: 22826518/9

BUSINESS PROMOTION BUREAU
8/1, Ritchie Street, Mount Road, CHENNAI-600002 Ph: 28410796, 28550491

BPB PUBLICATIONS
B-14, Connaught Place, NEW DELHI-110001
Ph: 23325760, 23723393, 23737742

BPB BOOK CENTRE
376, Old Lajpat Rai Market, DELHI-110006
PH: 23861747

MICRO MEDIA
Shop No. 5, Mahendra Chambers,150 D.N. Rd, Next to Capital Cinema V.T. (C.S.T.) Station, MUMBAI-400001 Ph.: 22078296, 22078297

DECCAN AGENCIES
4-3-329, Bank Street,
HYDERABAD-500195 Ph: 24756400, 24756967

INFO TECH
G-2, Sidhartha Building, 96 Nehru Place, NEW DELHI-110019
Ph: 26438245, 26415092, 26234208

INFO TECH
SHop No. 2, F-38, South Extension Part I, NEW DELHI-110049
Ph: 24691288

Published by Manish Jain for BPB Publications, B-14, Connaught Place, New Delhi-110 001 and Printed by him at Akash Press New Delhi

Dedication

Dedicated to
Neelima and Kamalakar Dani

\- Asang Dani

Dedicated to
Prabhakar Kanetkar

\- Yashavant Kanetkar

About the Authors

Asang Dani

Having worked with product development companies like Brocade, Microsoft, Veritas, Dow Jones, etc., Asang left USA a few years ago to create a product company of his own Together with Yashavant he has created several products under the aegis of KSET Pvt. Ltd. These products have become immensely successful in the marketplace with clientele around the world. Asang's current areas of interest include .NET Technologies, Window CE, Device Drivers and Embedded Linux. Asang is most recently noted for his significant contributions in Windows CD by "Most Valuable Professional" award from Microsoft. Asang holds a BE in Electronics Engineering from VRCE, Nagpur and ME in Computer Science from IISc, Bangalore. He can be reached at asang@ksetindia.com.

Yashavant Kanetkar

Yashavant is a pioneer in IT Education in India. A true entrepreneur, he has single-handedly set benchmarks for IT education and has played a major role in taking IT learning to every nook and corner of this country. He has authored several bestsellers over last 15 years and helped shape careers of millions of programmers throughout Asia. Most recently, he has created several interactive training titles for KSET's flagship "Quest" Content Delivery Platform which have become a stellar success. In recognition of his immense contribution to IT education in India, he has been most recently awarded the "Best .NET Technical Contributor" and "Most Valuable Professional" awards by Microsoft. His current passion is Internet Technologies, Device Drivers and Embedded Systems. Yashavant holds a B.E. from VJTI Mumbai and an M. Tech.

from IIT Kanpur. He can be reached at kanetkar@ksetindia.com.

Yashavant's and Asang's current activities can be tracked at http://goembedded.kicit.com.

Acknowledgments

Giving birth is a painful process. A process that is followed by so much joy that it makes the whole process with the effort. Creating this book, recording Quest Embedded Systems Courseware CDs and developing an Embedded Systems board gave us the same feeling. A feeling that is a mixture of pain and joy.

In our journey towards this goal we latched on to several helping hands that came our way. Those whom we would like to specially mention are:

Monali Nikhare for creating some of the exercises in this book; and Uday Mujumdar for helping us create the Embedded Systems Development Board.

Our parents who gave us the confidence that given a level playing field, armed with the knowledge and willingness to work hard, anything can be made possible Many thanks to them.

Our wives for sharing our joy when the programs worked. And when the programs didn't work the smiles on our kids faces told us that when everything is lost, hope remains.

Preface

As we release "Go Embedded" I have the same feeling today that I had a decade and half ago when I wrote Let Us C. At that time I wanted to write a book that would make even the last person in the programming chain feel that he too can learn C programming. Millions of satisfied users of Let Us C ratified my feeling that indeed such a book can be written. When I started writing "Go Embedded" with my colleague and coauthor Asang Dani, we had set ourselves one simple goal—make everybody feel and experience that Embedded Systems is his cup of tea.

If Embedded Systems have became so pervasive today, then it is natural that India as a software nation should have enough manpower with Embedded System skills. Towards that end, we have tried to create an ecosystem that will help create and nurture your Embedded Systems programming skills. The three pieces of this ecosystem are "Go Embedded" book, "Quest Embedded Systems Courseware CDs" and "KSET Embedded Systems Development Board". The book will help you understand how to build Embedded Systems software. The CDs will help you hone your Embedded Systems programming skills further, whereas the Embedded Systems Development board will give you an opportunity to soil your hands in seeing and experiencing the fruits of your programming labors. We are confident that you would find as much enjoyment in reading, viewing and using these products, as we had in creating them.

You are holding the book in your hands. The details of the Quest CDs and the KSET Embedded Systems Development board are available at http://quest.ksetindia.com/.

In this book, we don't expect or assume any Electronics Engineering background from the readers. In our opinion, Embedded Systems is an inter-disciplinary field. To become a good Embedded Systems developer one needs to possess skills in modern computer architecture, hardware interfacing, sensors, programming languages and more. In addition, you must possess tenacity and patience that will make you true Embedded System developer. Material in this book has been organized in easy to understand units that build these skills in systematic fashion. Exercises at the end of every chapter help you test the knowledge acquired on reading the chapter. The book contains numerous small and large programs to help you understand the theory behind the concepts discussed.

This book addresses the needs to students and professionals alike and ends with a working example of a serial-bootloader considered as a dreaded topic by most. Although we have chosen Atmel AVR ATmega32 microcontroller to teach Embedded Systems concepts, the knowledge gained can be easily applied to work with other popular microcontrollers like 8051, PIC, STAMP, 68xx etc. Every effort has been made to make the text and programs in this book as accurate as possible. Please send your suggestions and comments to goembedded@ksetindia.com.

Contents

1 Embedded C Programming

We are hopeful that all the readers of this book have more than just a nodding acquaintance with C language. If not, then we would advise that you do go through the "C Primer" in Appendix A to brush up your knowledge of the language before you read this chapter further. This chapter touches upon the nuances of C programming which are very relevant while doing Embedded Systems programming in C. Each sub-topic in the chapter is unrelated with the other, so you can read them in any order. But we would rather want that you read them sequentially since we have arranged them in the increasing order of difficulty.

Why C?

First things first! Why is C language so popularly used for building embedded systems? There are several reasons for this. These are as follows:

- Simple data types in C very closely resemble those supported in modern micro-processors and micro-controllers
- Simplicity of "C" language makes it easier for compiler to generate efficient machine-language instructions.
- C offers efficient bit manipulation using bitwise operators. These operations are often required in interacting with I/O devices that are connected to embedded systems.
- The pointer datatype available is C helps programmer access memory during program execution easily.
- There is hardly a processor for which "C" compiler and other tools are not available. Thus C is most widely supported "higher" level language.

These reasons makes C a language of choice for most embedded systems programmers.

Toolchain

The set of tools that one uses in creating programs is known as toolchain. A typical embedded system toolchain consists of:

- Compiler
- Assembler
- Linker
- Debugger
- Embedded system specific tools

The popular C language development tools in the PC world like TC, VC++ and BC++ cannot be used to create programs for Embedded Systems. The main reason for this is that these tools are meant to be used for development on Intel x86 processors. Most embedded systems use processors (microprocessors and microcontrollers) that are different than x86. Some examples of these processors are Intel 8051, AVR ATMega16, PIC Micro, etc. Each of these processors has its own machine language. The PC based C compilers and linkers cannot convert your C program to these machine languages. As a result, you have to use compilers and other tools that work with these processors.

Which toolchain to select for development with Embedded System is an important decision. Most embedded systems offer several choices. Commercial toolchains from companies like Keil, IAR Embedded Workbench, etc. are available. However, legally free toolchain from GNU is the most popularly used toolchain because of following features:

(a) They support large number of microprocessors and microcontrollers.

(b) They are well-supported by the community as they are commonly used.
(c) They generate good "optimized" code for most microcontrollers.

In this book we plan to use GNU toolchain for programming with embedded systems. Some of the prominent tools in this "toolchain" are as follows:

Compiler – gcc

Assembler – as

Linker – ld

Debugger - gdb

Another advantage of using GNU toolchain is its portability. It means that these tools can be used with numerous popular microcontrollers and microprocessors like Intel x86, Atmel AVR, ARM, PowerPC, MIPS, SPARC, etc. As a result, the knowledge of these tools will help you in building variety of embedded systems—big and small.

How to Use GNU Toolchain

Since we intend to use the GNU toolchain for building embedded systems in this book it is important to get yourself familiar this toolchain before we begin the development on a embedded system board. To get this basic familiarity I will demonstrate how to use this toolchain on a x86 PC. Consider the following simple program.

```
/* Program 1.1 */
# include <stdio.h>
int main( )
```

```
{
    printf ( "The First Embedded C Program!" ) ;
    return 0 ;
}
```

To execute this program we need to first type it, then compile it, then link it with the library and finally execute it. To type the program we would need an editor, to compile it we would need a compiler and to link it we would need a linker. In an integrated PC-based development environment like TC++ or VC++ all these programs are integrated into the development environment. However, there is no such integrated development environment available for GNU toolchain. While using this toolchain one has to edit the program using some editor and then compile and link the program at command line.

The editor, compiler and the linker are present in the CD accompanying this book. To install them on your machine, refer Appendix B. During installation the entire toolchain will be installed on your machine. You can access the tools through the two icons created on your desktop. One icon is for the editor called 'Programmer's Notepad' and the other icon is for a shell program called 'Cygwin'. The Cygwin shell is one of the free software tools originally developed by Cygnus Solutions. Cygwin shell provides a powerful command-line environment that can be used to do Embedded Systems development. Double click the 'Cygwin' icon on your desktop. This will launch a window which will display a **$** prompt. At the **$** prompt, type following command:

```
$ cd C:/myprograms
```

This command will take you inside the **C:/myprograms** directory. Once inside this directory, type the command shown below.

```
$ newproject hello
```

On doing this, a new directory called **hello** will get created. It will contain three files—**hello.c**, **hello.h** and **makefile**. The contents of **hello.c** and **hello.h** are shown below:

hello.h

```
/* hello.h */
#ifndef _hello_h_
#define _hello_h_

/* Include all system header files here */
#include <stdio.h>
#include <stdlib.h>

/* Structures / Classes ... */

/* Extern declarations, prototypes etc. ... */

#endif /* _hello_h_ */
```

hello.c

```
/* Program 1.2 */
/* hello.c */
#include "hello.h"

/* Global variables */
```

```
/* Function prototypes */

int main( int argc, char *argv[ ] )
{
	/* your code goes here */
	fprintf ( stdout, "Hello World!\n" ) ;
	return 0 ;
}
```

As you can see, these files contain skeleton code. You now need to edit the file **hello.c**. To do so, double click the 'Programmer's Notepad' icon on the Windows desktop. Once the editor is launched, open the file **hello.c** in it. Then type Program 1.1 shown above in it and then save it. Once saved, you are ready to compile and link it. To do this switch to Cygwin window and type the following commands at the $ prompt.

```
$ cd hello
$ make
```

Here **make** is a utility for compiling and linking our program. It uses the instructions given in the file called **makefile** present in the **hello** directory to carry out the compilation and linking. If there are any errors in the program they will be reported now. You can rectify them through the Programmer's Notepad, save the file and once again compile and link the program using the **make** command.

The end result of the compilation and linking process is creation of the file **hello.exe** in the directory **hello/obj**. Now you can execute **hello.exe** by using the command shown below:

```
$ obj / hello.exe
```

If you are able to execute the first program successfully, then you can begin with the next program. The starting point will be the commands shown below:

```
$ cd C:/myprograms
$ newproject  secondproject
```

You can then follow the steps mentioned above to create, compile, link and execute the program.

One last thing before we finish this topic. You can get additional help for the **make** command or the **gcc** compiler, using the following commands and explore their usage further.

```
$ make -h
$ gcc --help
```

Size of Chars and Integers

Consider the following code snippet...

```
char  ch ;
int I ;
printf ( "%d %d", sizeof ( ch ), sizeof ( I ) ) ;
```

What will be the output of this program? In all probaility, it will be 1 and 2. However, this is not guaranteed. The size of a char and int depends on two things—the CPU architecture and the compiler. For example, the CPU may treat an int as 2 byte, but the compiler can generate instructions to work with 4-byte or 8-byte long integers. Also, for the same CPU, one compiler may report an integer to be 2 bytes long, whereas another may report it to be only of 1 byte.

Hence we as embedded system programmers should not make any assumptions about sizes of chars and integers. Instead, we should use fixed width datatypes as shown below:

```
unit8_t a ;
uint16_t b ;
```

These declarations ensure that no matter what is the default size of integer assumed by the compiler and the architecture, the variable **a** will always by 1 byte long, whereas, the variable **b** would always be 2 bytes long.

Ideal Way To Implement if-else

How you write your decision control instructions, can have a profound impact on efficiency of your program. To understand why, you must understand how modern processors execute instructions in your program. The steps in execution are as follows:

- Fetch an instruction from memory [FETCH]
- Decode the instruction to find out what it means
- Execute the operation [EXEUCTE]
- Store the result in memory [WRITEBACK]

As you can clearly see, there are 4 distinct steps in execution of any instruction. Most embedded processors execute more than one instruction simultaneously. The above steps are carried out by independent hardware components within a CPU. This makes it possible for processors to fetch next instruction from memory even before the earlier one has been executed. This is known as "prefetch". This logic works fine when your program only has sequential instructions.

However, most real world programs have control instructions as well. Among them, decision control instructions i.e. **if-else** are most common. Let us see how the way of writing an **if-else** can impact the program's performance. Consider following example:

```
if ( condition == 1 )
    i++ ;
else
    i -- ;
```

When processor is executing the **if (...)** the next instruction to be executed might be either **i++** or **i--**. How does the processor know which out these two instructions should it "prefetch"? It certainly has no choice but to make a guess. This is called as "branch prediction". This prediction may not be accurate in all cases. For wrong prediction, "prefetch" will be wasted and another instruction will have to be fetched. This wastes processing time. Can we not help the processor in this regard? Of course we can. We can do this by writing that part of the code in if block which is more likely to get executed on evaluating the condition. Let us understand this with the help of the following example.

```
/* method - 1 */
fp = fopen ( "foo.txt", "w" ) ;
if ( fp == NULL )
{
    exit ( 0 ) ;
}
else
{
    /* read the file */
    .......
}
```

The same code can also be written as shown below:

```
/* method - 2 */
fp = fopen ( "foo.txt", "w" ) ;
if ( fp != NULL )
{
    /* read the file */
    ........
}
else
{
    exit ( 0 ) ;
}
```

Here method 2 is a better way of writing the **if-else**. This is because we know that in all probability **fopen( )** will be successful and will return a non-NULL value. With this technique, we are helping processors with branch prediction. Most processors assume that **if** evaluates to "true" more often and will decide to prefetch the first instruction in **if** block. Since this will indeed be a correct decision because of the way you wrote the condition, you program will work faster.

switch Versus *if-else* Ladder

There are some things that you simply cannot do with a **switch**. These are:

(a) A float expression cannot be tested using a **switch**
(b) Cases can never have variable expressions (for example it is wrong to say **case a +3 :**)
(c) Multiple cases cannot use same expressions. Thus the following **switch** is illegal:

```
switch ( a )
```

```
{
    case 3 :
        ...
    case 1 + 2 :
        ...
}
```

(a), (b) and (c) above may lead you to believe that these are obvious disadvantages with a **switch**, especially since there weren't any such limitations with **if-else**. Then why use a **switch** at all? For speed—**switch** works faster than an equivalent **if-else** ladder. How come? This is because the compiler generates a jump table for a **switch** during compilation. As a result, during execution it simply refers the jump table to decide which case should be executed, rather than actually checking which case is satisfied. As against this, **if-elses** are slower because the conditions in them are evaluated at execution time. Thus a **switch** with 10 cases would work faster than an equivalent **if-else** ladder. If the 10th **case** is satisfied then jump table would be referred and statements for the 10th **case** would be executed. As against this, in an **if-else** ladder 10 conditions would be evaluated at execution time, which makes it slow. Note that a lookup in the jump table is faster than evaluation of a condition, especially if the condition is complex.

If on the other hand, the conditions in the **if-else** were simple and less in number then **if-else** would work out faster than the lookup mechanism of a **switch**. Hence a **switch** with two **cases** would work slower than an equivalent **if**-else. Thus, you as an embedded system programmer should take a decision which of the two should be used when.

Myths About Standard C Library

Will the following code work correctly in every Embedded System?

```
char target[ 25 ] ;
char source[ ] = "Go Embedded!" ;
strcpy ( target, source ) ;
```

This seems to be a very standard code and should really work on any system. But when it comes to an embedded system, you need to think carefully. The **strcpy( )** function is present in the libray, amongst other library functions. So when we link the library, though we may not have used other functions in the library, won't they become part of executable code? If the answer to this question is yes, then the size of the executable code will increase unnecessarily. There are many microcontroller based embedded systems which have only 32 KB memory for program storage. When the executable code is placed into such an embedded system, most of the memory may be consumed by library functions which are linked into the executable but are not being used. In such a case, it would not be prudent to use the library functions. Instead, we would be better off implementing these functions ourselves. This will reduce the size of the executable drastically, as the unnecessary functions will not get linked.

Fortunately, you do not have to get into all this. This is because the linker links only those functions from the library that are being called from your program. Thus unnecessary functions never become part of the executable code.

Safe Functions

Consider the following program:

```
/* Program 1.3 */
# include <stdio.h>
# include <string.h>
int main( )
{
    char  source[ ] = "Raindrops on roses and whiskers on kittens" ;
    char  target[ 20 ] ;
    strcpy ( target, source ) ;
    printf ( "%s\n%s", target, source ) ;
    return 0 ;
}
```

On the face of it, this code seems to be quite alright. However, on closer examination you will realize that the **target[ ]** string is not big enough to hold what is being copied into it. As a result, when we do the copying using **strcpy( )**, the source string gets overwritten. Thus the output of the program would be:

```
Raindrops on roses and whiskers on kittens
on kittens
```

Though this program works, this is dangerous as in other programs some variables that may lie in between the two strings may also get overwritten.

Thus it is not safe to copy strings using **strcpy( )**. A better function for the same is **strncpy( )**. The following program shows how to use it.

```
/* Program 1.4 */
# include <stdio.h>
# include <string.h>
int main( )
```

```
{
    char  source[ ] = "Raindrops on roses and whiskers on kittens" ;
    char  target[ 20 ] ;
    target[ 19 ] = '\0' ;
    strncpy ( target, source, sizeof ( target ) - 1 ) ;
    printf ( "%s\n%s", target, source ) ;
    return 0 ;
}
```

strncpy( ) copies a specified number of characters from source string to target string. We have specified the number of characters to copied as **sizeof (target) - 1**. This value turns out to be 19 in our case. Thus only first 19 characters will get copied into the target string. Before copying the strings we have set the last character in the **target[ ]** string to '\0'. Thus even though only part of the **source[ ]** string gets copied to the **target[ ]** string, it is still properly terminated by a '\0'.

What would be the effect if the source string is smaller than the size of the target string? In this case **strncpy( )** stores a '\0' at the end of the target string after copying is over. As you can appreciate, this is a completely safe approach to deal with the strings.

Copying Other data types

String copying is done using the string library functions like **strcpy( )** or **strncpy( )**. What if we wish to copy an array of integers or an array of structures? Well, in such situations we can use the function **memcpy( )**. This is shown in the following program.

```
/* Program 1.5 */
# include <stdio.h>
# include <stdlib.h>
```

```
struct sample
{
    int i ;
    float a ;
};
int main( )
{
    struct sample source[ ] = {
                                { 15, 3.14 },
                                { 20, 6.28 },
                                { 25, 3.55 }
                              } ;
    struct sample target[ 3 ] ;
    int j ;

    memcpy ( target, source, sizeof ( source ) ) ;
    for ( j = 0 ; j <= 2 ; j++ )
        printf ( "\n%d %f", target[ j ].i, target[ j ].a ) ;
    return 0 ;
}
```

The **memcpy( )** function copies the bytes specified in the third argument from the source address in memory to the target address. Thus **memcpy( )** can be used to copy data types other than strings from one variable to another.

Inline Functions

One of the important advantages of using functions is that they help us save memory space. As all the calls to the function cause the same code to be executed; the function body need not be duplicated in memory.

Imagine a situation where a small function is getting called several times in a program. As you must be aware, there are certain overheads involved while calling a function. Time has to be spent in passing values, passing control, returning value and returning control. In such situations to save the execution time you may instruct the C compiler to put the code present in the function body directly at the place where the function is being called. That is, at each place where there's a function call in the source file, the actual code from the function would be inserted, instead of a jump to the function. Such functions are called **inline** functions. The in-line nature of the individual copy of the function eliminates the function-calling overhead of a traditional function. The following program shows **inline** function at work.

```
#include <stdio.h>
inline void reporterror ( char *str )
{
    printf ( "\n%s", str ) ;
    exit ( 1 ) ;
}
void main ( )
{
    // code to open source file
    if ( fileopeningfailed )
        reporterror ( "Unable to open source file" ) ;

    // code to open target file
    if ( fileopeningfailed )
        reporterror ( "Unable to open target file" ) ;

    // code to copy contents of source file into target file
}
```

Note that, the function must be declared to be **inline** before calling it. On compilation, the contents of the **reporterror( )** function would get inserted at two places within our program.

These obviously are the places where **reporterror( )** is being called.

One question that should occur to you is why ask the compiler to insert the code of the function in line with the other program code when we can easily do so ourselves? The trouble with repeatedly inserting the same code is, that you lose the benefits of program organization and clarity that come with using functions. The program may run faster and take less space, but the program listing becomes longer and more complex. Instead, if we write the code in an **inline** function the source file remains well organized and easy to read, since the function is shown as a separate entity. However, when the program is compiled, the function body is actually inserted into the program wherever a function call occurs.

You should use the **inline** function qualifier only when the function code is small. If the functions are large, you should prefer the normal functions since the savings in memory space is worth the comparatively small sacrifice in execution speed.

Note that, when we define the function **inline** there is no guarantee that its code would get inserted at the place where the call is being made. This is because we are just making a request to the compiler. The C language does not define under what conditions the compiler may choose to ignore our request. Because of this ambiguity in the language specification, compiler builders have flexibility in how they interpret the requirements.

Inline functions are similar to **#define** macros. However, they provide better type checking and do not have the side effects typically associated with macros. For example consider the following program:

```
/* Program 1.6 */
# define SQUARE( x ) x * x
inline float square ( float y )
{
    return y * y ;
}
int main ( )
{
    float a = 0.5, b = 0.5, c, d ;
    c = SQUARE ( ++a ) ;
    d = square ( ++b ) ;
    return 0 ;
}
```

During preprocessing the macro SQUARE gets expanded into

```
c = ++x * ++x ;
```

You can notice the undesirable side effect in this macro expansion: the variable is getting incremented twice even though we have used the incrementation operator only once. Such side effects would not occur in the **inline** function.

Static Variables and Functions

All variables that are defined inside a function are normally created on the stack each time the function is called. These variables die as soon as control goes back from the function. However, if the variables inside the function are defined as **static** then they *do not* get created on the stack. Instead they are created in a place in memory called 'Data Segment'. Such variables die only when program execution comes to an end.

A **static** variable can also be declared outside all the functions. For all practical purposes, it will be treated as an **extern** variable. However, the scope of this variable is limited to the same file in which it is declared. This means that the variable would not be available to any function that is defined in a file other than the file in which the variable is defined. Similarly, if a function is declared as **static** then the function too will be available only within the file in which it is defined.

If a variable is defined outside all functions, then not only is it available to all other functions in the file in which it is defined, but is also available to functions defined in other files. In the other files the variable should be declared as **extern**. This is shown in the following program:

```
/* Program 1.7 */
# include <stdio.h>
# include "functions.c"

int i = 35 ;
int fun1( ) ;
int fun2( ) ;

int main( )
{
    printf ( "%d", i ) ;
    fun1( ) ;
    fun2( ) ;
    return 0 ;
}

/* functions.c */
extern int i ;
int fun1( )
{
    i++ ;
    printf ( "\n%d", i ) ;
    return 0 ;
}
```

```
int fun2( )
{
    i-- ;
    printf ( "\n%d", i ) ;
    return 0 ;
}
```

The output of the program would be

```
35
36
35
```

If we place the keyword **static** in front of an external variable (**i** in our case), it makes the variable private and not accessible for use in any other file.

Macros versus Functions

Consider the following program...

```
/* Program 1.8 */
# include <stdio.h>
# define AREA(x) ( 3.14 * x * x )

int main( )
{
    float r1 = 6.25, r2 = 2.5, a ;

    a = AREA ( r1 ) ;
    printf ( "\nArea of circle = %f", a ) ;
    a = AREA ( r2 ) ;
    printf ( "\nArea of circle = %f", a ) ;
    return 0 ;
```

```
}
```

Here's the output of the program...

```
Area of circle = 122.656250
Area of circle = 19.625000
```

In this program, wherever the preprocessor finds the phrase **AREA(x)**, it expands it into the statement **(3.14 * x * x)**. However, that's not all that it does. The **x** in the macro template **AREA(x)** is an argument that matches the **x** in the macro expansion **(3.14 * x * x)**. The statement **AREA(r1)** in the program causes the variable **r1** to be substituted for **x**. Thus the statement **AREA(r1)** is equivalent to:

```
( 3.14 * r1 * r1 )
```

After the above source code has passed through the preprocessor, what the compiler gets to work on will be this:

```
# include <stdio.h>
int main( )
{
     float  r1 = 6.25, r2 = 2.5, a ;

     a = 3.14 * r1 *r1 ;
     printf ( "Area of circle = %f\n", a ) ;
     a = 3.14 *r2 * r2 ;
     printf ( "Area of circle = %f", a ) ;
     return 0 ;
}
```

In the above example, a macro was used to calculate the area of the circle. You will agree that even a function can be written to calculate the area of the circle. Though macro calls are 'like' function calls, they are not really the same things. Then what is the difference between the two?

In a macro call, the preprocessor replaces the macro template with its macro expansion, in a stupid, unthinking, literal way. As against this, in a function call the control is passed to a function along with certain arguments, some calculations are performed in the function, and a useful value is returned back from the function.

This brings us to a question: when is it best to use macros with arguments and when is it better to use a function? Usually macros make the program run faster but increase the program size, whereas functions make the program smaller and compact.

If we use a macro hundred times in a program, the macro expansion goes into our source code at hundred different places, thus increasing the program size. On the other hand, if a function is used, then even if it is called from hundred different places in the program, it would take the same amount of space in the program.

But passing arguments to a function and getting back the returned value does take time and would therefore slow down the program. This gets avoided with macros since they have already been expanded and placed in the source code before compilation. Thus the trade-off is between memory space and time.

Moral of the story is—if the macro is simple and sweet, it makes nice shorthand and avoids the overheads associated with function calls. On the other hand, if we have a fairly large macro and it is used fairly often, perhaps we ought to replace it with a function.

If memory space in the machine in which the program is being executed is less (like a mobile phone or a PDA), then it may make sense to use functions instead of macros. By doing so, the program may run slower, but will need less memory space.

Bounds Of An Array

Consider the following program which finds average of all numbers present in the array **arr**.

```
/* Program 1.9 */
# include <stdio.h>
void main( )
{
    int arr[ ] = { 12, 3, 4, 5, 23, 11, 10, 15, -24, 23 } ;
    int i, sum = 0 ;

    for ( i = 0 ; i <= 9 ; i++ )
        sum = sum + arr[ i ] ;

    printf ( "Sum = %d", sum ) ;
}
```

This program seems to be correct at first glance. However, on closer look you will realize that the program has been hard-coded to work only with an array of 10 elements. Tomorrow if the array size changes, then the **for** loop will have to be appropriately modified to deal with the modified array size.

This can be avoided in two ways. These are shown below:

```
/* method – 1 */
#define MAX 9
for ( i = 0 ; i <= 9 ; i++ )
    sum = sum + arr[ i ] ;

/* method – 2 */
for ( i = 0 ; i <= sizeof ( arr ) / sizeof ( arr[ 0 ] ) ; i++ )
    sum = sum + arr[ i ] ;
```

In method 1 if the size of the array changes then the **MAX** macro should be changed to reflect the new size. Method two is better, since now the change in array size doesn't call for change in the **for** loop.

The *volatile* Keyword

When a C program is compiled to generate machine language instructions, a compiler might do optimizations to make the program execute as fast as possible. One of these optimizations involves postponing writing of a variable to its memory location. Consider following code snippet:

```
int i, s = 0 ;
for ( i = 0 ; i <= 10 ; i++ )
    sum = sum + i ;
printf ( "%d", s ) ;
```

When this program is compiled, compiler may optimize variables i and sum. It knows that **i** and **sum** are required during each iteration of the loop. It loads them from memory only once - i.e. for the first iteration. Afterwards, it simply keeps their current values in internal registers. Only when the loop terminates, it will write these values back to their locations in memory. This is definitely faster than accessing memory to load these variables during each iteration. There are many cases in embedded systems programming which require that variables get loaded from memory and stored into memory immediately after an operation. To ensure this, C language provides a keyword **volatile**. Using **volatile**, among other things ensure that **load**, **use**, **store** sequence is followed for that variable every single time, and compiler optimization is disabled. Following snippet shows the changed code:

```
volatile int i, s = 0 ;
for ( i = 0 ; i <= 10 ; i++ )
    sum = sum + i ;
printf ( "%d", s ) ;
```

Attribute-based Programming

While doing serious C programming, at times we come across requirements which cannot be fulfilled using the ANSI C. For example, ANSI C standard had no provision to specify that a variable be stored in any place other than RAM. Similarly, ANSI C standard has no provision for specifying the function that you may want to execute before **main( )**, or after returning from **main( )**. If we wish to do any of these jobs, we have to rely on extensions provided by the compiler to achieve this. Note right away that these extensions are completely compiler specific. Hence what works with one compiler may not work with another.

Let us now see how we can execute a function before **main( )** and after **main( )**. Here is the program that demonstrates this.

```
/* Program 1.10 */
#include <stdio.h>

int i = 0 ;

void init ( ) __attribute__ ( ( constructor ) ) ;
void deinit ( ) __attribute__ ( ( destructor ) ) ;

void init( )
{
    i = 10 ;
    printf ( "init: i = %d\n" , i ) ;
}
```

```
void deinit( )
{
    i = 0 ;
    printf ( "deinit: i = %d\n" , i ) ;
}

int main( )
{
    i = i * 2 ;
    printf ( "main i = %d\n", i ) ;
    return 0 ;
}
```

The output of the program will be as follows:

```
init: i = 10
main i = 20
deinit: i = 0
```

From this output, it is clear that the function **init( )** got called before **main( )**, whereas the function **deinit( )** got called after **main( )**. To achieve this all that we had to was mark these functions as *constructor* and *destructor* respectively. This was done in the declarations as shown below:

```
void init ( ) __attribute__ ( ( constructor ) ) ;
void deinit ( ) __attribute__ ( ( destructor ) ) ;
```

Here **__attribute__** is an identifier that is used to specify special attributes to a function. Here we have used it do declare a function as constructor or destructor. As their names suggest, the constructor is typically used to do initialization, whereas the destructor is used to perform the cleanup. Note that the attribute has to be applied only in the declaration of the function, not in its definition. Also, the two pairs of parentheses after **__attribute__** are compulsory.

Packing & Aligning Structures

Consider the following program...

```
/* Program 1.11 */
#include <stdio.h>
int main( )
{
    struct data
    {
        int a ;
        char ch ;
        float s ;
    } ;
    struct data e ;
    printf ( "\n%u %u %u", &e.a, &e.ch, &e.s ) ;
    printf ( "\n%d", sizeof ( e ) ) ;
    return 0 ;
}
```

If we execute this program using gcc compiler, we get the output as:

```
2280656 2280660 2280664
12
```

It can be observed from this output that the **float** doesn't get stored immediately after the **char**. In fact there is a hole of three bytes after the **char**. Let us understand the reason for this. gcc is a 32-bit compiler targeted to generate code for a 32-bit microprocessors. The architecture of this microprocessor is such that it is able to fetch the data that is present at an address, which is a multiple of four much faster than the data present at any other address. Hence the gcc compiler aligns every element of a structure at an address that is multiple of four. That's the reason why there were three holes created between the **char** and the **float**.

However, some programs need to exercise precise control over the memory areas where data is placed. For example, suppose we wish to write an **int** which is part of a structure to flash memory. Flash memory is a type of persistent memory used extensively in today's embedded systems. If the **int** is of one byte, then a hole of three bytes would be created if the structure elements are aligned on a 4-byte boundary. This would lead to wastage of memory.

This wastage can be avoided by using the attribute called **packed**. The following code snippet shows how to use this directive.

```
/* Program 1.12 */
#include <stdio.h>
int main( )
{
    struct data
    {
        int a ;
        char ch ;
        float s ;
    } __attribute__( ( packed ) ) ;
    struct data e ;
    printf ( "\n%u %u %u", &e.a, &e.ch, &e.s ) ;
    printf ( "\n%d", sizeof ( e ) ) ;
    return 0 ;
}
```

The **packed** attribute specifies that a structure field should have the smallest possible alignment, i.e. one byte. Hence each structure element begins on a 1-byte boundary as justified by the output of the program given below:

```
2280656 2280660 2280661
9
```

Instead of packing structure elements, if we want we can align them at specific byte boundaries using the **aligned** attribute as shown in the following program.

```
/* Program 1.13 */
#include <stdio.h>
int main( )
{
    struct data
    {
        int a       __attribute__( ( aligned ( 8 ) ) ) ;
        char ch  __attribute__( ( aligned ( 1 ) ) ) ;
        float s     __attribute__( ( aligned ( 4 ) ) ) ;
    } ;
    struct data e ;
    printf ( "\n%u %u %u", &e.a, &e.ch, &e.s ) ;
    printf ( "\n%d", sizeof ( e ) ) ;
    return 0 ;
}
```

The **aligned** attribute specifies minimum alignment for a structure field. The number of bytes is specified as its argument. Here is the output of the program...

```
2280624 2280640 2280656
16
```

Exercise

[A] Pick up the correct alternative for each of the following questions:

[1] Which of the following utility is used for compiling and linking the program?

(a) make
(b) makefile
(c) compiler
(d) linker

[2] Which of the following command is used to get help on the make file and gcc compiler?

(a) $ make -h
$ gcc --help

(b) $ make
$ gcc

(c) # -h make
-help gcc

(d) # make
gcc

[3] What do the following declarations indicate?

```
uint8_t a ;
unit16_t b ;
```

(a) The variable a is always 1 byte long, whereas, the variable b is always 2 bytes long.

(b) The variable a is always 8 bytes long, whereas, the variable b is always 16 bytes long.

(c) The variable a is always 4 byte long, whereas, the variable b is always 8 bytes long.

(d) The variable a is always 2 byte long, whereas, the variable b is always 4 bytes long.

[4] Which of the following things cannot be done with a **switch**?

(i) A float expression cannot be tested using a switch
(ii) Cases can never have variable expressions
(iii) Multiple cases cannot use same expressions

(a) Only (i) and (ii)
(b) Only (i) and (iii)
(c) Only (ii) and (iii)
(d) (i), (ii) and (iii)

[5] Which of the following function copies a specified number of characters from source string to the target string?

(a) strncpy( )
(b) copy( )
(c) strcopy( )
(d) copystring( )

[6] Which of the following function is used to copy data types other than strings from one variable to another?

(a) memcpy( )
(b) strcpy( )
(c) objcpy( )
(d) datacpy( )

[7] Which of the following statement is correct about all the variables defined inside a function that are not static?

i. They are normally created in the Data Segment each time the function is called.
ii. These variables die as soon as control goes back from the function.

(a) Only i is correct.
(b) Only ii is correct.
(c) Both i and ii are correct.
(d) Both i and ii are incorrect.

[8] Which of the following is the correct sequence of execution of the functions **main( )**, **init( )** and **deinit( )** if the function **init( )** is marked as constructor and **deinit( )** is marked as destructor?

(a) init( ), main( ) and deinit( )
(b) main( ), init( ) and deinit( )
(c) main( ), deinit( ) and init( )
(d) init( ), deinit( ) and main( )

[9] Which of the following is the correct declaration of functions **init( )** and **deinit( )**?

(a) void init( ) __attribute__((constructor)) ;
void deinit( ) __attribute__((destructor)) ;

(b) void init( ) __attribute__(constructor) ;
void deinit( ) __attribute__(destructor) ;

(c) void init( ) ((constructor)) ;
void deinit( ) ((destructor)) ;

(d) void init( ) (constructor) ;
void deinit( ) (destructor) ;

[10] Which of the following attribute specifies that the structure field should have the smallest possible alignment?

(a) packed
(b) alignment
(c) packattr
(d) alignattr

[11] C Compiler converts the expanded source code into which of the following forms?

(a) Relocatable Object code
(b) Executable code
(c) Assembly code
(d) Source code

[B] Answer the following:

(a) Write a simple program to convert a string of number to a corresponding unsigned long integer. Its prototype will be as follow:

```
unsigned int mystrtoul ( const char *str )
```

(b) Write a "logging" function that takes number indicating "logging level" as input and variable number of arguments starting with a "format" string (like **printf**( )). This function should be exactly like **printf( )**, however it should print the argument only if "level" is less than a LOG_LEVEL

```
#define LOG_LEVEL 4
int mylog ( int level, const char *str, ... )
```

(c) Write a **memmove( )** function that moves specified number of bytes from source to destination. You should handle the scenario where source and destination addresses contain "overlapping addresses".

```
int mymemmove ( void *dst, const void *src, int nbytes )
```

(d) Explain with example the 3 most important advantages of using arrays. Explain possible disadvantages of using array in Embedded Systems programming.

(e) How are arrays passed as function parameters? How is passing arrays different than passing other types of variables?

(f) What is make? What happens when you type make in cygwin shell window? Why do we use it for development of C programs?

(g) Locate stdio.h on your system. Inside each system header file you will find #ifndef __XXX_ .... #endif. What is the purpose of that?

(h) Locate stdio.h on your system. Inside each system header file you will find #ifndef __XXX_ .... #endif. What is its purpose?

(i) Create a new project using newproject command. Which files are created as a result of this and what are their purposes?

(j) Why does one need to create new datatypes in C? Why built-in data types are not enough?

(k) What is the purpose of aligning fields/members of a structure? Will different compilers like Turbo C++, Microsoft Visual C and GNU C compiler handle alignment issues differently? Can you control how member variables are aligned - explain in detail.

(l) Strings and arrays are not very different in C. Then why are strings treated differently than normal arrays?

(m) What is the purpose of the volatile keyword?

2 Operations On Bits

While building embedded systems we are frequently required to deal with individual bits of a byte. So far we haven't attempted to access or manipulate individual bits of a byte. Being able to operate on a bit level will help you immensely because hardware tends to be bit oriented. Let us now delve inside the byte and see how it is constructed and how it can be manipulated effectively. So let us take apart the byte... bit by bit.

Bitwise Operators

One of C's powerful features is a set of bit manipulation operators. These permit the programmer to access and manipulate individual bits within a piece of data. The various Bitwise Operators available in C are shown in Figure 2.1.

Operator	Meaning
~	One's complement
>>	Right shift
<<	Left shift
&	Bitwise AND
|	Bitwise OR
^	Bitwise XOR(Exclusive OR)

Figure 2.1: Bitwise Operators

These operators can operate upon **int**s and **char**s but not on **float**s and **double**s. Before moving on to the details of the operators, let us first take a look at the bit numbering scheme in integers and characters. Bits are numbered from zero onwards, increasing from right to left as shown below:

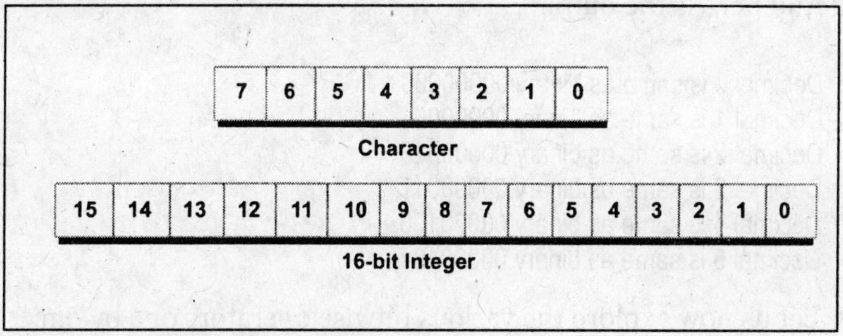

Figure 2.2: Bit numbering

Throughout this discussion of bitwise operators, we are going to use a function called **showbits( )**, but we are not going to show you the details of the function immediately. The task of **showbits( )** is to display the binary representation of any integer or character value.

We begin with a plain-jane example with **showbits( )** in action.

```
/* Program 2.1 */
/* Print binary equivalent of integers using showbits( ) function */
# include <stdio.h>
void showbits ( unsigned char ) ;
int main( )
{
    unsigned char  j ;

    for ( j = 0 ; j <= 5 ; j++ )
    {
        printf ( "\nDecimal %d is same as binary ", j ) ;
        showbits ( j ) ;
    }
```

```
    return 0 ;
}
```

And here is the output...

```
Decimal 0 is same as binary 00000000
Decimal 1 is same as binary 00000001
Decimal 2 is same as binary 00000010
Decimal 3 is same as binary 00000011
Decimal 4 is same as binary 00000100
Decimal 5 is same as binary 00000101
```

Let us now explore the various bitwise operators one by one.

One's Complement Operator

On taking one's complement of a number, all 1's present in the number are changed to 0's and all 0's are changed to 1's. For example, one's complement of 1010 is 0101. Similarly, one's complement of 1111 is 0000. Note that, here when we talk of a number, we are talking of binary equivalent of the number. Thus, one's complement of 65 means one's complement of 0100 0001, which is binary equivalent of 65. One's complement of 65 therefore would be 1011 1110. One's complement operator is represented by the symbol ~ (tilde). Following program shows one's complement operator in action.

```
/* Program 2.2 */
# include <stdio.h>
int main( )
{
    unsigned char j, k ;

    for ( j = 0 ; j <= 3 ; j++ )
    {
        printf ( "\nDecimal %d is same as binary ", j ) ;
```

```
        showbits ( j ) ;

        k = ~j ;
        printf ( "\nOne's complement of %d is ", j ) ;
        showbits ( k ) ;
    }
    return 0 ;
}
```

And here is the output of the above program...

```
Decimal 0 is same as binary 00000000
One's complement of 0 is 11111111
Decimal 1 is same as binary 00000001
One's complement of 1 is 11111110
Decimal 2 is same as binary 00000010
One's complement of 2 is 11111101
Decimal 3 is same as binary 00000011
One's complement of 3 is 11111100
```

Right Shift Operator

The right shift operator is represented by >>. It needs two operands. It shifts each bit in its left operand to the right. The number of places the bits are shifted depends on the number following the operator (i.e. its right operand).

Thus, **ch >> 3** would shift all bits in **ch** three places to the right. Similarly, **ch >> 5** would shift all bits 5 places to the right.

For example, if the variable **ch** contains the bit pattern 11010111, then, **ch >> 1** would give 01101011 and **ch >> 2** would give 00110101.

Note that as the bits are shifted to the right, blanks are created on the left. These blanks must be filled somehow. They are always filled with zeros. The following program demonstrates the effect of right shift operator.

```
/* Program 2.3 */
# include <stdio.h>
void showbits ( unsigned char ) ;
int main( )
{
    unsigned char i = 225, j, k ;

    printf ( "\nDecimal %d is same as binary ", i ) ;
    showbits ( i ) ;

    for ( j = 0 ; j <= 5 ; j++ )
    {
        k = i >> j ;
        printf ( "\n%d right shift %d gives ", i, j ) ;
        showbits ( k ) ;
    }
    return 0 ;
}
```

The output of the above program would be...

```
Decimal 225 is same as binary 11100001
5225 right shift 0 gives 11100001
5225 right shift 1 gives 01110000
5225 right shift 2 gives 00111000
5225 right shift 3 gives 00011100
5225 right shift 4 gives 00001110
5225 right shift 5 gives 00000111
```

Note that if the operand is a multiple of 2, then shifting the operand one bit to right is same as dividing it by 2 and ignoring the remainder. Thus,

```
64 >> 1 gives 32
```

64 >> 2 gives 16
128 >> 2 gives 32

but,

27 >> 1 is 13
49 >> 1 is 24 .

A Word of Caution

In the expression **a** >> **b** if **b** is negative the result is unpredictable. If **a** is negative then its left most bit (sign bit) would be 1. On right shifting **a** it would result in extending the sign bit. For example, if **a** contains -1, its binary representation would be 11111111. If we right shift it by 4 then the result would still be 11111111. Similarly, if **a** contains -5, then its binary equivalent would be 11111011. On right shifting it by 1 we would get 11111101, which is equal to -3. Thus on right shifting 11111011 the right-most bit, i.e. 1, would be lost; other bits would be shifted one position to the right and the sign which was negative (1) will be extend, i.e. it would be preserved as 1. The following program, would help you get a clear picture of this.

```
/* Program 2.4 */
# include <stdio.h>
void showbits ( unsigned char ) ;
int main( )
{
    char i = -5, j, k ;

    printf ( "\nDecimal %d is same as binary ", i ) ;
    showbits ( i ) ;

    for ( j = 1 ; j <= 3  ; j++ )
    {
```

```
        k = i >> j ;
        printf ( "\n%d right shift %d gives ", i, j ) ;
        showbits ( k ) ;
    }
    return 0 ;
}
```

The output of the above program would be...

```
Decimal -5 is same as binary 11111011
-5 right shift 1 gives 11111101
-5 right shift 2 gives 11111110
-5 right shift 3 gives 11111111
```

Left Shift Operator

This is similar to the right shift operator, the only difference being that the bits are shifted to the left, and for each bit shifted, a 0 is added to the right of the number. The following program should clarify my point.

```
/* Program 2.5 */
# include <stdio.h>
void showbits ( unsigned char ) ;
int main( )
{
    unsigned char  i = 225, j, k ;

    printf ( "\nDecimal %d is same as binary ", i ) ;
    showbits ( i ) ;

    for ( j = 0 ; j <= 4 ; j++ )
    {
        k = i << j ;
        printf ( "\n%d left shift %d gives ", i, j ) ;
        showbits ( k ) ;
```

```
    }
    return 0 ;
}
```

The output of the above program would be...

```
Decimal 225 is same as binary 11100001
225 left shift 0 gives 11100001
225 left shift 1 gives 11000010
225 left shift 2 gives 10000100
225 left shift 3 gives 00001000
```

Bitwise AND Operator

This operator is represented as **&**. Remember it is different than **&&**, the logical AND operator. The **&** operator operates on two operands. While operating upon these two operands they are compared on a bit-by-bit basis. Hence both the operands must be of the same type (either **char** or **int**). The second operand is often called an AND mask. The **&** operator operates on a pair of bits to yield a resultant bit. The rules that decide the value of the resultant bit are shown below:

First bit	Second bit	First bit & Second bit
0	0	0
0	1	0
1	0	0
1	1	1

Figure 2.3: Bitwise And operation

This can be represented in a more understandable form as a 'Truth Table' shown in Figure 2.4.

&	0	1
0	0	0
1	0	1

Figure 2.4: Truth table of & operator

The example given below shows more clearly what happens while ANDing one operand with another. The rules given in the Figure 2.5 are applied to each pair of bits one by one.

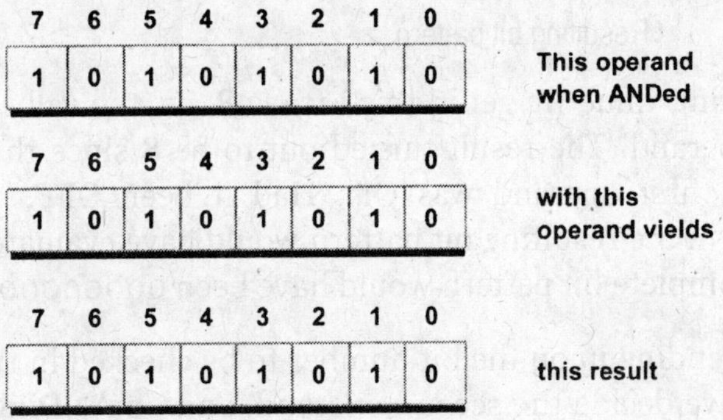

Figure 2.5: Example of & operation

Work through the Truth Table and confirm that the result obtained is really correct.

Thus, it must be clear that the operation is being performed on individual bits, and the operation performed on one pair of bits is completely independent of the operation performed on the other pairs.

Probably, the best use of the AND operator is to check whether a particular bit of an operand is ON or OFF. This is explained in the following example.

Suppose, from the bit pattern 10101101 of an operand, we want to check whether bit number 3 is ON (1) or OFF (0). Since we want to check the bit number 3, the second operand for the AND operation should be 1 * 2^3, which is equal to 8. This operand can be represented bitwise as 00001000.

Then the ANDing operation would be,

```
10101101        Original bit pattern
```

```
00001000        AND mask
--------------
00001000        Resulting bit pattern
```

The resulting value we get in this case is 8, i.e. the value of the second operand. The result turned out to be 8 since the third bit of the first operand was ON. Had it been OFF, the bit number 3 in the resulting bit pattern would have evaluated to 0 and the complete bit pattern would have been 00000000.

Thus, depending upon the bit number to be checked in the first operand, we decide the second operand, and on ANDing these two operands the result decides whether the bit was ON or OFF. If the bit is ON (1), the resulting value turns out to be a non-zero value, which is equal to the value of second operand. If the bit is OFF (0), the result is zero, as seen above. The following program puts this logic into action.

```
/* Program 2.6 */
/* To test whether a bit in a number is ON or OFF */
# include <stdio.h>
void main( )
{
    int i = 65, j ;

    printf ( "\nvalue of i = %d", i ) ;
    j = i & 32 ;

    if ( j == 0 )
        printf ( "\nand its fifth bit is off" ) ;
    else
        printf ( "\nand its fifth bit is on" ) ;

    j = i & 64 ;

    if ( j == 0 )
        printf ( "\nwhereas its sixth bit is off" ) ;
```

```
    else
        printf ( "\nwhereas its sixth bit is on" ) ;
}
```

And here is the output...

```
Value of i = 65
and its fifth bit is off
whereas its sixth bit is on
```

Let's now summarize the uses of bitwise AND operator:

It is used to check whether a particular bit in a number is ON or OFF.

It is used to turn OFF a particular bit in a number.

Bitwise OR Operator

Another important bitwise operator is the OR operator which is represented as |. The rules that govern the value of the resulting bit obtained after ORing of two bits is shown in the truth table below.

|	0	1
0	0	1
1	1	1

Figure 2.6: Truth table of | operator

Using the Truth table confirm the result obtained on ORing the two operands as shown below.

```
11010000    Original bit pattern
00000111    OR mask
-------------
11010111    Resulting bit pattern
```

Bitwise OR operator is usually used to put ON a particular bit in a number.

Let us consider the bit pattern 11000011. If we want to put ON bit number 3, then the OR mask to be used would be 00001000. Note that all the other bits in the mask are set to 0 and only the bit, which we want to set ON in the resulting value is set to 1.

Bitwise XOR Operator

The XOR operator is represented as ^ and is also called an Exclusive OR Operator. The OR operator returns 1, when any one of the two bits or both the bits are 1, whereas XOR returns 1 only if one of the two bits is 1. The truth table for the XOR operator is given below.

^	0	1
0	0	1
1	1	0

Figure 2.7: Truth table of ^ operator

XOR operator is used to toggle a bit ON or OFF. A number XORed with another number twice gives the original number. This is shown in the following program.

```
/* Program 2.7 */
# include <stdio.h>
void main( )
{
    int b = 50 ;

    b = b ^ 12 ;
    printf ( "\n%d", b ) ; /* this will print 62 */

    b = b ^ 12 ;
    printf ( "\n%d", b ) ; /* this will print 50 */
}
```

The *showbits( )* Function

We have used this function quite often in this chapter. Now we have sufficient knowledge of bitwise operators and hence are in a position to understand it. The function is given below followed by a brief explanation.

```
void showbits ( unsigned char n )
{
    unsigned char i, k, andmask ;

    for ( i = 7 ; i >= 0 ; i-- )
    {
        andmask = 1 << i ;
        k = n & andmask ;

        k == 0 ? printf ( "0" ) : printf ( "1" ) ;
    }
}
```

All that is being done in this function is, using an AND operator and a variable **andmask**, we are checking the status of individual bits. If the bit is OFF we print a 0, otherwise we print a 1.

First time through the loop, the variable **andmask** will contain the value 1000000000000000, which is obtained by left-shifting 1, fifteen places. If the variable **n**'s most significant bit is 0, then **k** would contain a value 0, otherwise it would contain a non-zero value. If **k** contains 0, then **printf( )** will print out 0, otherwise it will print out 1.

On the second go-around of the loop, the value of **i** is decremented and hence the value of **andmask** changes, which will now be 0100000000000000. This checks whether the next most significant bit is 1 or 0, and prints it out accordingly. The same operation is repeated for all bits in the number.

While working with embedded systems we are often required to use hexadecimal numbers. The reason for this is—everything a embedded system does is based on binary numbers, and hexadecimal notation is a convenient way of expressing binary numbers. Before justifying this statement let us first discuss what numbering systems are, why computers use binary numbering system, how binary and hexadecimal numbering systems are related and how to use hexadecimal numbering system in everyday life.

Hexadecimal Numbering System

When we talk about different numbering systems we are really talking about the base of the numbering system. For example, binary numbering system has base 2 and hexadecimal numbering system has base 16, just the way decimal numbering system has base 10. The base represents number of digits you can use before you run out of digits. For example, in decimal numbering system, when we have used digits from 0 to 9, we run out of digits. That's the time we put a 1 in the column to the left–the ten's column–and again start constructing numbers. This results into numbers from 10 to 99. Once we reach 99, we again run out of digits. That's when we go one column to the left–the hundred's column–and again start constructing numbers like 100, 101, 102, ..., etc. up to 999.f

Since decimal numbering system is a base 10 numbering system any number in it is constructed using some combination of digits 0 to 9. This seems perfectly natural. However, the choice of 10 as a base is quite arbitrary, having its origin possibly in the fact that man has 10 fingers. It is very easy to use other bases as well. For example, if we wanted to use base 8 or octal numbering system, which uses only eight digits (0 to 7), here's how the counting would look like:

0, 1, 2, 3, 4, 5, 6, 7, 10, 11, 12, .., .., 77, 100, 101, 102, .., .., 777, 1000, ..

Similarly, a hexadecimal numbering system has a base 16. In hex notation, the ten digits 0 through 9 are used to represent the values zero through nine, and the remaining six values, ten through fifteen, are represented by symbols A to F. The hex digits A to F are usually written in capitals, but lowercase letters are also perfectly acceptable. Here is how the counting in hex would look like:

0, 1, 2, 3, 4, 5, 6, 7, 8, 9, A, B, C, D, E, F, 10, 11, 12, .., .., FF, 100, .., .., FFF

The hex numbers are built out of hex digits in much the same way the decimal numbers are built out of decimal digits. For example, when we write the decimal number 342, we mean,

```
  3 times 100 (square of 10)
+ 4 times 10
+ 2 times 1
```

Similarly, if we use number 342 as a hex number, we mean,

3 times 256 (square of 16)
+ 4 times 16
+ 2 times 1

Relation between Binary and Hex

In binary numbering system, there are only two digits 0 and 1. Here is how the counting in binary would look like:

0, 1, 10, 11, 100, 101, 110, 111, 1000, 1001, 1010, .., .., 1111, 10000, ..

Binary numbering system is a natural system for computers because each of the thousands of electronic circuits in the computer can be in one of the two states—on or off. Thus, binary numbering system corresponds nicely with the circuits in the computer—0 means off, and 1 means on. 0 and 1 are called bits, a short-form of binary digits.

Hex numbers are used primarily as shorthand for binary numbers that the computers work with. Every hex digit represents four bits of binary information as shown in Figure 2. 8.

Hex	Binary	Hex	Binary
0	0000	8	1000
1	0001	9	1001
2	0010	A	1010
3	0011	B	1011
4	0100	C	1100
5	0101	D	1101
6	0110	E	1110
7	0111	F	1111

Figure 2.8: Hexadecimal Digits and their Binary equivalents

In binary numbering system 4 bits taken at a time can give rise to sixteen different numbers, so the only way to represent each of these sixteen 4-bit binary numbers in a simple and short way is to use a base sixteen numbering system.

Suppose we want to represent a binary number 11000101 in a short way. One way is to find it decimal equivalent by multiplying each binary digit with an appropriate power of 2 as shown below:

$$1 * 2^7 + 1 * 2^6 + 0 * 2^5 + 0 * 2^4 + 0 * 2^3 + 1 * 2^2 + 0 * 2^1 + 1 * 2^0$$

which is equal to 197.

Another method is much simpler. Just look at Figure 2.8. From it, find out the hex digits for the two four-bit sets (1100 and 0101). These happen to be C and 5. Therefore, the binary number's hex equivalent is C5. You would agree this is an easier way to represent the binary number than to find its decimal equivalent. In this method neither multiplication nor addition is needed. In fact, since there are only 16 hex digits, it's fairly easy to memorize the binary equivalent of each one. Quick now, what's binary 1100 in hex? That's right C. You are already getting the feel of it. With a little practice it is easy to translate even long numbers into hex. Thus, 1100 0101 0011 1010 binary is C53A hex.

As it happens with many unfamiliar subjects, learning hexadecimal requires a little practice. Try your hand at converting some binary numbers and vice versa. Soon you will be talking hexadecimal as if you had known it all your life.

More Complex Bitwise Operations

In embedded systems programming you are often required to work with bits of registers (internal memory of microprocessor). Instead of every time using bitwise operators to do so the preferred way is to #define macros that would do the same job. This makes it easy to write, understand and maintain the program. For example, we can define a macro that sets a bit in a byte to a value 1. Likewise, another macro can be defined to clear a bit (i.e. set its value to 0). The following program demonstrates how to define some of the commonly required macros and how to use them in a program.

```
# define CHARSIZE 8
# define MASK( y ) ( 1 << y % CHARSIZE )
# define BITSLOT( y ) ( y / CHARSIZE )
# define SET( x, y ) ( x[ BITSLOT( y ) ] |= MASK( y ) )
# define TEST( x, y ) ( x[ BITSLOT( y ) ] & MASK ( y ) )
# define NUMSLOTS( n ) ( ( n + CHARSIZE – 1 ) / CHARSIZE )
```

Given the above macros suppose we wish to:

declare an array *arr* of 50 bits
put the 20th bit on
test whether the 40th bit is on or off

This can be achieved as follows:

```
char arr[ NUMSLOTS( 50 ) ] ;
SET ( arr, 20 ) ;
if ( TEST ( arr, 40 ) )
```

Note that the |= operator is a bitwise compound assignment operator. It offers a shortcut for carrying out the bitwise operation and then assigning the result. Thus the following two operations are same:

```
a = a | 20 ;
a |= 20 ;
```

On similar lines if we are to define a macro that will clear a given bit in a bit array, we can do so as follows:

```
#define CLEAR( x, y ) ( x[ BITSLOT( y ) ] &= ~MASK( y ) )
```

Some More Macros

Can we use control instructions while defining macros? Yes. But when would be required to do so? While defining macros which let you run a loop till a condition is satisfied. This is illustrated in the following example.

```
#define _BV( bit ) ( 1 << ( bit ) )
#define bit_is_set( ch, bit ) ( ch & _BV( bit ) )
```

```
#define bit_is_clear( ch, bit ) ( ! ( ch & _BV( bit ) ) )
#define loop_until_bit_is_set ( ch, bit ) do { } while ( bit_is_clear( ch, bit ) )
#define loop_until_bit_is_clear ( ch, bit ) do { } while ( bit_is_set( ch, bit ) )
```

As the name suggests, **bit_is_set( )** macro tests whether a particular bit in **ch** is set or not. This macro returns a non-zero number if the bit is set and a 0 if the bit is clear. Similar is the working of the macro **bit_is_clear( )**. It test whether a bit in **ch** is clear. It returns a non-zero if the bit is clear, and a 0 if the bit is set. The other two macros **loop_until_bit_is_set( )** and **loop_until_bit_is_clear( )** continue in a loop until a bit is set/cleared.

Exercise

[A] Pick up the correct alternative for each of the following questions:

[1] Which of the following statement is correct about the << operator?

(a) It multiplies a value by a power of two until overflow occurs.
(b) It divides a value by a power of two.
(c) It adds a value with a power of two until overflow occurs.
(d) It subtracts from a value a power of two.

[2] Which of the following statement is correct about the >> operator?

(a) It divides a positive value by a power of two.
(b) It multiplies a positive value by a power of two.
(c) It adds a positive value with a power of two.
(d) It subtracts from a positive value a power of two.

[3] Which of the following statement is correct?

(a) int a = 64 << 2 ;
(b) float a = 6.42 << 2 ;
(c) double a = 3.33 << 2 ;
(d) long double a = 3.67 << 2 ;

[4] What would be the result of the expression a ^ a?

(a) 0
(b) 1
(c) Sum of two operands
(d) Multiplication of two operands

[5] Which of the following statement is correct about the >> operator?

(a) The second operand of >> operator specifies the number of bit positions the value of first operand is to be right shifted.

(b) The second operand of >> operator specifies the number of bit positions the value of both operands is to be left shifted.

(c) The second operand of >> operator specifies the number of bit positions the value of both operands is to be right shifted.

(d) The second operand of >> operator specifies the number of bit positions the value of first operand is to be left shifted.

[6] Which of the following statement is correct about the << operator?

(a) The second operand of << operator specifies the number of bit positions the value of first operand is to be left shifted.

(b) The second operand of << operator specifies the number of bit positions the value of both operands is to be right shifted.

(c) The second operand of << operator specifies the number of bit positions the value of both operands is to be left shifted.

(d) The second operand of << operator specifies the number of bit positions the value of first operand is to be right shifted.

[7] What will be the output of the code snippet given below?

```
# include <stdio.h>
void main( )
{
    int a = 10, b = 65 ;
    printf ( "%d", a << ( a & b ) ) ;
}
```

(a) 65
(b) 10
(c) 0
(d) 1

[8] What will be the output of the code snippet given below?

```
#include <stdio.h>
void main( )
{
    unsigned int i = 0xb5, j, res ;
    int n = 0 ;
    if ( n == 0 )
```

```
            res = i ;
        else
        {
            n = -n ;
            j = i >> ( 16 - n ) ;
            res = i << n | j ;
        }
        printf ( "%X", res ) ;
    }
```

(a) B5
(b) oxb5
(c) 5
(d) 181

[9] What will be the output of the code snippet given below?

```
#include <stdio.h>
void main( )
{
    char ch = 'A' ;
    prlnlf ( "%d", ch | 'A' & 'z' ) ;
}
```

(a) 65
(b) A
(c) z
(d) 122

[10] What will be the output of the code snippet given below?

```
# include <stdio.h>
void main( )
{
```

```
    unsigned int i = 077, k ;
    int n = -6 ;

    if ( n > 0 )
        k = i >> n ;
    else
        k = i << -n ;
    printf ( "%o", k ) ;
}
```

(a) 7700
(b) 77
(c) -677
(d) -776

[B] Answer the following:

(a) The information about colors is to be stored in bits of a char variable called color. The bit number 0 to 6, each represent 7 colors of a rainbow, i.e. bit 0 represents violet, 1 represents indigo, and so on. Write a program that asks the user to enter a number, and based on this number, it reports which colors in the rainbow does the number represents.

(b) A company planning to launch a new newspaper in market conducts a survey. The various parameters considered in the survey were, the economic status (upper, middle, and lower class) the languages readers prefer (English, Hindi, Regional language) and category of paper (daily, supplement, tabloid). Write a program, which reads data of 10 respondents through keyboard, and stores the information in an array of integers. The bit-wise information to be stored in an integer is given below:

Bit Number	Information
0	Upper class
1	Middle class
2	Lower class
3	English
4	Hindi
5	Regional Language
6	Daily
7	Supplement
8	Tabloid

At the end give the statistical data for number of persons who read English daily, number of Upper class people who read Tabloid and number of Regional Language readers.

(c) In an inter-college competition, various sports like cricket, basketball, football, hockey, lawn tennis, table tennis, carom and chess are played between different colleges. The information regarding the games won by a particular college is stored in bit numbers 0, 1, 2, 3, 4, 5, 6, 7 and 8 respectively of an integer variable called **game**. The college that wins in 5 or more than 5 games is awarded the Champion of Champions trophy. If a number representing the bit pattern mentioned above is entered through the keyboard then write a program to find out whether the college won the Champion of the Champions trophy or not, along with the names of the games won by the college.

(d) An animal could be a canine (dog, wolf, fox, etc.), a feline (cat, lynx, jaguar, etc.), a cetacean (whale, narwhal, etc.) or a marsupial (koala, wombat, etc.). The information whether a particular animal is canine, feline, cetacean, or marsupial is stored in bit number 0, 1, 2 and 3 respectively of a integer variable called **type**. Bit number 4 of the variable **type** stores the information about whether the animal is Carnivore or Herbivore.

For the following animal, complete the program to determine whether the animal is a herbivore or a carnivore. Also determine whether the animal is a canine, feline, cetacean or a marsupial.

```
struct animal
{
    char name[30] ;
    int type ;
}
struct animal a = { "OCELOT", 18 } ;
```

(e) In order to save disk space, information about student is stored in an integer variable. If bit number 0 is on then it indicates I[st] year student, bit number 1 to 3 stores IInd year, IIIrd year and IVth year student respectively. Bits 4 to 7 store the stream Mechanical, Chemical, Electronics and IT. Rest of the bits store room number. Based on the given data, write a program that asks for the room number and displays the information about the student, if its data exists in the array. The contents of array are,

```
int data[ ] = { 273, 548, 786, 1096 } ;
```

(f) What will be the output of the following program:

```
# include <stdio.h>
void main( )
{
```

```
    int i = 32, j = 65, k, l, m, n, o, p ;
    k = i | 35 ;
    l = ~k ;
    m = i & j ;
    n = j ^ 32 ;
    o = j << 2 ;
    p = i >> 5 ;
    printf ( "\nk = %d l = %d m = %d", k, l, m ) ;
    printf ( "\nn = %d o = %d p = %d", n, o, p ) ;
}
```

(g) What is hexadecimal equivalent of binary number 0101 1010?

(h) Consider an unsigned integer in which rightmost bit is numbered as 0. Write a function **checkbits (x, p, n)** which returns true if all "n" bits starting from position "p" are turned on. For example, **checkbits (x, 4, 3)** will return true if bits 4, 3 and 2 are 1 in number x.

```
int checkbits ( unsigned int x, int p, int n )
```

3 Embedded System Programming

As we have already seen, an embedded system consists of a combination of software and hardware other than a Computer. In the PC world one can afford to learn hardware and software in isolation. Unlike this, in the embedded systems world, the hardware and software interact so closely with one another to provide the desired functionality that it is impossible to learn them as two isolated streams. So anyone learning embedded systems has two options:

(a) Focus on software aspects and learn hardware on 'need to know' basis.
(b) Focus on hardware aspects and learn software on 'need to know' basis.

In this book, we have decided to take the first approach. There are two reasons for this:

(a) Experience with PC world has proved several times that it is the software that brings maximum flexibility. For example, radically different Operating Systems like Windows and Linux run on same PC hardware. On the other hand same Linux operating system also runs on radically different hardware like Intel's Pentium family, Sun's Ultra-Sparc family and IBM's PowerPC family of Microprocessors.

(b) If we learn how to program one embedded system hardware, we can apply the knowledge gained, in programming other embedded systems. Unlike this, most of the hardware design for embedded systems is highly processor specific. It takes much more effort to apply the knowledge gained, to design an embedded system based on different processor.

Language Choice

An embedded system can be programmed using either Assembly language or C language. In the early days, people used assembly since it was closest to hardware. However, over the years, C language has become the top favorite with embedded system programmers worldwide. There are several reasons for this choice. These are as under:

Easy to learn - C language is much easier to learn as compared to Assembly language.

Easy to organize data - With the availability of constructs like structures and unions it is easier to organize related data.

Easy to organize programs - Organization of a program becomes extremely important as the program size goes on increasing. Unless properly organized, it becomes difficult to maintain the program. It is easier to organize a large C program into functions and libraries as compared to an equivalent Assembly language program.

Easy to debug - It is much easier to debug a C language program in comparison to debugging an equivalent assembly language program.

Easy to work with different microprocessors - Different embedded systems use different microprocessors. Each microprocessor has its own assembly language. Hence, a program written for a specific microprocessor to achieve desired functionality has to be modified suitably to make it work on a different microprocessor. All these issues are eliminated while using C language.

Hence every program in this book is written in C language. This book expects you to know C language. Those readers who are not so comfortable with C programming can refer 'The C Primer' in Appendix A.

Before We Begin

Though you might have written quite a few C programs by now, you may not have bothered too much about the terminologies that are associated with them. The discussion that follows makes use of terminologies like local variables, uninitialised global variables, etc. It would be a good idea to identify them in a program before we begin any further discussion. So go through the program given below and note the comments carefully.

```
/* Program 3.1 */
#include <stdio.h>  /* preprocessor directive */
int i, j ;   /* uninitialised global variables */
char *p = "Hello" ; /* initialised global variables */
int main( )
{
    int x = 1, y = 2 ;   /* initialised global variables */
    char str[ ] = "World!" ;   /* constant string */
    printf ( "%d %d", i, j ) ;   /* library function call */
    printf ( "%d %d", x, y ) ;
    printf ( "%s %s", p, str ) ;
    return 0 ;
}
```

PC Programming

Though we write programs, compile them and get them executed on a daily basis, often we do not have a crystal clear idea about what is happening under the hood. We think it is necessary to get a clear picture of this process as it will help you understand the parallel process for embedded systems.

In a PC when we run the program the program makes use of a set of services provided by the Operating System. Hence this execution environment is known as a "Hosted" environment. Contrasted with this, in many embedded systems there is no operating system. This execution environment is called "Freestanding" execution environment. In this section we will concentrate on hosted execution environment.

There are many steps involved in converting a C program into an executable form. These are shown in Figure 3.1.

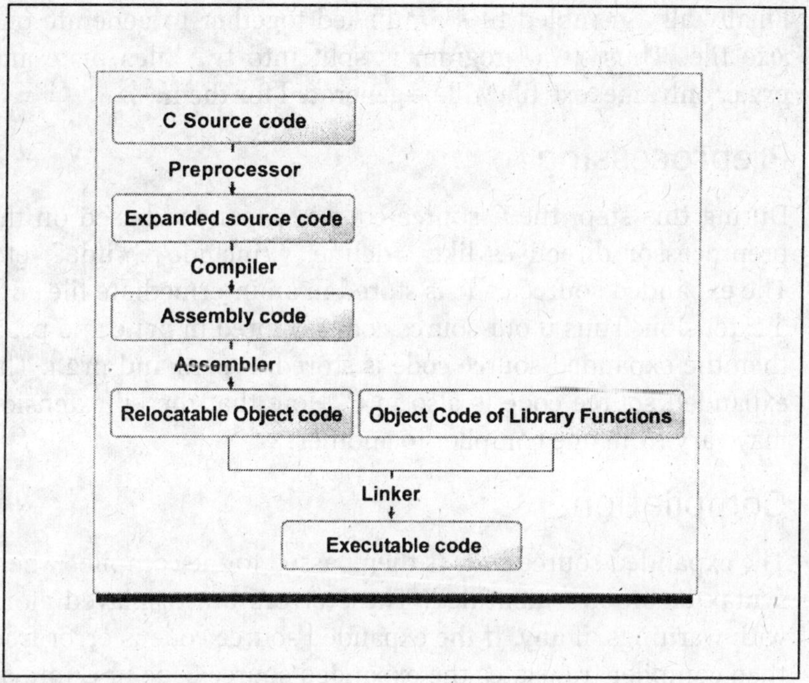

Figure 3.1: PC Build process

Software development tools like TC++ and VC++ hide many of the steps shown in Figure 3.1 from us. However, it is important to understand these steps for two reasons:

(a) It would help you understand the process much better than just believing that some kind of 'magic' generates the executable code.

(b) If you are to alter any of these steps then you would know how to do it.

Let us now understand the steps mentioned in Figure 3.1 in detail. Though most elementary programs are written in one .c file, any program of reasonable size is split into multiple .c files. Each of these files are preprocessed, compiled and assembled. Finally all assembled files are linked together to generate one .exe file. Thus, if a program is split into two files pr1.c and pr2.c, only one .exe file will be generated for them.

Preprocessing

During this step, the C source code is expanded based on the preprocessor directives like '#define', '#include', '#ifdef', etc. The expanded source code is stored in an intermediate file with .i extension. Thus if our source code is stored in pr1.c and pr2.c then the expanded source code is stored in pr1.i and pr2.i. The expanded source code is also in C. Note that the '.i' extension may vary from one compiler to another.

Compilation

The expanded source code is then passed to the compiler where syntax errors are identified. These errors are displayed along with warnings, if any. If the expanded source code is error free, then compiler translates the expanded source code in C into an equivalent assembly language code. Different microprocessors support different set of assembly language instructions using which they can be programmed. Hence a compiler for Intel Pentium II microprocessor will generate the assembly instructions using the instructions understood by it. Likewise, the same C program when compiled for Intel Pentium IV microprocessor is likely to generate different assembly language instructions. The assembly instructions are typically stored in .s file. Thus for pr1.i and pr2.i, the assembly instructions would be stored in pr1.s and pr2.s.

Assembling

The job of the Assembler is to translate .s program into Object Code. The assembler also creates a table called **Symbol Table**. This table contains following information:

(a) Name, type and size of each global variable
(b) Name and address of each function defined in the program
(c) Name of external functions like **printf( )** and **scanf( )**

Note that addresses of the external functions are undefined at this stage. They are later filled in by the linker. The Object Code and the Symbol Table are stored in .o file. Thus the assembler converts pr1.s into pr1.o.

The .o file is a specially formatted binary file. It contains a header that describes the object file contents. It also has different sections. Most important sections in an object file are:

(a) Code / Text section – This section contains machine language code equivalent to the expanded source code.

(b) Data Section – This section contains global variables and their initial values.

(c) Bss (Block Started by Symbol) section – This section contains uninitialized global variables.

(d) Symbol Table – This section contains information about symbols found during assembling of a program.

Although part of the .o file contains machine language instructions, it cannot be executed directly because of following reasons:

(a) The external functions like **printf( )** are not present in .o file.

(b) The .o file may use some global variables defined in another .o file. For example, pr1.o may use a global variable **count2** which is defined in the file pr2.o.

(c) The .o file may use a function defined in another .o file. For example, pr2.o may use a function **display( )** defined in the file pr1.o.

Linking

Linking is the final stage in creating an executable program. It has to do the following important things:

(a) Find definition of all external functions—those which are defined in other .o files, and those which are defined in Libraries (like **printf( )**).

(b) Find definition of all global variables—those which are defined in other .o files, and those which are defined in Libraries (like **errno** which is a commonly used global variable that is defined in Standard C Library).

(c) Combine Data Sections of different .o files into a single Data Section.

(d) Combine Code Sections of different .o files into a single Code Section.

Addresses of all variables and functions in the Symbol Table of the .o file are Relative addresses. This means that address of a Symbol (variable or function) is in fact only an offset from start of the Section (Data or Code Section) to which it belongs. For example, if there are two 4-byte wide global integer variables **count1** and **index1** in pr1.o, then the Symbol Table will have addresses 0 and 4 for them. Similarly, if pr2.o has two similar variables **count2** and **index2** then Symbol Table in pr2.o will have addresses 0 and 4 for these variables. Same addressing scheme is used with functions present in each .o file.

When linker combines the two .o files, it has to re-adjust the addresses of global variables and functions. Thus, the variables **count1**, **index1**, **count2** and **index2** will now enjoy addresses 0, 4, 8 and 12 respectively.

Similar re-adjustment of addresses will be done for functions. Even after re-adjustment the addresses of variables and functions are still *relative* in the combined Data and Code sections of the .exe file.

Execution

Once the .exe file is created and stored on the disk, it is ready for execution. When we execute it, it is first brought from the disk into the memory (RAM) by an Operating System component called Program Loader.

Program Loader can place the .exe anywhere in memory depending on its availability. Since all the addresses in the .exe file are *relative* addresses, exact *position* where .exe is loaded in memory doesn't matter. No further adjustment of addresses is necessary. Thus, the Code and Data in .exe file are 'Position Independent'.

Once the *loading* process is completed, the loader reserves memory for stack to be used by the program (for storing local variables and function addresses) and calls a system startup function. The name of this function is different under different Operating Systemns. Under Windows environment the name is is **mainCRTStartup( )**, **WinMainCRTStartup( )**, or **_DllMainCRTStartup( )** depending on which type of Windows application is being created. Don't worry too much about the name of the function. What is important is, this function is added to our code by the linker. This function provides a set of services to a program during execution. Some of these services are as follows:

(a) Making available a special set of variables called environment variables to our program.

(b) Initializing the uninitialized global variables to a value 0 or NULL.

Once the system startup function executes, it initializes the global variables and then calls **main( )**. Once execution of the program is over, the control returns to the system startup function, which performs the cleanup and returns the control to the OS. The OS now unloads the program and its associated resources from memory.

Figure 3.2 summarizes the role played by each processor program during the build process.

Program	Input	Output
Editor	Program typed from keyboard	C source code containing program and preprocessor commands
Preprocessor	C source code file	Source code file with the preprocessing commands properly sorted out
Compiler	Source code file with preprocessing commands sorted out	Assembly language code
Assembler	Assembly language code	Relocatable Oject code in machine language
Linker	Object code of our program and object code of library functions	Executable code in machine language

Figure 3.2: Role of programs in Build process

One final word before we end this topic. Like a .o file, a .exe file is also a formatted binary file. The format of these binary file differs from one Operating System to another. For example, Windows Operating System uses Portable Executable (PE) file format, whereas, Linux uses Executable and Linking Format (ELF). Hence an .o or .exe file created for Windows cannot be used on Linux and vice-versa.

Embedded System Programming

Having seen in sufficient detail the complete build and execution process for 'PC Programming', let us now turn our attention to Embedded System Programming (ES Programming). In PC programming, the system on which the development is done and the system on which the program is executed are same.

As against this, in Embedded Systems the development is done on a PC and the execution is carried out on a separate Embedded device as shown in Figure 3.3. The development PC is often known as the *host* and embedded device is known as the *target*. For example, the program that runs in a mobile phone is developed on a *host* (PC) but executed on the target (mobile phone). Note that the PC has a different microprocessor than the one in mobile phone. This fact has a direct impact on the build process as discussed below.

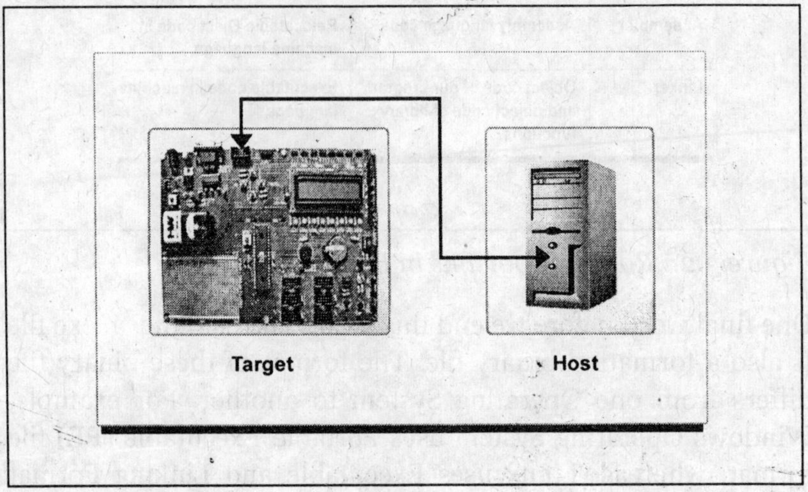

Figure 3.3: ES programming model

Preprocessing

The preprocessing step is same as that in PC programming. During preprocessing the typed source is converted into expanded source code.

Compilation

Compiler translates expanded source code in C into an equivalent assembly language code. There is a major deviation here. The assembly language code generated would not contain instructions for the PC's processor. Instead, it will contain instructions for the processor of the embedded device on which the program is finally going to get executed. Hence this compilation process is often known as 'cross-compilation'. A compiler that is capable of generating assembly instructions for processor other than the one on which it is running is known as a cross-compiler.

Assembling

As described earlier, an Assembler translates .ASM program into Object Code. In ES programming, assembler produces Object Code for the processor in target device.

Linking

In ES programming, linker creates an executable for the target device. The executable produced by linker is stored on the hard disk of the host system.

Program Transfer / Burning

This is an additional step necessary while working with every embedded system. In this step, the executable generated by a linker has to be physically transferred from hard disk of host system to the target embedded device. This is commonly done using a serial cable or a network cable connecting the host and the target device. The details of this transfer process will be explained when we do our first ES program.

Most embedded systems do not have a hard drive to store the executable program. Needless to say, there has to be some other storage medium to store the executable. For most embedded systems "Flash Memory" is used for this purpose. Some embedded systems may also store the program in

NVRAM (Non-Volatile RAM), EEPROM (Electrically-Erasable Programmable Read-Only Memory), PROM (Programmable Read-Only Memory). No matter which storage medium is used, the program is stored at a fixed location, commonly at the beginning of the storage medium.

Execution

In PC programming, code and data section for the program have to the transferred to RAM before execution begins. Unlike this, in most ES, code section is not transferred to RAM. However, data section must be loaded in RAM before execution begins. There are several reasons for this:

(a) In most ES, RAM is smaller than the combined size of code and data sections. Hence the code and data together cannot be accommodated in RAM.

(b) Code sections for most programs is quite large compared to data section. By executing the program directly from Flash memory, the startup performance of a program is improved. This is because time required to copy code from Flash memory to RAM gets eliminated.

Most small ES do not have an Operating System. As a result, there is no Program Loader component that loads the program into memory. The program straight away starts executing the instructions from the location where it is stored.

Two Questions About ES Programming

After going through the above discussion about embedded system development process you are likely face following questions:

Why Flash Memory Is Used?

While designing an Embedded System the three important design goals are:

(a) Keep the size of the embedded device small.
(b) Keep the power requirement of the embedded device to a minimum.
(c) Ensure a good system performance.

All these design goals cannot be met if a hard disk is used for storage in an embedded system. This is because a typical hard disk is bulky and consumes far too much power than what an embedded device can afford. Also, the storage space available on the hard disk is much larger than what may be needed by an ES. Hard disk being a electro-mechanical component, using it leads to delays due to the time spent in mechanical movement of the parts of a hard disk. All these disadvantages can be overcome by using flash memory.

Flash memory is a form of EEPROM. In normal RAM, when we write a value to memory location, the earlier value is simply "overwritten". Unlike this, in flash and EEPROM, the current value in the memory location is erased, before writing a new value at that location. Flash and EEPROM are non-volatile, i.e. their contents are not lost when power is turned off. Normal EEPROM only allows writing to one location at a time. Unlike this, flash memory allows multiple memory locations to be written in one operation. Flash memory and EEPROM offer faster read access times as compared to a hard disk. Also, due to absence of any moving parts, EEPROM and flash have better shock resistance as compared to a hard disk. Figure 3.4 shows some popular Flash and EEPROM memories.

Figure 3.4: EEPROM and Flash memories

Though flash memory offers advantages mentioned above, it has a few limitations too. Firstly, information has to be written to it as a chunk of bytes (often known as block) rather than a byte at a time. Typical block-size is 512 bytes. In contrast to this, reads can happen a byte at a time. Another downside is, there is a limit to number of times a particular block can be written. This is also known as "endurance" of a flash memory.

Why Data Section Is Brought Into RAM?

During execution of any program, its instructions never need to be changed. This means that code section can remain in read-only memory. However, most realistic programs use variables and pointers to access data memory. They modify these variables during execution. It clearly means that if data section is not brought into read/write memory before execution starts, programs will not work correctly. Therefore, in most ES data section is copied to the only read/write memory available — RAM. A detailed discussion of various forms of memories and their usage will be done in chapters to follow.

There is no point in copying the code section to RAM as it is not going to change. As seen earlier, writing to flash happens in blocks, whereas, the program may want to modify only a few bytes of data at a time.

Exercise

[A] Answer the following:

(a) Why C language is the preferred choice for Embedded System programming?

(b) What are the steps involved in the build process on a PC?

(c) What are the different sections of an Object file?

[B] Pick up the correct alternative for each of the following questions:

[1] What is an embedded system?

(a) IBM PC Computer
(b) Computer system hidden inside a device
(c) Software
(d) Hardware

[2] What does "C" compiler do?

(a) Converts "assembly language" to "machine language"
(b) Converts "C language" to "machine language"
(c) Converts "machine language" to "object language"
(d) Converts "Java language" to "assembly language"

[3] Which one of the following is not a memory?

(a) RAM
(b) ROM
(c) Flash
(d) ALU

[4] Which of the following is NOT part of an object file?

(a) Code section
(b) Data section
(c) Preprocessor section
(d) BSS

[5] Which of the following activities are carried out during linking?

(i) Finding definition of all external functions

(iii) Finding definition of all global variables

(iii) Combining Data Sections of different .OBJ files into a single Data Section

(iv) Combining Code Sections of different .OBJ files into a single Code Section

(a) Only (i) and (ii)
(b) Only (ii) and (iv)
(c) Only (i), (ii) and (iii)
(d) (i), (ii), (iii) and (iv)

[6] Which of the following is responsible for bringing the executable program from disk into memory during execution?

(a) Loader
(b) Compiler
(c) Linker
(d) Preprocessor

[7] C Compiler converts the expanded source code into which of the following forms?

(a) Relocatable Object code

(b) Executable code
(c) Assembly code
(d) Source code

[8] Which of the following are present in the symbol table?

(i) Name, type and size of each global variable

(ii) Name and address of each function defined in the program

(iii) Name of external functions like **printf( )** and **scanf( )**

(a) Only (i)
(b) Only (ii)
(c) Only (i) and (ii)
(d) (i), (ii) and (iii)

[9] Which of the following function will be called by the loader once the loading process is completed?

(a) WinMain( )
(b) main( )
(c) mainCRTStartup( )
(d) Startup( )

[10] Which of the following memories are non-volatile?

(i) Flash

(ii) EEPROM

(iii) RAM

(a) Only (i) and (iii)
(b) (i), (ii) and (iii)

(c) Only (i) and (ii)
(d) Only (ii)

[11] Which of the following is not brought into RAM in most embedded systems during execution?

(i) Data section

(ii) Instructions

(a) Only (i)
(b) Only (ii)
(c) (i) and (iii)
(d) Neither (i) nor (ii)

4 Introduction To Embedded System

Software development as a profession has come a long way since E. W. Dijkstra first wrote about it in his famous essay EWD340. Ironically, not much has changed when it comes to developing good software. What has changed radically over last several decades is computer programming has reached masses. It allowed all those "lone attic" inventors to feel empowered and saw various revolutionary works in the form of Linux Operating System, Open Source community based software development etc. Over the years, "systems" used to run these programs have also changed dramatically. From "formidable" UNIX Servers and Workstations, programming today is done on "Desktop"s i.e. PCs and Laptops that are everywhere.

One more form of "computing system" has gained tremendous popularity and acceptance in industry and Consumer Electronic markets. These systems are generally known as "Embedded Systems" because more often than not, they get "embedded" into a larger "system". As with regular "computers", software makes these systems flexible and "reusable". This book aims to bring these "Embedded Systems" to your household. After studying this book you will be able to work with a wide variety of embedded systems. Asia has built a name for itself as a Software Development powerhouse. This is the era of Embedded Systems. Developing software for Embedded Systems is generally not covered in a typical University course. If we are to emerge as a global player in Embedded Systems Development, we must begin on a firm foundation. One of the reasons why Embedded Systems is not taught in Universities is because of lack of a good book on the subject. We hope this book will fill that void.

What Is An Embedded System?

A general-purpose computing system like a PC is not designed to perform a specific function. In fact, it has the ability to do many different things.

While manufacturing such a system, the Manufacturer does not know what will be the end use(s) of the machine. One person may use the same system for storing inventory data, someone else may use it for playing movies and music and some may put it to use as a web server. Contrasted with this, an Embedded System is typically designed with a specific purpose in mind. For example, one Embedded System may be designed to control flow coal on a conveyor belt in a Power Plant. Another Embedded System detects and reports the height of an airplane.

Yet another Embedded System is a Firewall that protects corporate network from hackers. Many Consumer Electronic devices, like music players (iPOD), remote controls, TV Set-Top boxes, digital cameras, medical diagnostics like Ultra-sonograph, microwave ovens, washing machines, cell-phones etc. also contain Embedded Systems. Often, several Embedded Systems may be contained in one large system. For example, an airplane may contain hundreds of Embedded Systems performing variety of tasks like Communication, Navigation, Fuel monitoring etc. As you can see, Embedded Systems have applications in wide ranging fields. Figure **Error! No text of specified style in document.**.1 shows few examples of Embedded Systems.

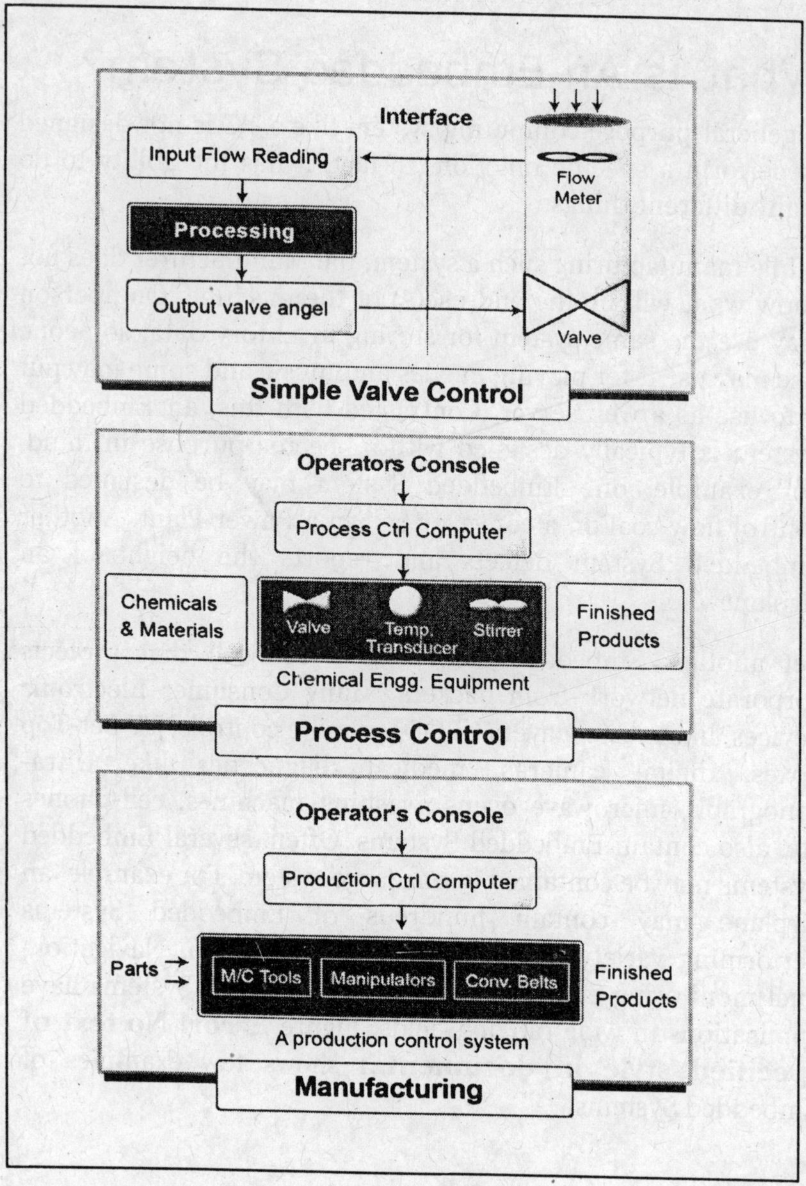

Figure 4.1: Examples of Embedded Systems

Thus the simplest definition of an embedded system can be a combination of hardware and software in which the software runs on hardware other than a Computer.

The whole idea behind designing a system that would do a specific job is to reduce the cost of hardware and software design process. Once the special-purpose hardware and software is built, an Embedded System typically manufactured in millions of units.

Though millions of such Embedded Systems are manufactured each for carrying our specific tasks, increasingly, there is a trend towards building "General Purpose Embedded Systems". The motive behind this is to ensure that some the same hardware can be used to perform numerous tasks. Once manufactured, the hardware obviously cannot be changed. So the flexibility required to perform numerous tasks on the same hardware can be accomplished only through the ability to run different software on it. For this to be feasible, an Operating System Software must first be installed on the hardware, and subsequently different software can be made to run on it. Perfect example of this scenario is a Mobile Phone. Every Nokia™ phone has Symbian Operating System installed on it and then several applications like Dialer, Calendar, Contacts, Alarm, Music Player, Camera, Games etc. run on top of it. An added advantage of this trend is that newer applications can be installed on same Mobile Phone once it is in the hands of a user. Such Embedded Systems enhance the end-user experience.

Figure 4.2 shows the three types of systems that discussed above.

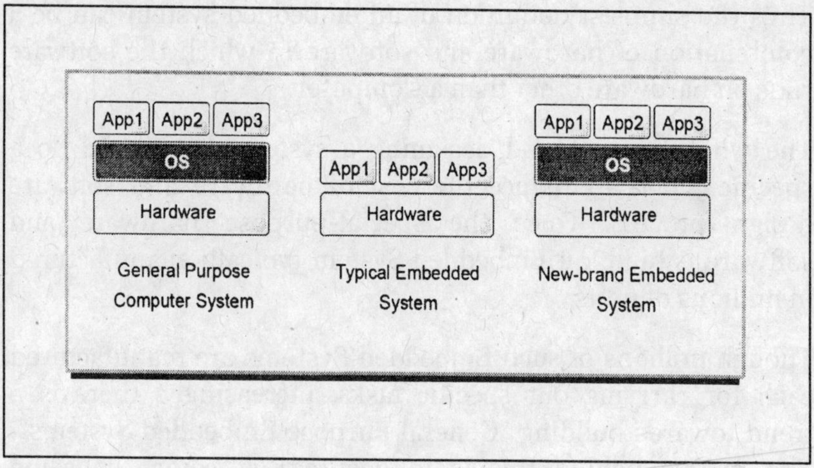

Figure 4.2: Types of Embedded Systems

Characteristics Of Embedded Systems

Though different Embedded Systems carry out fundamentally different tasks, they still share the following common characteristics which distinguish them from General Purpose computing systems.

Constraints

Embedded Systems must be designed to work under more severe constraints on resources than their General Purpose counterparts. They generally have much lesser processing power, memory, storage space, cost and size. Most of them are battery powered, and are designed to obtain best possible processing power per unit of energy consumed. To top it all, in spite of all these constraints, it is supposed to complete its assigned task at a reasonable speed.

Single Purpose

Most Embedded Systems do one job and do it well. They are optimized to perform a single action repeatedly. For example, most Mobile Phones don't allow accessing any other application during a voice call. Of course, there are exceptions to this where one action can be put on 'hold' while some other action is being carried out. In such scenarios, only application is actively running and receiving inputs and controlling output of the system. Explicit user request is needed to 'switch' between applications.

Real-time And Non Real-time

Embedded Systems used in process control and machine automation environments must be designed to complete the assigned task in fixed time (deterministic). Failure to do so might result in a disaster. For example, in an engine assembly line, a robot must complete a welding operation in a predetermined time and move the engine to the next station; otherwise there may be accidents in the engine assembly process.

In non real-time Embedded Systems, a delay in completing a particular task might cause inconvenience, but is not catastrophic. For example, a network router takes longer to decide outgoing path for received packets, the transmission of packets may get delayed. This may cause inconvenience but not disaster.

A typical Embedded System

A typical Embedded System consists of a processor, memory, and an optional input/output subsystem. Let us now understand each of these in detail.

Processor

At the heart of any Embedded System is a "processor" that executes the program stored in memory. Three categories of processors are commonly used in an Embedded System—Microprocessor (MP), Microcontroller (MC) and Digital Signal Processor (DSP). Factors like Performance and Cost govern the selection of one of these processors in any Embedded System.

Microprocessor

Although an MP is a General Purpose processor, it is still popularly used in Embedded Systems to carry out a specific task. Major reasons for their use in building Embedded System are their continuously falling costs and increasingly smaller sizes. Using General Purpose Microprocessors like Intel Pentium-IV or IBM PowerPC 705 is usually overkill, since the processing power that they offer is not needed by most Embedded Systems. Their lower-end cousins like Intel 80386 and PowerPC 440 are popularly used in Embedded Systems. Other commonly used Microprocessors specifically designed for use in Embedded Systems are: Hitachi SH-4, ARM (Advanced RISC Machines), MIPS.

Microcontroller

Microcontrollers are an offshoot in the evolution of Microprocessors. In all microcontrollers a processor, memory, input/output subsystem and many more features are integrated into a single chip. Industrial automation was a prime mover for this processor technology. Major criteria for Embedded Systems used in industrial controls are, lower cost and larger numbers of these systems. Most of these Systems are also very small in size and must be built with as few chips as possible. Microcontrollers fit these requirements very well. Most popular

Microcontrollers of today include Intel 8051, Motorola 6812, Atmel AVR series, Microchip PIC series etc.

DSP

Most common form of signals encountered in everyday life are audio and video. Public airwaves bring broadcast television and radio to every household. Increasingly, these signals are being transmitted in digital rather than analog form. Digital Signal Processors are specifically designed to work with such signals and carry out complex mathematical computations on these signals, to enhance their quality. e.g. a picture taken by a digital camera is processed by a DSP to remove effects like red-eye, over/under exposure, etc. before storing it on an internal storage card. DSP is a processor which is tuned to do this intensive computation, efficiently. In absence of a DSP, if a MP/MC is used to do this computation, it would take considerably longer and affect the system performance adversely.

Figure 4.3 shows different processors used in Embedded Systems.

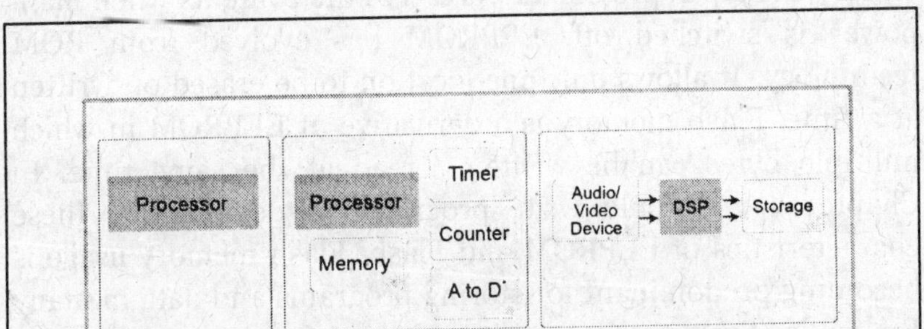

Figure 4.3: Processor Types

Memory

In plain english, memory is "recollection of past". In Embedded Systems, different types of memories are used. These include SRAM, DRAM, NVRAM, ROM, EEPROM, Flash etc. Ultimately, all memories fall under two broad categories:

Volatile Memory

Contents of volatile memory are lost when power is switched off. SRAM (Static RAM) and DRAM (Dynamic RAM) fall under this category. SRAM is a form of memory whose contents remain valid indefinitely as long as power is continuously applied. DRAM memory on the other hand requires its contents to be refreshed periodically.

Persistent Memory

Contents of persistent memory are preserved even after power is switched off. NVRAM (Non-Volatile RAM), EEPROM (Electrically Erasable Read Only Memory) and Flash fall under this category. NVRAM is a descendant of SRAM in which battery backup is provided to preserve the contents when main power is switched off. EEPROM has evolved from ROM technology. It allows only one location to be erased on written at a time. Flash memory is a derivative of EEPROM in which multiple bytes can be written / read at the same time. In Chapter 9 we would write programs to demonstrate these characteristics of EEPROM and Flash. Flash memory usage is becoming predominant for storing programs and data in many Embedded Systems.

Input/Output Subsystem

Most Embedded Systems have ability to process "inputs". These inputs may be in the form of external controls like knobs, keyboards, or built-in sensors that change in response to their environment. For example, a temperature sensor may be used by a centralized air conditioning system to control compressor power. Similarly, most Embedded Systems also provide some user-visible "output". Examples include, displays for Mobile Phones, LCD screen for a DVD player etc. One must remember that although most Embedded Systems have at least one input, they need not have a "display" (output) device connected. Such Embedded Systems are called as "Headless" systems.

Design Considerations

Designing an embedded system is a challenging proposition. This is because not only should the system achieve the desired functionality, it must meet several other goals. Commonly used design metrics are:

Cost - There are two components to the cost of an embedded system—Fixed cost and Variable cost. The fixed cost pertains to the cost of designing the systems whereas the variable cost is the cost of manufacturing the embedded system. The variable cost goes down as the number of units manufactured goes on increasing.

Size - Size of an embedded system is very important. There is no point in creating a mobile phone studded with features if it's size is so big that it cannot fit in a shirt pocket.

Memory Requirement - The memory required by the software (and OS) should be minimum, since it has a direct impact on size and cost of an embedded system. On the other hand, it should be enough to provide reasonable performance and data storage capacity.

Power - Since many embedded systems are battery powered, higher the power requirement, lesser is the battery life. Also, if the power requirement of the embedded system is more, then cooling requirement of the system would also have to be scaled up proportionately.

Performance - The execution time of the system is an important design consideration. For example, a portable media player which takes longer to process audio/video signals before storing them, is undesirable.

Flexibility - The software running inside an embedded system provides flexibility to it. It should be possible to change the functionality of the embedded system in response to last minute changes in functional requirements and market forces. For example, if a mobile phone has Bluetooth and InfraRed (IrDA) capability then it should be possible enhance it's functionality by adding new applications like TV remote control, latest games etc.

Development Time - There are several components to the development time—time to create a prototype, time to manufacture and time to develop necessary software components. Another dimension to this issue is that during software development, target hardware may not be available. As a result, most of the software development is done using emulators. With increasing competition in embedded system markets, there is always a race against time to get the systems to the markets and into the hands of customers in smallest possible time. Due to this, the time from conceptualization to realization is continuously shrinking.

Software Reliability - As we all know most of the PC software today has to be continually kept up-to-date by downloading periodic updates from the Internet. In stark contrast, once sold, software on most embedded systems is never updated. Hence it is all the more important that embedded software be much more reliable and error free.

Figure 4.4 shows various metrics involved in ES design.

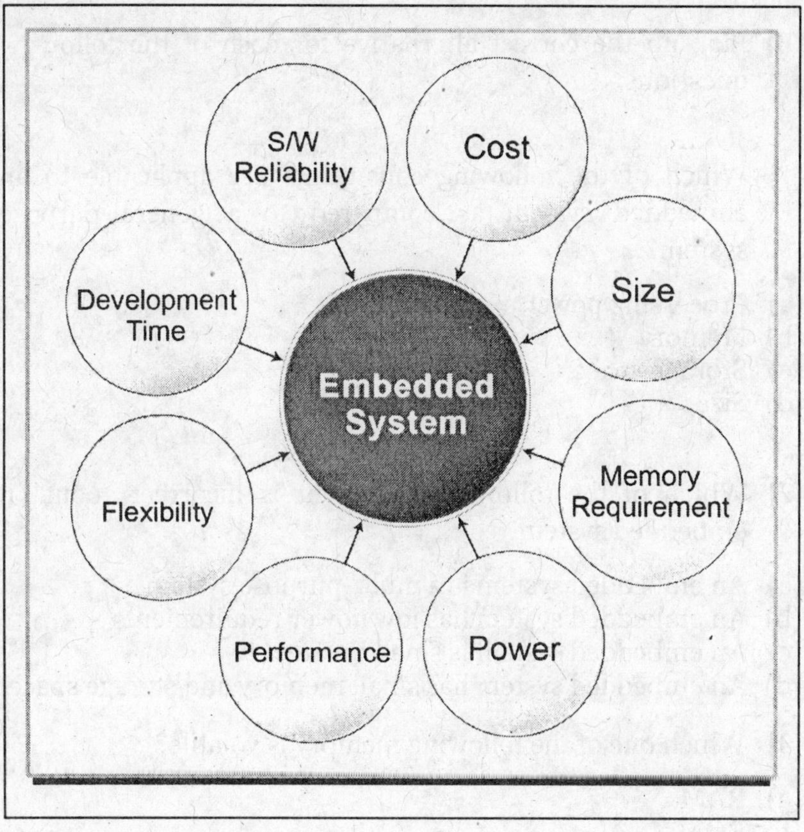

Figure 4.4: Embedded System Design Metrics

Exercise

[A] Answer the following:

(a) Name two embedded systems (other than mobile phones) that you have seen. Identify characteristics of these systems like Processor used, type of memory used, amount of program memory etc.

(b) Describe most important design considerations for creating an embedded system.

[B] Pick up the correct alternative for each of the following questions:

[1] Which of the following constraints are applicable to an embedded system as compared to a general-purpose system?

(a) Processing power
(b) Memory
(c) Storage space
(d) Size

[2] Which of the following statement is incorrect about an embedded system?

(a) An embedded system is a multi-purpose system
(b) An embedded system has low power requirements
(c) An embedded system is small in size
(d) An embedded system has small memory and storage space

[3] Which one of the following memory is volatile?

(a) RAM
(b) ROM
(c) Flash
(d) EEPROM

[4] Which of the following memory is odd one out?

(a) SRAM
(b) Flash
(c) EEPROM
(d) NVRAM

[5] Which of the following is used in an embedded system?

(i) Microprocessor
(ii) Microcontroller
(iii) Digital Signal Processor

(a) Only (i) and (ii)
(b) Only (ii) and (iii)
(c) Only (i) and (iii)
(d) (i), (ii) and (iii)

[6] In which of the following categories all types of memories fall?

(i) Volatile memory
(ii) Persistent memory

(a) Only (i)
(b) Only (ii)
(c) Both (i) and (ii)
(d) Neither (i) nor (ii)

[7] Which of the following statements are correct?

(i) Contents of persistent memory are lost when power is switched off.
(ii) Contents of volatile memory are preserved even after power is switched off.

(a) Only (i) is correct.
(b) Only (ii) is correct.
(c) Both (i) and (ii) are correct.
(d) Both (i) and (ii) are incorrect.

[8] In which of the following memory contents remain valid indefinitely as long as power is continuously supplied to it?

(i) SRAM

(ii) DRAM

(a) Only (i)
(b) Only (ii)
(c) Both (i) and (ii)
(d) Neither (i) nor (ii)

[9] In which of the following memory contents required to be refreshed periodically?

(i) SRAM
(ii) DRAM

(a) Only (i)
(b) Only (ii)
(c) Both (i) and (ii)
(d) Neither (i) nor (ii)

[10] Which of the following is a persistent memory?

(i) NVRAM
(ii) EEPROM
(iii)Flash

(a) Only (i) and (ii)
(b) Only (i) and (iii)
(c) Only (ii) and (iii)
(d) (i), (ii) and (iii)

5 Embedded System Boards

In order to master embedded systems, it is very important that you learn hands-on programming with embedded systems. The hardware used in embedded systems in practice is very diverse. Most Embedded System hardware is designed with a specific product in mind. There are companies like Intel, AMD, Cirrus Logic, Motorola that create 'Reference Boards' which serve as a starting point for designing an embedded system of your choice. They are also called as SDBs (Standard Development Boards) or simply Reference Designs or Evaluation Kits.

It is important that you choose a right standard development board. As a developer you must choose a board that allows you freedom in design and lets you explore several possibilities. Whenever you plan to build an embedded system, you must study the features a board offers and then decide to use it in your design/application.

There are several embedded system boards available in the market. Which board to choose is a difficult choice to make since the application domains for embedded systems are varied and numerous. Some examples of these domains are Industrial controllers, Digital Media Servers, Integrated home media gateways, Set-top boxes, Streaming media players, Point Of Sales terminals, Medical Equipment, Automobiles, etc. Hence it is important to study some reference boards available in the market. This chapter discusses some of them.

Kwikbyte 9202

Kwikbyte 9202 is a popularly used embedded system development board (Refer Figure 5.1). It contains 32 MB SDRAM memory (outside the CPU), 16 MB flash memory, 16k on-chip RAM. It is based on ARM9 microprocessor running at 180 MHz. The board has LCD interface and support for USB and LAN/Ethernet. A temperature sensor is also present on the board. This can be used in a typical handheld-device in industrial and consumer applications. Cost of this board at the time of this writing is around Rs. 13,000. Since it contains ARM9 processor it is clear that this board is overkill for building small embedded systems. Cost of the board is also quite high.

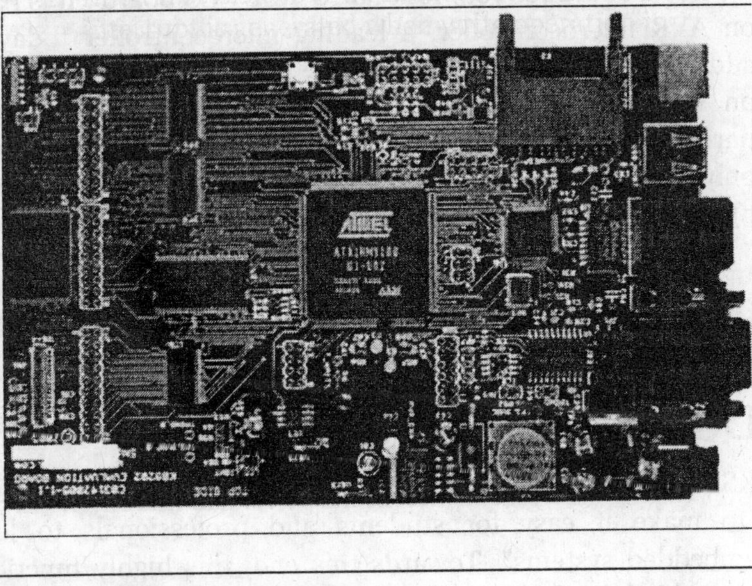

Figure 5.1: Kwikbyte 9202 SDB

Cirrus Logic EP9302

Cirrus Logic is a leading semiconductor equipment manufacturer. It has created the EP9302 embedded systems board for multimedia applications. It has 200 MHz ARM920T processor, 128 kB internal ROM, two serial port controllers, USB, Ethernet and infra-red support. It also contains a separate floating point co-processor. These features make it ideal for pocket based music players. Its price is around Rs. 16,000. That makes it difficult to use in smaller embedded systems.

KSET Embedded System Board

The standard development boards are way too complex and costly for a learner of embedded systems. Hence, to make it simpler for you to learn and design embedded systems, we have created a board for you. It is called 'KSET ES Board'. It is based on AVR microcontroller, a leading microcontroller today. In addition, it contains several sensors, LCD screen, LEDs, etc. all on same board. You don't need to connect any additional hardware to start using it. Importantly, the cost of the board is only Rs. 3000. It can be ordered online through http://quest.ksetindia.com.

In this book, we will use KSET ES Board as a reference. However, concepts that you learn here will be useful in working with other microcontrollers and boards as well.

Details of KSET ES board

KSET ES board has been designed with a single goal in mind - "to make it easy for students and professionals to learn embedded systems". Towards this end, this highly functional embedded development board has following features:

- AVR ATmega32 microcontroller
- 2-line LCD display
- 8 LEDs
- Temperature sensor
- RTC (Real Time Clock) chip

- Light sensor
- Buzzer
- Four on-board keys for input
- External interrupt pins
- Operation using 9V battery or AC adapter
- Complete toolchain for programming the board
- Videos indicating how to use the board

Figure 5.2: KSET ES Board

The programming environment for KSET ES board is extremely simple and intuitive. This makes embedded systems fun to learn and interesting. The board also comes with pin headers to enable users to attach external devices and build projects in embedded systems.

Microcontroller

A microprocessor has three parts—Arithmetic Logic Unit, Control Unit and registers (like memory). The control unit is the circuitry that directs the operations of the CPU. As the name suggests, the ALU performs arithmetic operations (addition, subtraction, and sometimes multiplication and division, though this is more expensive), bitwise logic operations (AND, NOT, OR, XOR) and bit-shifting operations (shifting or rotating a word by a specified number of bits to the left or right, with or without sign extension).

A microcontroller (or MCU) is a computer-on-a-chip. Apart from CPU a microcontroller also has the following:

- RAM for data storage during program execution
- ROM, EPROM, EEPROM or Flash memory for program storage
- Input/output interfaces such as serial ports (UARTs)
- Other serial communications interfaces like I^2C
- Internal devices like Counters
- Peripherals such as timers and watchdog
- Clock generator - often an oscillator for a quartz timing crystal, resonator or RC circuit
- Analog-to-digital converters

Thus a microcontroller emphasizes self-sufficiency and cost-effectiveness, in contrast to a general-purpose microprocessor (the one used in a PC).

Selecting a correct microcontroller is one the most important tasks in creating good embedded systems. We have chosen AVR ATmega32 microcontroller for the KSET ES board. Although several other microcontrollers are available in the market today, AVR is the best one in our opinion for following reasons:

- It uses RISC design - proven to be better technology for embedded processors. Support for 32 general purpose registers makes it very appealing for programming using higher level languages like C.

- It has very simple instruction set "designed for C" - which makes it possible for us to write all our programs in C - rather than assembly language.

- It is a high-performance, low-power consumption microcontroller.

- Although it is an 8-bit microcontroller, it supports 16-bit and 32-bit arithmetic.

- It contains flash, RAM and EEPROM all inside the same chip resulting in more compact designs.

- AVR microcontrollers range from small "Tiny" series with 8-pin chips to higher end Mega series with much larger flash and memory for more demanding applications.

- Tools for AVR are available from Open Software community. No commercial compiler and other tools and needed for development. This makes it ideal for use for a student.

- AVR microcontroller supports In-System Programming. In-System Programming is the ability of the microprocessor to be programmed while installed in a complete system, rather than requiring the chip to be programmed prior to installing it into the system.
- Operating voltage can be between 1.8 - 5.5 volts. As a result, it can be used on a board which is powered by a battery whose operating voltage fluctuates commonly.

Memory

How memory in the system is connected to the processor has a significant impact on the performance of an embedded system. Over the years, two models for such interconnection have been established. These are, Princeton Architecture and Harvard Architecture. Both these names come from the Universities in United States of America where extensive research was done on this topic. Let us understand these architectures in short.

Princeton Architecture

In this architecture, the memory for program's instructions and data is same. This model is widely used in today's PC, where instructions as well as data for the program occupy space in same RAM. For executing instructions or performing calculations on data, the instruction and the data have to be brought from memory to CPU.

The advantages of this approach are as follows:

(a) Better utilization of available memory as instructions and data share same memory space.
(b) Less complex interconnections are required between processor and memory.

This approach has its disadvantages as well.

(a) At any given time either instructions or data can be fetched from memory.
(b) There is more contention for available memory as instructions and data compete for same memory.

Harvard Architecture

In this model, there is separate memory for instructions and data of a program. These two memories are connected to processor independently. The advantages of this approach are as follows:

(a) Better memory bandwidth utilization as instructions and data can be fetched in parallel.
(b) No contention between program's data and instructions for same memory.

Designer of an embedded system can choose different technologies for instruction memory and data memory. With advancements in technology, flash memory has become very cheap compared to static RAM. Also, most programs contain 90% instructions and 10% data. As a result, many embedded system designers prefer to use Flash memory for instructions and the more expensive Static RAM for data memory.

However, this approach has following disadvantages:

(a) The data memory and the instruction memory cannot be shared.
(b) Fragmentation may occur thereby wasting some space in respective memories.
(c) Interconnection between memories and processor is more complex.

Advantages of Harvard Architecture far outweigh its disadvantages; as a result, most embedded systems today use this model.

Registers

A microprocessor has several registers. A register is nothing but a small amount of very fast memory. Registers are used to speed up the execution of programs by providing quick access to commonly used values—typically, the values being used for calculations at a given point in time.

AVR microcontroller architecture uses the load-store principle. This means that it moves the data from main memory into registers, operates upon it and then moves the result back into main memory.

Registers are normally measured by the number of bits they can hold, for example, an '8-bit register' or a '16-bit register'. There are several classes of registers according to their content. For example, Data registers are used to store data, whereas Address registers hold memory addresses and are used to access memory. General purpose registers (GPRs) can store both data and addresses, i.e., they are combined Data/Address registers. There also exist Special purpose (function) registers (SFRs) that can hold program state. For example, a SFR can hold address of the instruction begin executed. Another SFR can hold address of current top of stack.

General Purpose I/O ports

Most embedded systems are designed to interact with external devices. There are two types of devices—input and output. Devices like keyboard, mouse, temperature sensor etc. are input devices. The signals they generate are read by microcontroller. Devices like motor, lathe machine, LCD

(Liquid Crystal Display), LEDs (Light Emitting Diodes) are output devices. Microcontroller generates signals that are communicated to these devices. Most interactive embedded systems contain several input and output devices. Number of input and output devices is not fixed. As a result, a microcontroller designer must make provision for reasonably large number of I/O (input/output) devices to be connected to it. The microcontroller pins where these devices can be connected are known as I/O pins. These pins are grouped together and often called as 'ports'. Each port typically consists of 8 I/O pins. These ports are *general purpose* in the sense that they can be configured by the programmer to act either as input or as output port.

AVR I/O ports

AVR ATmega32 MC consists of 4 I/O ports. They are referred to as port A, B, C and D respectively. Each port consists of 8 pins. Each pin is bi-directional, i.e. it can be independently configured as Input or Output. At any given moment a pin can be either input or output, never both. Each port has a register associated with it. These registers are called as PORTA, PORTB, PORTC and PORTD respectively. Direction (input/output) of each pin for a port is configured with a direction register for that port. For each port there is one direction register. They are named DDRA (Data Direction Register A), DDRB, DDRC and DDRD respectively. To make a pin output, binary value 1 has to be written to its position in direction register. For example, writing 1 to bit 7 of DDRA makes pin 7 of PORTA output. Similarly, writing FFF0 to pin 4 of DDRA make it an input pin.

Each microcontroller has a datasheet that is supplied by the manufacturer. The datasheet contains detailed description of each pin of a microcontroller. ATmega32 microcontroller that we have used with KSET ES board is available in 40-pin DIP

(Dual In-line Package) with 20-pins to each side. Out of these, 32 pins are for ports A, B, C and D. Keep in mind that DDRA, B, C & D are not pins of microcontroller. They are simply internal I/O control registers that let a programmer control direction of a port's pin. We will later see how I/O ports are used to interact with different type of external devices.

Exercise

[A] Answer the following:

(a) What is the main difference in Harvard and Princeton memory architectures?

(b) What are Registers? What are different types of registers?

[B] Pick up the correct alternative for each of the following questions:

[1] Which of the following statement is incorrect about an AVR ATmega32 microcontroller?

(a) It uses CISC design
(b) It can be programmed in C
(c) It has a low power consumption
(d) It supports In System Programming

[2] AVR ATmega32 Microcontroller consists of how many 8-bit I/O ports?

(a) 4
(b) 8
(c) 16
(d) 32

[3] Each AVR ATmega32 has how many pins?

(a) 8

(b) 16
(c) 40
(d) 64

[4] Direction of each pin for a port is configured using which of the following?

(a) Direction register
(b) Input register
(c) Output register
(d) I/O register

[5] What is a register?

(a) It is external memory connected to Microcontroller
(b) Magnetic memory
(c) Internal memory of Microcontroller
(d) Area in PROM

[6] How many general-purpose registers does AVR AtMega32 have?

(a) 12
(b) 16
(c) 8
(d) 32

[7] In which of the following architecture the memory for program's instructions and data is same?

(i) Princeton architecture
(ii) Harvard architecture

(a) Only (i)
(b) Only (ii)
(c) Both (i) and (ii)
(d) Neither (i) nor (ii)

[8] Which of the following statements are correct?

(i) In Princeton architecture, there is a better utilization of available memory as instructions and data share same memory space.

(ii) In Princeton architecture, there is less complex interconnections are required between processor and memory.

(a) Only (i) is correct.
(b) Only (ii) is correct.
(c) Both (i) and (ii) are correct.
(d) Both (i) and (ii) are incorrect.

[9] In which of the following architecture, there is separate memory for instructions and data of a program?

(i) Princeton architecture
(ii) Harvard architecture

(a) Only (i)
(b) Only (ii)
(c) Both (i) and (ii)

(d) Neither (i) nor (ii)

[10] Which of the following statements are correct?

(i) In Harvard architecture, there is better memory bandwidth utilization as instructions and data can be fetched in parallel.

(ii) In Harvard architecture, there is no contention between program's data and instructions for same memory.

(a) Only (i) is correct.
(b) Only (ii) is correct.
(c) Both (i) and (ii) are correct.
(d) Both (i) and (ii) are incorrect.

6 First Embedded System Program

Embedded Systems are vastly different than a PC-based computing system. The embedded system boards are much smaller. They are customized to do one task, and do that well. For all the programs to follow in this book, we will use KSET Embedded System Board. Using a specific board allows us to test our knowledge of embedded systems hands-on. In this chapter, we will demonstrate how to use the board to run our first embedded system program on it.

Embedded System Programming

Once the embedded system board is selected, there are four steps involved in the embedded system programming sequence:

Create - Write a the Program

Build - Compile the Program to obtain machine language code

Burn - Transfer the program to ES internal memory

Execute - Run the program

Figure 6.1 shows these options. Most programmers would use one of the following four options to perform these steps.

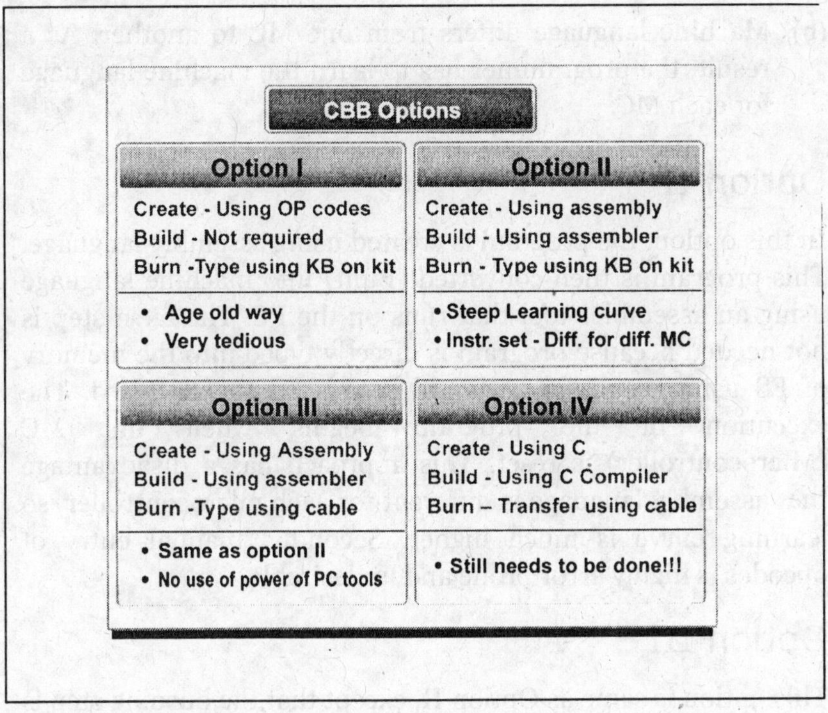

Figure 6.1: CBB Options

Option I

In this option the programmer can create the program using low-level Opcodes (operation codes) in machine language. The build step will not be required as the program directly uses machine language. The burn step is also not needed because program is directly typed into the memory of ES using a special keyboard connected to the ES Board. Execution of the program begins when the MC (Microcontroller) is reset. This approach has several disadvantages. These are:

(a) It's an age old and tedious method as the programming has to be done using opcodes.

(b) Machine language differs from one MC to another. As a result, the programmer has to learn the machine language for each MC.

Option II

In this option, the program is created using assembly language. This program is then converted (Built) into machine language using an assembler tool that runs on the PC. The burn step is not needed because program is directly typed into the memory of ES using a special keyboard connected to ES Board. The execution of the program begins when the MC (Microcontroller) is reset. This approach has a disadvantage that assembly language is different for each microcontroller, so learning curve is much higher. Secondly, manual entry of opcodes is highly error prone and undesirable.

Option III

This option is same as Option II, except that the burning step is different. The burning step is done by connecting a special cable between ES Board and the PC. Then by executing a burning program on the PC, the program is transferred from the PC to the embedded system. Execution once again begins when the MC (Microcontroller) is reset. This approach has same disadvantages as option II.

Option IV

In this option, the program is created using C language. This program is then built using a cross-compiler and linker on the PC. Then program is transferred to the ES Board using a special cable. Special burning program installed on the PC does this job. Execution begins when the MC (Microcontroller) is reset. This is the best approach, as it uses full power of today's PC-based embedded system tools and portable language like C.

This approach makes it easier for developers to work with a variety of embedded systems.

Naturally, out of these options, we will be using Option IV for building embedded systems in this chapter and the chapters to follow. But to be able to reach there, we must first create an embedded system program. It is time we begin with the same.

The "Hello World!" Program

Unlike the color monitors for PCs, the display units of most embedded systems are quite different. Most embedded systems have limited display capabilities and as a programmer, you must be able to convey your messages to a user in concise manner. For example, everything that you do with your home CD or DVD player is displayed on a small LCD unit present on the front-panel of the CD / DVD player.

The KSET ES Board also has a LCD display unit fixed on it. This LCD display has following characteristics:

- The LCD is an output device connected to ATmega32 MC
- It has a two-line black and white display
- Each line can display 16 characters each
- Each character has a width of 5 x 8 dots (or pixels)

Let us now write a program that will display a **Hello World!** string on the LCD of the KSET ES board. Here is the program...

```
#include <avr/io.h>
#include "lcd_io.h"

/* function prototype */
void hello_world ( void ) ;
```

```
int main ( void )
{
    lcd_init( ) ;
    hello_world( ) ;
    return 0 ;
}

void hello_world ( void )
{
    /* Clear LCD Screen */
    lcd_clrscr( ) ;

    /* Goto top left corner of LCD Screen. (x, y). (0, 0) indicates origin */
    lcd_gotoxy ( 0, 0 ) ;

    lcd_putc ( 'H' ) ;
    lcd_putc ( 'e' ) ;
    lcd_putc ( 'l' ) ;
    lcd_putc ( 'l' ) ;
    lcd_putc ( 'o' ) ;

    /* Print string on LCD screen */
    lcd_puts ( " World!\n" ) ;
}
```

Let us now try to understand this program. Interfacing with an LCD is quite complex. Hence we have used a LCD library written in C language rather than working with LCD directly using low-level commands to interface with it. Prototypes for various functions in the LCD library are available in header file **lcd_io.h**. Hence we have included this header file at the top.

Before using LCD we need to initialize it. For this we have called **lcd_init( )** function. This function sends a 'control word' to the LCD informing it how the MCU will communicate with it. This control word includes information like:

- Wait for 50 milli-seconds for LCD power on.
- Communication between LCD and MC be done using 4 bits.
- LCD be put in entry mode for output. When set in this mode a character can be displayed in LCD.
- On writing a character, cursor be moved from left to right.

To display a character in LCD screen, **lcd_putc( )** function is used. This is similar to standard C library routine **putc( )**. To display entire string we can use the **lcd_puts( )** function. Note that after a character is displayed on LCD screen, the cursor moves to next location on it. If cursor is already at the end of first line, it goes to the first character on second line.

If we wish to display a number it can be accomplished using the **lcd_puti( )** function. This function takes two arguments—number to be displayed and the number of digits from right-hand side after which decimal point is displayed. The following calls can display the numbers 2 and 2.15.

```
lcd_puti ( 2, 0 ) ;
lcd_puti ( 215, 2 ) ;
```

There are many other useful functions in LCD library. Some of these are as follows:

lcd_home( ) - Returns the cursor to first character on first line.

lcd_clrline( ) - Clears the current line.

lcd_getxy( ) – Returns current cursor position as an unsigned short. Lower byte of this unsigned short int contains column number, whereas, higher-byte contains the row number.

lcd_command (cmd) - Accepts various command codes to display cursor, blinking cursor, turn-off cursor, cursor movement direction (Left to Right or Right to Left).

Now that our first embedded system program is ready let us see how we can create it, build it, burn it and execute it.

Creating The Program

First step in working with KSET ES Board is to create a project. A project consists of all the necessary files needed for working with the embedded system. To make it easier to locate the files, all files for a project should be placed in the project directory. To create the project directory and to create the skeleton files in it, we have created a simple program called **newavrproject**. This program is present in the CD accompanying this book.

To run this program, all that you have to do is start a command window by typing **cmd** in the Start | Run dialog. Once you get the command window change to the directory where you want to create your programs as shown below:

```
$cd C:/myprograms
```

Next, type the following command:

```
$newavrproject helloavr
```

This will create a folder called **helloavr**. Inside this folder, files **helloavr.c**, **helloavr.h** and **makefile** would get created.

Now you can type our program in helloavr.c file using the Programmer's Notepad. 'helloavr.c' contains some initial code for getting started. You must add all your shown above, inside **main( )** function. Next, add the prototypes in 'helloavr.h'. A separate header file makes it easier for you to understand and maintain your programs. It also ensures that your function prototypes, macros etc. remain in a different file.

Building The Program

When you are finished typing the program, you must save it, go back to **cmd** window and type:

```
$ cd helloavr
$make
```

The **make** utility will now use the commands present in 'makefile' to compile and link our program. The command window will display the sequence of steps that would be carried out. If you have made a mistake while typing the program, compiler will indicate the line number and name of the file where you have made a mistake. You must correct these mistakes using Programmer's Notepade editor, save the file and retype **make** to build the program once again. If everything goes well, a file called **helloavr.hex** would be generated inside the folder **helloavr**. Note that, unlike the PC environment, the output of this build process is a .hex file and not an .exe file. We would learn more about the hex file format in a later chapter. This is the file that must be now transferred to ATmega32 MC present on the KSET ES board.

Burning The Program

In this step executable program generated on your PC is transferred to KSET ES board using a process called In System Programming (ISP). To do this, you have to use the parallel-port programming dongle and the ISP ribbon cable. Both of these come with the KSET ES board kit. You should connect the parallel-port programming dongle to the parallel port connector present at the back of your PC. At the back of this dongle, you should connect one end of ISP ribbon cable. The other end of the ISP cable must be connected to pin-header marked 'ISP' on the KSET ES board. Once this is done, you are now ready to transfer the program from PC to ATmega32's internal flash memory. To do this, type the following command in the **cmd** window (you must be inside c:/myprogram/helloavr directory when you type this command):

```
$make program
```

The messages on the screen should indicate that the program has been successfully transferred to ATmega32's flash memory. What if there is a problem? Don't panic! Please read the messages on the screen carefully. Check the ISP cable connection between parallel-port dongle on PC end and ISP pin-header on board side to ensure that there is no loose connection. Do not ever touch any components on the board with bare hands. Static electricity from your body parts may damage sensitive IC (Integrated Circuit) chips on the board.

How does the program get transferred to ATmega32's flash memory? – This is done using a tool called "avrdude". This is a PC based tool that takes generated program as input and uses the ISP cable to transfer it to ATmega32 using special "In System Programming" procedure. We will explore this tool in greater detail later.

Running The program

If your program is transferred successfully to the AVR microcontroller present on the KSET ES board, then it is ready for execution. In fact, if transfer was successful, ATmega32 would be reset at the end of Burn phase and you should see your program display **Hello World**! on the LCD screen.

Frequently Asked Questions

Many people get the feeling at this stage that this was too simple. Certainly it has been made simple so that you can learn embedded systems one step at a time. Understanding everything at the outset is certainly not feasible. Some of the commonly asked questions and their answers are mentioned below:

Question: Who created LCD library?

Answer: Chris Efstathiou (hendrix@otenet.gr). People like Chris create such software for the community free of cost for the benefit for students and professionals alike. Hats off to them!

Question: Who wrote makefile.inc? Where is it?

Answer: This is a master makefile. We have created it for you. Your makefile includes this file. Most of the instructions to build a program arc inside this master makefile. One day you will be able to create your own master makefile. Don't rush right now - you are likely to get overwhelmed.

Question: Do I have to understand all this right now?

Answer: Of course not. One of the most important things while learning a new technology is to manage complexity. We will help you in this process by teaching you everything it takes to master embedded systems, one step at a time. Have patience and you will be rewarded! Writing makefiles and libraries like LCD library require you to read the datasheets and a lot of documentation. With experience and maturity you too can do it.

Exercise

[A] Answer the following:

(a) Write a program that displays “Hello” in one line and “World!” in another line of the 2-line LCD display.

(b) Write a program that blinks a message “Hello World!” on the LCD display.

(c) Write a program that displays “Hello World!” in the pattern shown below in the 2-lin LCD display:

```
H   L   O   O   L   !
  E   L   W   R   D
```

[B] Pick up the correct alternative for each of the following questions:

[1] Which form of memory is used by AVR ATmega32 to store automatic variables during execution?

(a) Flash
(b) EEPROM
(c) SRAM
(d) DRAM

[2] AVR ATmega32 executes the program from

(a) Flash
(b) ROM
(c) SRAM
(d) PC

[3] What is the best way for developing an embedded system?

(a) Create using Assembly, Build using assembler, Load using keyboard on kit
(b) Create using C language, Build using make, Load using In-System Programming
(c) Create using Opcodes, Build, Load using In-System Programming
(d) Create using Assembly, Build using Assembler, Load using In-System Programming

[4] Which of the following is the correct embedded system programming sequence?

(e) Create, Build, Burn and Execute
(f) Create, Build, Execute and Burn
(g) Create, Burn, Build and Execute
(h) Create, Execute, Burn and Build

[5] Which of the following statements are correct?

(i) The LCD is an output device connected to ATmega32 MC.
(ii) The LCD display has a one-line black and white display.

(a) Only (i) is correct.
(b) Only (ii) is correct.
(c) Both (i) and (ii) are correct.
(d) Both (i) and (ii) are incorrect.

[6] Which of the following statements are correct?

(i) Each line of the LCD display can display 16 characters.

(ii) Each character of the LCD display has a width of 8 x 8 dots or pixels.

(a) Only (i) is correct.
(b) Only (ii) is correct.
(c) Both (i) and (ii) are correct.
(d) Both (i) and (ii) are incorrect.

[7] In which of the following header file the prototypes for various functions in the LCD library are available?

(a) lcd.h
(b) lcd_io.h
(c) io.h
(d) io_lcd.h

[8] Which of the following function is called to initialize the LCD?

(a) lcd_init( )
(b) init( )
(c) initialize_lcd( )
(d) initialize( )

[9] Which of the following statement is correct about the code snippet given below?

```
void delay ( void ) ;
int main ( void )
{
    int i ;
    while ( 1 )
    {
        lcd_gotoxy ( i, 0 ) ;
        lcd_puts ( "Hello world" ) ;
        delay( ) ;
        lcd_clrscr( ) ;
        if ( ++i > 16 )
            i = 0 ;
```

```
        }
        return 0 ;
}

void delay ( void )
{
        unsigned char i, j, k ;
        for ( i = 0 ; i < 255 ; i++ )
        {
                for ( j = 0 ; j < 255 ; j++ )
                        for ( k = 0 ; k < 123 ; k++ ) ;
        }
}
```

(a) The code display Hello World on the LCD in a banner like fashion in the first row.
(b) The code displays Hello World only once.
(c) The code first displays Hello World on the first row and then on the second row.
(d) The code display Hello World on the LCD in a banner like fashion in the second row

7 Blinking LEDs

In the last chapter, we saw how we can use LCD to display a message. In this chapter, we will see how to control LEDs (Light Emitting Diodes) through an embedded system program. LEDs are used quite commonly for visual displays. For example, the DVD player or television set has several small LEDs on the front-panel. Each LED is used to indicate certain status. For example, a DVD may have a green LED that glows when the DVD disc is loaded inside it. It may have a red LED to indicate that the drive is busy and cannot be ejected right now. Let us now see how we can use the LEDs present on the KSET ES Board.

LEDs And How To Glow Them?

LEDs are used for visual display needs. In simplest words LED is like a bulb with two pins. If current flows between these pins, the LED can glow. For the current to flow, there must be voltage difference between two pins of LED. We must do the following to achieve this:

(a) Connect the LED pins to form a circuit.

(b) Through an embedded system program, generate a voltage difference between two pins of the LED connected to the circuit.

These steps are discussed below in detail.

Creating The LED Circuit

To establish the circuit one pin of the LED should be connected to a 5V power supply. The other pin of the LED should be connected to a pin on ATmega32 microcontroller. The ATmega32 microcontroller has 40 pins. Of these, 32 pins are reserved for input/output with external devices. In our case, this device happens to be LED. Instead of numbering these I/O pins from 0 to 31, they are combined into 4 groups, each of 8 pins. These groups are called ports. These ports are named as Port A, Port B, Port C and Port D. Microcontroller identifies these ports using addresses. These addresses are used to send/receive value to/from an I/O ports. For each port, multiple addresses may be allocated. For example, 3 addresses are allocated for Port B, 3 for port C and 3 for port D.

Do not confuse the port addresses with memory addresses. What is written to a memory address is retained till it is overwritten. Same is not true about a port address. Thus memory is *recollection of past*. Memory preserves what was last written to it and returns same content whenever we read from that address in memory. Unlike this, I/O ports have values that depend on external inputs or conditions inside the MC. If you read an input port two times in a row, each time the value at these pins may be different. Hence addresses of memory locations (in RAM) and those for I/O devices like ports are different.

Another term that is used loosely with port address is 'register'. So instead of saying that a value is sent to a port address, many texts say that a value is sent to a port register. In reality, registers are present only inside the CPU of the microcontroller and there doesn't exist anything like a port register.

Controlling The LED Circuit

To glow the LED, we should ensure that the voltage at the microcontroller pin to which the second pin of the LED is connected is 0V. To achieve this we should first configure the port to which this pin belongs for output. Next, we should write a value 0 to the address of this pin. Port configuration is done by sending a suitable value to the appropriate address of the port.

For example, suppose that the LED is connected to Pin 1 of PORTA. To glow this LED we must first set the Bit 1 at port address (configure) to 1 and then set Bit 1 at port address to 0 (write). It is common to say the same thing as—set bit 1 of DDRA register and write 0 to bit 1 in PORTA register.

LED Blinking Setup On KSET ES Board

KSET ES Board has 8 LEDs on it. They are arranged in the sequence—one yellow LED, one green LED, one red LED followed by 5 yellow LEDs. As mentioned in the previous section, to make these LEDs blink, one pin of each of the 8 LEDs is connected to 5V power supply, whereas the other pin should be connected to one of the port of ATmega32 MC. Note that on KSET ES Board, the LED pins are not connected to any of the AVR I/O ports permanently. This gives us flexibility to connect them to any of the 4 ports. To establish connection between LEDs with one of the I/O ports, we should use the small ribbon cable (this comes with KSET ES Board) to connect LED pin header (with the cable notch in correct orientation) to PORTA pin header (with notch in correct orientation). The value that we write to PORTA will determine whether LEDs glow or not.

ATMega32 has provision for 64 I/O addresses. Out of these, 3 addresses are assigned to each of the I/O ports. For example, addresses 0x3A, 0x3B and 0x3C are assigned to Port A. Of these, for blinking LEDs we need to use only two addresses—0x3A and 0x3B. First we need to configure the pins of Port A for output by writing a suitable value at address 0x3A and then send a value to Port A that makes the LEDs blink by writing a suitable value at address 0x3B. The following section discusses the program that shows how this can be achieved.

LED Blinking Program

We intend to write a program that makes all 8 LEDs on the KSET ES board to turn on and off at one second intervals. Here is the program...

led_blinking.h

```
#ifndef led_blinking_h_
#define led_blinking_h_

/*
 * This header file contains all AVR specific port, memory and other I/O
 * addresses.
 */
#include <avr/io.h>

typedef unsigned char  u08 ;

/* function prototypes */
void led_blink ( void ) ;
void delay ( void ) ;

#endif /* led_blinking_h_ */
```

led_blinking.c

```
# include <compat/deprecated.h>
# include "led_blinking.h"

# define MYDDRA   ( * ( volatile u08 * )( 0x3A ) )
# define MYPORTA  ( * ( volatile u08 * )( 0x3B ) )

int main ( void )
```

```
{
    led_blink( ) ;
    return 0 ;
}

/* Lights 4 LEDs at a time and after a delay lights remaining four */
void led_blink( )
{
    u08 num = 0 ;
    MYDDRA = 0xFF ;
    for ( ; ; )
    {
        MYPORTA = num ;
        num ^= 0xFF ;
        delay( ) ;
    }
    return ;
}

void delay( )
{
    u08 i, j, k ;
    for ( i = 0 ; i < 255 ; i++ )
    {
        for ( j = 0 ; j < 255 ; j++ )
        {
            for ( k = 0; k <= 59 ; k++ )
            {
                ;
            }
        }
    }
    return ;
}
```

The program has been designed to make all 8 LEDs turn on and off at one second intervals. In order to do this, we must first configure 8 pins of port A as output. For this we must write a value 0xFF to DDRA (Data Direction Register) for port A. How do you do this in C language? It is simple enough. We simply have to cast the address of DDRA (in I/O memory) to **unsigned char pointer** datatype, and then use * (value at address) operator to assign a value to it. This is shown in the following statement:

```
*( ( volatile unsigned char * ) 0x3A ) = 0xFF ;
```

You would agree that this is a bit clumsy. Hence we have #defined a macro called MYDDRA to get the same effect. Once this macro is defined, it becomes very easy to assign a value to DDRA or PORTA. It can be achieved through simple statements like:

```
MYDDRA = 0xFF ;
MYPORTA = num ;
```

Thus the definitions of **MYDDRA** and **MYPORTA** let you use them in an assignment expression as if they are variables. This technique is very commonly used in embedded systems programming.

led_blink( ) routine implements the blinking functionality. It uses bitwise operator ^ (xor) for inverting the bits written to port A. Between two consecutive writes to port A, there is a delay of 1 second. **delay( )** function provides the delay. To make the LEDs turn on and off, values **0** and **0xff** are written to port A at 1 second intervals in an endless loop.

Why Use Volatile

Do you think that our program would work in all cases? Well, it may not. The reason is that a C compiler cannot distinguish between I/O memory addresses and addresses in normal memory (RAM). This leads to an issue when compiler optimizes memory accesses. If a compiler detects that we are using an address in memory frequently, it will try and assign an register inside the CPU for caching value at that address (for better performance). This is not acceptable for I/O memory addresses. If we write a value to DDRA address and instead of that value being written to it directly, it gets cached in CPU registers, Port A doesn't get configured as output register. So when the following statement is executed

```
// Write value to Port A - make the LEDs glow
* ( ( unsigned char *) 0x3B ) = 0 ;
```

you would expect to see all the LEDs glow because voltage at second pin of all 8 LEDs is 0V. When you actually execute the program, this may not happen! Reason is simple, value **0xFF** was never written to DDRA. It is still cached in CPU's internal register. To prevent this, you must use a C language keyword **volatile**. This keyword ensures that access to any memory location is in the sequence **load**, **modify**, **store**. So the correct way to write this expression (for modifying DDRA) is:

```
* ( ( volatile unsigned char * ) 0x3A ) = 0xFF ;
```

How To Delay Execution?

Why do we need a delay between two consecutive writes to port A? The reason is very simple. The program executes quite fast. If the LEDs blink so rapidly, they will appear to be turned on at all times—making it impossible to detect the fact that they are indeed blinking. Delaying program execution is the simplest option in cases like these. It is ok to waste time (i.e. delay) because a simple program like this cannot do anything else in the meantime. In a real-world embedded system, this waste of time would be unacceptable.

We wish to change the state of the LEDs every one second. To ensure this, we have called the **delay( )** function. Once called, control returns from it after approximately one second. Let us now understand the calculations involved in computing a one-second delay.

ATmega32 MC running at frequency of 8MHz, executes $8*10^6$ instructions in one second. This is because in most ATmega32 instructions are executed in a single clock cycle. Hence, we must execute 8000000 instructions before returning from **delay( )** function. A simple way to do this would be executing a no-operation instruction within 3 **for** loops as shown below.

```
for ( i = 0 ; i < 255 ; i++ )
{
    for ( j = 0 ; j < 255 ; j++ )
    {
        for ( k = 0; k <= 59 ; k++ )
        {
            ;
        }
    }
}
```

The outermost **for** loop has two instructions in it—testing (i < 255) and incrementation (i++). Similarly j loop and k loop also have two instructions in them. Thus total number of instructions that are getting executed are :

256 * 2 + (256 * 2) * 256 + ((60 * 2) * 256) * 256

This expression evaluates to 7995904, which is approximately 8,000,000. Hence this function produces a delay of approximately 1 second.

Port Address-related Macros

Interaction with I/O ports and other I/O memory registers is a frequent necessity when working with ATmega32 or any other MC. We have used two such macros in our program—MYDDRA and MYPORTA. However, finding addresses of each I/O port and creating macros for them can be fairly time consuming and error-prone process. To simplify our life, AVR GCC toolchain provides a set of standard header files that contain these macro definitions. All that we have to do is include the header file **avr/io.h** at the top of our program so that these macros become available to us. These macros are named as **PORTA**, **DDRA**, **PORTB**, **DDRB,** etc. In the programs to follow, we would use these macros rather than our hand-crafted macros.

Standard Header Files

Now that we are through with a few programs on the KSET ES Board, it is time to dig a little deeper. It's important at this time to locate some of the important header files and look inside them. This will be a great learning experience for you. All AVR related header files will be installed in **C:\WinAVR\avr\include** folder. Some of the important files to look at are:

avr/io.h - General header file that includes other important header files

avr/sfr_defs.h - Contains macros that make the I/O memory addressing work

avr/iom32.h - Contains definitions specific to ATmega32 MC.

Other useful files that you commonly use can be found in **C:\myrograms\topdir\avr** folder. It contains master makefile (**makefile.inc**), header files, C files, and datasheets for ATmega32 MC, and many other files that provide a wealth of information and knowledge. As we move deeper into the world of embedded systems, we will start using these files more and more. At this stage we would want to urge you to go through these files frequently, so that you get a better hang of how things work.

Exercise

[A] Answer the following:

(a) KSET ES Board has 8 LEDs. Write a program to turn on one LED at a time. Switch to next pattern should happen after ½ second. The pattern for blinking should be:

LED7, LED6, LED5, LED4, LED3, LED2, LED1, LED0, LED7, LED6,...

(b) Write a program to turn on alternate LEDs. Switch to next pattern should happen after 2 seconds. The pattern for blinking should be:

<LED7 LED5 LED3 LED1>, <LED6 LED4 LED2 LED0>, <LED7 LED5 LED3 LED1>, ...

(c) To generate a delay of 400 milli-seconds, how many no-op instructions will have to be executed?

(d) Display "Hello World" on LCD one character at a time with a "space" between each character and a delay of 0.6 seconds between displaying each character.

(e) Modify the program (d) above to wait for 2 seconds after displaying the string. Then clear the LCD screen and repeat the entire logic.

(f) What is the difference between I/O addresses and memory addresses?

(g) Can we use PORTB on the KSET ES Board for blinking LEDs? If yes, what changes will you make in the program given in the chapter?

(h) Write a program to blink LEDs 0, 1, 2, 3, 4, 5, 6 and 7 one by one using left shift operator?

[B] Pick up the correct alternative for each of the following questions:

[1] Which of the following statements are correct?

(i) LEDs are bulb with two pins.
(ii) When the current flows between the pins of LED, the LED can glow.

(a) Only (i) is correct.
(b) Only (ii) is correct.
(c) Both (i) and (ii) are correct.
(d) Both (i) and (ii) are incorrect.

[2] Which of the following statements are correct?

(i) To establish the circuit both the pins of the LED should be connected to a 5V power supply.
(ii) The ATmega32 microcontroller has 40 pins.

(a) Only (i) is correct.
(b) Only (ii) is correct.
(c) Both (i) and (ii) are correct.
(d) Both (i) and (ii) are incorrect.

[3] Out of 40 pins of ATmega32 microcontroller, how many pins are reserved for communication with external devices?

(a) 32
(b) 16
(c) 8
(d) 4

[4] Which of the following statements are correct?

(i) To glow the LED we should ensure that the voltage at the microcontroller pin to which the second pin of the LED is connected is 0V.

(ii) If the LED is connected to Pin 1 of PORTA, to glow this LED we must first set the Bit 1 of DDRA register and write 0 to bit 1 in PORTA register.

(a) Only (i) is correct.
(b) Only (ii) is correct.
(c) Both (i) and (ii) are correct.
(d) Both (i) and (ii) are incorrect.

[5] Which of the following header file contains macros that make the I/O memory addressing work?

(a) avr/sfr_defs.h
(b) avr/io.h
(c) avr/iom32.h
(d) avr/sfr.h

[6] Which of the following header file contains definitions specific to ATmega32 MC?

(a) avr/sfr.h
(b) avr/iom32.h
(c) avr/sfr_defs.h
(d) avr/io.h

[7] Which of the following statement is correct about the code snippet given below?

```
void delay ( void ) ;
int main( void )
{
    DDRA = 0xFF ;
    int num = 0XFF ;
    while ( 1 )
    {
        PORTA = num ;
        num = num ^ 0XAA ;
        delay( ) ;
    }
    return 0 ;
}

void delay ( void )
{
    unsigned char i, j, k ;
    for ( i = 0 ; i < 255 ; i++ )
    {
        for ( j = 0 ; j < 255 ; j++ )
            for ( k = 0 ; k < 123 ; k++ ) ;
    }
}
```

(a) The LEDs 0, 2, 4 and 6 remain off and LEDs 1, 3, 5 and 7 blink after every 1 second delay.
(b) The LEDs 1, 3, 5 and 7 remain off and LEDs 0, 2, 4 and 6 blink after every second.
(c) All the LEDs blink after every second.
(d) First the LEDs 0, 2, 4 and 6 blink and then LEDs 1, 3, 5 and 7 blink alternately after every 1 second.

[8] Which of the following statement is correct about the code snippet given below?

```
void delay ( void ) ;
int main( void )
{
    DDRA = 0xFF ;
    int num = 0XAA ;
    while ( 1 )
    {
        PORTA = num ;
        num = num ^ 0XFF ;
        delay( ) ;
    }
    return 0 ;
}

void delay ( void )
{
    unsigned char i, j, k ;
    for ( i = 0 ; i < 255 ; i++ )
    {
        for ( j = 0 ; j < 255 ; j++ )
            for ( k = 0 ; k < 123 ; k++ ) ;
    }
}
```

(a) First LEDs 0, 2, 4 and 6 blink and then LEDs 1, 3, 5 and 7 blink alternately after every 1 second.
(b) First LEDs 1, 3, 5 and 7 blink and then LEDs 0, 2, 4 and 6 blink alternately after every 1 second.
(c) All the LEDs blink after every 1 second delay.
(d) The LEDs 0, 2, 4 and 6 remain off and LEDs 1, 3, 5 and 7 blinks after every 1 second delay.

[9] Which of the following statement is correct about the code snippet given below?

```
void delay ( void ) ;
int main( void )
{
    DDRA = 0xFF ;
    int num = 0X01 ;
    while ( 1 )
    {
        PORTA = ~num ;
        num = num * 2 ;
        delay( ) ;
        if ( num > 128 )
            num = 0x01 ;
    }
    return 0 ;
}
void delay ( void )
{
    unsigned char i, j, k ;
    for ( i = 0 ; i < 255 ; i++ )
    {
        for ( j = 0 ; j < 255 ; j++ )
            for ( k = 0 ; k < 123 ; k++ ) ;
    }
}
```

(a) The LEDs 0, 1, 2, 3, 4, 5, 6 and 7 blinks one by one continuously.
(b) Only the LED 0 blinks continuously.
(c) The LEDs 0, 2, 4 and 6 remain off and LEDs 1, 3, 5 and 7 blinks after every 1 second delay.
(d) All the LEDs blink after every 1 second delay.

8 EEPROM Programming

Now that we have developed a couple of programs for the KSET ES board, we are sure you are now familiar with the basics of working in an embedded system development environment. Time has come to understand ATmega32 MC a bit more closely. This is what we intend to do in this chapter.

AVR ATmega32

ATmega32 MC is a MC created by Atmel Corporation. This company was started by two students of Norwegian Institute of Technology, Norway. They named their microcontroller AVR (**A**dvanced **V**irtual **R**ISC). Later they started Atmel corporation that created an entire series of MCs based on their original design. All AVR microprocessors have common instruction set and allow users to choose a MC that is right for their ES.

We have chosen ATmega32 for KSET ES board. It has 32 general purpose registers and a simple instruction set. That makes it easy for programmers to use high-level language like C to program it. It contains 2 KB RAM, 1 KB EEPROM and 32 KB Flash memory all on the same chip. In addition, it has 32 GPIO (General Purpose I/O) pins. They allow large number of external devices to be connected to ATmega32. It has a built-in Serial communication unit, 2 8-bit timers and 1 16-bit timer, an Analog to Digital Converter with 8 channels and 10-bit resolution all inside the same chip. We will study these peripherals during in later chapters. On top of all this there is an internal oscillator that provides accurate clock signal that is necessary for synchronizing the activities of all internal units (including ALU) of the MC. This compactness allows very powerful embedded systems to be created using ATmega32 MC with very little additional circuitry and components.

ATmega32 Memories

Apart from 32 registers (R0 - R31) that are used by ALU, ATmega32 contains 3 different on-chip memories.

Program Memory (Flash) – This is non-volatile i.e. persistent memory. It cannot be modified during program execution. It is largest of all with 32 KB of storage. It stores the program that you transfer from PC to the microcontroller. ALU will fetch instructions from this memory directly - hence the name program memory. We will study flash memory in much more detail later in this book.

Data Memory (RAM) – It is volatile memory and fast because it uses static RAM technology. Data is read from it and written to it during program execution. Size of RAM is 2 KB. It is used to store most of your program's variables when program executes. It is also used for stack and dynamic memory needs of your program. Its limited size means that you must use it prudently.

Configuration Memory (EEPROM) – This is a non-volatile persistent memory. It allows fast reads, but can also be written during program execution. This makes it ideal for storing some configuration parameters/information related with your embedded application. Its size is smallest of all—1 KB. We will study EEPROM in greater detail later in this chapter.

A good embedded system developer must make prudent use of each of these memories. Only through experience one can master these techniques. Managing available memory is one of the key design goals while building an embedded system.

ATmega32 Program Memory

Flash memory of ATmega32 is also called program memory as it stores the program persistently. In most embedded systems, flash acts as the "hard-disk" for persistent storage of program and data. ATmega32 flash is divided into two sections—Application Section and Boot Section.

Size of each section is controlled through some special fuse registers (they can be modified by a programmer using a special technique used for modifying the fuses inside the MC). Application section stores your program. The program execution normally begins in this section. Boot section is optionally used to store a special program called boot-loader. By changing settings of ATmega32 fuses, we can force the execution to begin in boot section. Normally, a boot-loader checks things like—is a new application program ready or updates are necessary, etc. If required, it can initiate a transfer of new application program to the application flash section, burn it and then jump to the application flash section to start normal sequence of execution.

Most embedded systems today use boot-loaders to implement functionality like "automatic updates" to enable devices to update their internal application section if some defect (bug) is found in it. Having a boot-loader program is a very good idea in today's embedded systems.

ATmega32 Data Memory Layout

It is quite common for programmer to believe that an address must always belong to RAM. This is quite natural, because in PC based programming environment, RAM is the only form of memory that is available to the programmer. Microcontrollers on the other hand have lot of diversity when we refer to the term 'address'. It may seem surprising to most of you to know that the smallest address in memory is not zero. You must be wondering how this can be true. The fact is that in order for us to refer to different forms of internal memories and I/O registers of a Microcontroller in a uniform manner, designers of ATmega32 MC have implemented a technique known as 'memory mapping'. In this technique, CPU's internal registers (R0 - R31) and 64 I/O registers are assigned addresses which are adjacent to one another i.e. 0, 1, 2, ..., 31 and 32, 33,...., 95 respectively. Whenever you read/write to any address between 0 - 31, you are in fact referring to CPUs registers and not locations in RAM. Similarly whenever you read/write from/to addresses 31 - 95 you are referring to corresponding I/O registers like PORTA, DDRA, PINA, PORTB etc. and not corresponding RAM addresses. In fact the RAM addresses range from 96 - 2143! All this might appear confusing at the very least for some of you. But rest assured, it is for our own good. By allowing us to refer to CPU registers and I/O registers as if they are normal addresses ensures that a normal C programmer has access to them by merely using * (value at address) operator through our programs. This is precisely what we did when we wrote values to DDRA and PORTA in the LED blinking program in the last chapter.

Now that we have seen how R0 - R31, I/O registers and RAM all enjoy adjacent locations in memory, why wasn't same approach taken for Flash and EEPROM memories? The reason is that these memories have different access characteristics. Flash memory cannot be written to during program execution. EEPROM can be written but it is very slow during these writes. Besides, there is set of steps before we can read/write data from/to flash or EEPROM. A normal * operator generates a memory read access, which is insufficient to access these memories. As a result, these two memories have access methods of their own. We will see this shortly in this book.

ATmega32 EEPROM Memory

ATmega32 contains 1 KB EEPROM. It's a non-volatile memory. i.e. its contents are preserved even if power is lost. It allows single byte reads and writes at a time. There is a limit on how many times a location in EEPROM can be written. For ATmega32, it is 100,000 writes. At 8 MHz frequency EEPROM read time is ~ 0.5 μsec. Writes are slower by almost 2000 times and 1 byte write takes ~ 1.056 msec.

EEPROM cannot be accessed using 'value at address' (*) operator in C language. It requires use of three special I/O registers devoted for this purpose. They are:

EEAR - EEPROM Address Register

EEDR - EEPROM Data Register

EECR - EEPROM Control Register

All internal functional units inside ATmega32 involve one or more I/O registers like these and one must use Control Register in conjunction with other registers to manage I/O with it. Next few sections explain the usage of these I/O registers.

EEPROM Registers

The purpose of each EEPROM register is as follows:

EEDR - This is an 8-bit register. Data from a location in EEPROM cannot be transferred to location in RAM directly when reading from EEPROM. Similarly, data to be written to EEPROM must be first placed in this register. As a programmer you have to know this and manage this register correctly for reading/writing from/to EEPROM.

EEAR - Address of location in EEPROM from/to which data is to be read/written has to be first transferred to this register. ATmega32 EEPROM has 1024 bytes. So this register has two parts - **EEARH** (High-Byte) and **EEARL** (Low-Byte). The highest address is $2^{10} - 1$. As a result, 10 bits are enough to hold highest address in EEPROM. Top 6 bits in **EEARH** are unused and must be set to 0.

EECR - This register controls operation of EEPROM. It has 8 bits—each having a special meaning. A programmer must use this register correctly to control operations. This register also has bits that indicate the status of an operation like read/write. In that sense it acts as a status register.

Top level header file **avr/io.h** contains macros to manipulate these I/O registers just like port registers (PORTA, DDRA etc.)

EEPROM Address Register

This register has two parts—high-byte and low-byte of EEPROM memory location for which read/write is to be performed. As explained earlier, you must set address in these two 8-bit register pair correctly before read/write is performed. Top 6 bits in **EEARH** must be set to 0 as they are reserved and unused for ATmega32 MC.

EEPROM Data Register

For write operation, this register contains data to be written at address specified in **EEAR**. As a programmer you must transfer the byte into this register and then use **EECR** to initiate a write operation.

For read operations, data read from address specified in **EEAR** is made available in **EEDR**. It is your responsibility as a programmer to transfer it from this register to any variable of your choice.

EEPROM Control Register

This is an 8-bit register that is used for controlling EEPROM and indicating status of read/write operation. Each bit in this register has a special meaning. Most important bits and their meanings are as follows:

EERE (bit 0) - If written 1, read operation on address specified in **EEAR** is started.

EEWE (bit 1) - If this bit is written 1 (after setting bit **EEMWE**), write operation on address specified in **EEAR** is started in next CPU cycle. After write operation is completed, ATmega32 will clear this bit automatically.

EEMWE (bit 2) - If this bit is written 1, prior to setting **EEWE** to 1, EEPROM write is started. Otherwise, write operation is not started.

EERIE (bit 3) - If this bit is written 1, an interrupt is generated when write operation is completed. We will discuss interrupts in detail later in this course.

EEPROM Read Function

We can now write a simple function that reads one byte from specified address in EEPROM. Here is the function...

```
unsigned char EEPROM_read ( unsigned int addr )
{
  while ( EECR & ( 1 << EEWE ) )
```

```
    ;
  EEAR = addr ;
  EECR = EECR |  ( 1 << EERE ) ;
  return EEDR ;
}
```

This function takes address as a parameter. It firsts waits for previous EEPROM operation to be completed. This is indicated by clearing of bit **EEWE** in **EECR** register. Once an earlier write operation is completed, address is written to **EEAR** register. Thereafter, bit **EERE** in **EECR** register is set to 1. This starts an EEPROM read operation, result of which is made available in data register **EEDR**. This result is then returned to the caller.

EEPROM Write Function

On similar lines we can write a simple function that writes one byte to a specified address in EEPROM. This function is shown below:

```
unsigned char EEPROM_write ( unsigned int addr, unsigned char data )
{
  while ( EECR & ( 1 << EEWE ) )
    ;
  EEAR = addr ;
  EEDR = data ;
  EECR = EECR | ( 1 << EEMWE ) ;
  EECR = EECR | ( 1 << EEWE ) ;
}
```

This function takes address and byte of data to be written as parameters. It firsts waits for previous EEPROM operation (if pending) to be completed. This is indicated by clearing of bit **EEWE** in **EECR** register. Once an earlier write operation is completed, address is written to **EEAR**. Thereafter, bit **EEMWE** in **EECR** register is set to 1. In next statement, bit **EEWE** in **EECR** register is set. This starts an EEPROM write operation. The function returns immediately without waiting for write operation to be completed as it is substantially slower than a read operation. If this function is called again, next write will not begin unless earlier write operation is completed.

Standard EEPROM Access Functions

In the previous section we saw two functions—one for reading from and another for writing to EEPROM. In practice, we need various functions to interact with EEPROM and check its status. All the necessary support for this is available with GCC AVR toolchain through standard header file **avr/eeprom.h**. It contains numerous macros, typedefs and prototypes with detailed comments explaining the purpose of each. Another advantage in using these versus our own macros and typedefs is that it hides difference in access of EEPROM for other AVR MCs. If you use other AVR MC other than ATmega32, you can still use the same set of functions.

avr/eeprom.h provides functions to read/write EEPROM in units of bytes, words and blocks. For reading a set of consecutive memory locations it provides:

```
eeprom_read_block ( void * pointer_ram, const void *pointer_eeprom,
                    size_t  sz )
```

This function will read an array of bytes from address **pointer_eeprom** in EEPROM memory to an address **pointer_ram** in RAM. Number of bytes copied will be **sz**. **size_t** is a typedef that represents unsigned number. Similarly, the function **eeprom_write_block( )** provides ability to transfer an array of bytes from RAM into EEPROM memory. Keep in mind that reads/writes to EEPROM are always done one byte at a time. Although these functions make it appear that block read/writes are possible, internally they use byte-by-byte approach.

Important Lessons Learnt

Most important points to remember about EEPROM in ATmega32 are as follows:

(a) EEPROM is moderately big - 1024 bytes and should be used well.

(b) EEPROM should be used to store data that changes less frequently and needs to be persistent.

(c) Writes to EEPROM are slower than reads by a factor of 2000.

Storing Variables In EEPROM

It would be nice if we can directly instruct the compiler that a certain variable be stored and accessed from EEPROM directly. But why would we want to do this? Imagine if a mobile company wants to store its name and the number of hours of usage of that phone in memory. If it decides to use flash memory for this purpose there is a problem. The flash can be overwritten by the user easily. However, if this information is stored in EEPROM, it is relatively safe, as the user has no direct access to EEPROM.

There is no mechanism in ANSI C to store variables in EEPROM. This is because it doesn't consider the possibility of multiple types of memory in a system where a C program executes. However, GCC compiler provides extensions to ANSI standard and allows a programmer to do this. Using this extension, variable of any type—char, int, float, string, structure etc. can be stored in EEPROM.

One thing that you have to remember is that these variables cannot be accessed later like normal RAM based variables using ***variable**. You have to use **eeprom_read_xxxx( )** and **eeprom_write_xxxx( )** functions for that. Also not that, if these variables are initialized to some value, then these initial contents must be transferred to correct locations in EEPROM when ISP programming is used to transfer the program to flash.

To instruct a compiler to store a variable a in EEPROM, you must use the following declaration:

```
char ch __attribute__( (section ( ".eeprom" ) ) ) = 'A' ;
```

This instructs the compiler to create a new section called **.eeprom** inside the generated object file. Let us now write a program that would write a variable into EEPROM memory and then read it back. Here is the program...

Program file – eerw.c

```
#include <avr/eeprom.h>
#include "lcd_io.h"

char ech EEMEM = 'A' ;

int main ( int argc , char *argv[ ] )
{
   char   rch = eeprom_read_byte ( & ech ) ;
```

```
    lcd_putc ( rch ) ;
    rch += 1 ;
    eeprom_write_byte ( & ech, rch ) ;

    return 0 ;
}
```

Here we have included **avr/eeprom.h** at the top. This file provides us all necessary EEPROM access functions and macros. A global variable **ech** is declared and initialized as usual, except that an attribute is applied to it. This attribute is GCC's way of indicating that a variable is to be stored in different section of the executable file and not in data section to be loaded in RAM. Instead of writing the complete attribute syntax we can simply use a macro **EEMEM** which is #defined as **__attribute__((section (".eeprom")))** in the header file **avr/eeprom.h**. This makes the code look more compact. When the program is transferred to the KSET ES board the EEPROM memory will now be stored with the value 'A' for the variable **ech**.

Let's now see how we access the variable. Inside function **main**, we have called **eeprom_read_byte( )** with **&ech** as the argument. This reads a byte from specified location in EEPROM and stores the returned value in local variable **rch**. The variable is then printed on LCD using **lcd_putc( ).** Next line increments this variable's value by 1 and then uses **eeprom_write_byte (&ech, rch)** to write the new value to its address in EEPROM.

If you transfer this program to KSET ES board and run the program repeatedly, you will see next character being printed on the LCD each time. This proves that EEPROM is non-volatile memory. Its contents are preserved even if you reset the power to the board.

Internals Of EEPROM Access

How does this work? How does initial value of **ech** ('A') get written to EEPROM? These questions must be bothering you. Here is the explanation. We saw how the attribute instructs compiler to create a new section named **.eeprom** inside the executable. All variables that are marked with this attribute are stored in this section. After the program is linked, two files are created from it—**eerw.hex** and **eerw.eep**. Of these, **eerw.hex** contains the normal program + data to be written to flash memory and **eerw.eep** contains initial contents to be written to EEPROM during ISP (In System Programming) stage.

When you type **make program**, **avrdude** executes a command-line as follows:

```
avrdude -p atmega32 -P lpt1 -c pony-stk200 -u –U flash:w:eerw.hex -u -U
eeprom:w:eerw.eep
```

You can clearly see that this command-line contains arguments for both **eerw.hex** and **eerw.eep** to be written to flash and EEPROM memories respectively. This is how initial values of EEPROM variables are transferred to it. Once program is transferred to ATmega32, it uses current values of variables in EEPROM.

Storing An Array In EEPROM

If we can store a variable in EEPROM, can we not store an array in it? We can. Here is the program to do so...

Header File - eearray.h

```
#ifndef _eearray_h_
#define _eearray_h_

/* Include all system header files here */
#include <avr/io.h>
#include <avr/eeprom.h>
#include "lcd_io.h"

/* Structures/Classes ... */

/* Extern declarations, prototypes etc. ... */

#endif /* _eearray_h_ */
```

Program file - eearray.c

```
#include "eearray.h"

char ehw[ ] EEMEM = { "Hello KSET\n" } ;
void print_ees ( const char *ep ) ;

int main ( int argc , char *argv [ ] )
{
   print_ees ( ( const char *) ehw ) ;
   return 0;
}

void print_ees ( const char *ep )
{
   char   rch ;
   while ( ( rch = eeprom_read_byte ( ep ++ ) ) )
      lcd_putc ( rch ) ;
}
```

The declaration of array is as usual. You must write **EEMEM** after the name of the array. In this case it is initialized to string **Hello KSET\n**. Inside **main( )**, we have called the function **print_ees( )** to walk through the array and print all the characters to LCD screen one by one. It would be quite tempting to use the pointer notation and * operator to do this. However, you must keep in mind that direct access to EEPROM is not possible. So each byte must be obtained explicitly with a call to **eeprom_read_byte( )**.

Exercise

[A] Answer the following:

(a) Store your name in EEPROM and display it on LCD by reading it from EEPROM.

Hint: When program runs for the very first time it should write your name to EEPROM. Write a number to EEPROM when your program runs for the first time. For subsequent invocations of same program you can check if that number is present in EEPROM and not write your name to EEPROM second run onwards.

(b) Why should we not use our versions of read / write functions to read from and write to EEPROM?

(c) For what purpose are RAM, Flash and EEPROM used in embedded system programming?

[B] Pick up the correct alternative for each of the following questions:

[1] In AVR microcontroller family, following types of memory are not present 'in system' ?

(a) DDR RAM
(b) SRAM
(c) Flash
(d) EEPROM

[2] Which form of memory is used to store automatic variables during program execution?

(a) Flash
(b) EEPROM
(c) SRAM
(d) DDR RAM

[3] Which form of AVR memories is fastest?

(a) RAM
(b) ROM
(c) EEPROM
(d) Flash

[4] What is the size of in-system flash for AVR ATmega32 MC?

(a) 32 KB
(b) 1 KB
(c) 512 Bytes
(d) 1 MB

[5] Size of EEPROM for AVR ATmega32 MC is:

(a) 512 Bytes
(b) 1 KB
(c) 2 KB
(d) 256 Bytes

[6] Size of SRAM for AVR ATmega32 MC is:

(a) 512 Bytes
(b) 1 KB
(c) 2 KB
(d) 256 Bytes

[7] For AVR ATmega32, which of the following is EECR?

(a) Flash control register
(b) SRAM control register
(c) USART control register
(d) EEPROM control register

[8] Out of the different on-chip memories present in ATmega32, which of the following memories are persistent memories?

(i) Program memory
(ii) Data memory
(iii) Configuration memory

(a) Only (i) and (ii)
(b) Only (i) and (iii)
(c) Only (ii) and (iii)
(d) (i), (ii) and (iii)

[9] Which of the following EEPROM register has high-byte and low-byte parts for which reading/writing is to be performed?

(e) EEPROM Address register
(f) EEPROM Data register
(g) EEPROM Control register
(h) EEPROM Data Address register

[10] Which of the following statements are correct?

(i) In bit 0 of EEPROM Control register, if 1 is written, read operation on address specified in EEAR is started.

(ii) In bit 1 of EEPROM Control register, if 1 is written, write operation on address specified in EEAR is started.

(iii) In bit 2 of EEPROM Control register, if 1 is written, an interrupt is generated when write operation is completed.

(a) Only (i) and (ii) are correct.
(b) Only (i) and (iii) are correct.
(c) Only (ii) and (iii) are correct.
(d) (i), (ii) and (iii) are correct.

9 Flash Programming

In the last chapter we saw what is EEPROM memory and how to program it. Another commonly used form of memory in embedded system is flash memory. In this chapter we would discuss the details of this memory and write a few programs to use it.

What Is Flash Memory?

Flash memory is a non-volatile memory that has evolved from EEPROM (E^2PROM) memory. Over the years, flash memory capacity has increased and the prices have gone down. It is significantly cheaper than EEPROM. Major difference between flash and EEPROM is that write to flash memory must be done in "blocks" i.e. multiples of 64 or 128 bytes at a time. If you want to modify just one byte, you will have to read all 64 bytes in a block, change one byte that you want inside a buffer in RAM and then erase and write entire block back into flash memory. As a result, flash memory is optimized for large writes and is very poor in performance for small writes. Today, flash memory is very commonly used in pen drives, mobile phones, digital cameras, TV Set-top boxes, industrial applications etc.

Why Is It Popular?

In a typical embedded system, flash serves the same role that a hard-disk serves in a PC based computing system. Advantage of flash is that it has no moving parts and it is much more compact than a hard-disk. Even if it is dropped on floor it doesn't get damaged. Some flash enclosures are designed to work even underwater. Another advantage of flash memory over a hard-disk is faster read times.

Physical Characteristics

When it comes to storing information in flash memory, there are two major types—Single-cell and Multi-cell. Single-cell technology permits 1-bit of information to be stored per cell. Multi-cell technology allows more than one bits to be stored inside same cell, hence allow much higher capacities.

In single-cell as well as multi-cell, there are two major categories—NOR flash and NAND flash. We will study each of these memories in detail in following sections. Choosing a right flash memory for an embedded system is critical. Very often, internal flash memory inside MC is not enough for all the storage needs and external flash memory is required. We will discuss later in this chapter how you should go about choosing right kind of flash memory.

NOR Flash

NOR flash has longer erase and write times than NAND flash. However, it allows 'random-access' to any cell in memory for read operation. Each block in NOR flash has endurance of 10,000 - 100,000 erase + write cycles. After these many erase + write cycles the flash memory may fail. Since the read access is allowed randomly and fast, such flash is suitable for storing program's instructions. In a program when you call a function i.e. jump to another location a fast fetch from a non-adjacent memory location is needed. NOR flash allows this access efficiently. It is commonly used in TV (Television) set-top boxes, PC's BIOS, handheld barcode scanners etc. The cost of NOR flash is lower than that of NAND flash.

NAND Flash

In contrast to NOR flash, NAND flash allows faster erase and write performance. I/O interface of NAND flash doesn't allow 'random' access even for read operations. NAND flash provides sequential access for read operations. This makes it slower than comparable NOR flash for read operations. It is much more compact and provides much better packing density on a semiconductor chip. Write endurance is 10 times more than NOR flash. As a result, it is used in mass storage devices like camera, mobile phones, etc. for storing data where capacity is large and lower price is a big factor.

NOR Flash - Low-level Access

NOR flash is divided into erase segments or blocks. All cells in a block must be erased together. It provides same kind of 'read' access as RAM. It means cells can be accessed at random. Internal flash memory of ATmega32 is NOR flash. Reason for this is, NOR flash is more suitable for storing programs. It provides a specific protocol for erase and writes which will be explained later in this chapter.

NAND Flash - Low-level Access

NAND flash is divided into erase segments or blocks. All cells in block must be erased together. It provides same kind of 'read' access as hard-disk. This means that the cells can be accessed sequentially. It is typically used in embedded systems with large data storage requirement. In certain embedded systems where MC or Microprocessor supports 'Virtual Memory' concept, NAND can also be used to store programs—as program is loaded in RAM prior to execution and 'block' read is not an issue.

ATmega32 Flash Memory

ATmega32 flash is 32 KB of on-chip In System Programmable (ISP) flash memory. It has endurance of 10,000 erase/write cycles. i.e. each block in the flash memory can be erased/written at least 10,000 times. Flash is divided into two sections—Application section and Boot section. Size of each section can be controlled by designer of the embedded system. Application flash holds normal application program, whereas boot flash section may hold boot-loader program. The Boot-loader section is normally unused, unless you create a boot-loader program and transfer it there.

ATMega32 flash supports e**X**ecute **I**n-**P**lace i.e. instructions are executed directly from flash. Application programs cannot write to flash when their execution is in progress. As a result, you must treat flash as read-only memory in all application programs. However, boot-loader program can write to application flash section during its execution.

In System Programming

This is a process in which both application section and boot section of flash memory can be erased and written from an external system (typically your PC). We carry out this process via a utility called **avrdude**. This utility is used in the make program that we have been using in the previous chapters to burn our programs onto the KSET ES board. The avrdude program erases existing flash contents and transfers our program into ATmega32's flash memory. There are two possible ways of doing ISP (In System Programming). These are explained below:

(a) Parallel Transfer – In this method all 8 pins of port B are used to transfer data and all port D pins are used for controlling the ISP process. This is faster because 8-bits of data are transferred at a time.

(b) Serial Transfer – In this method 3 pins of port B are used for data transfer and control operations during ISP process. This is slower because data is transferred 1 bit at a time.

With KSET ES board we use the second approach as it results in much simpler interconnections and circuitry. Secondly, transferring programs of sizes up to 32 KB takes very small time even with this approach.

Reading From Flash Memory

We saw in Chapter 8 how EEPROM uses three registers in order to read from and write to it. Flash memory access also requires a special method for reading and writing. It is provided using two instructions—**LPM** (Load Program Memory) for reading and **SPM** (Store Program Memory) for writing. **SPM** is not very useful, as application programs cannot use this instruction (only boot-loader program can). **LPM** loads one byte at a specified address in flash memory into a variable/address in RAM. GCC AVR tool-chain has a header file called **avr/pgmspace.h** that provides useful functions and macros for accessing flash memory. Most commonly used functions are:

```
pgm_read_byte( )
pgm_read_word( )
pgm_read_dword( )
```

"pgm" is an short-form for "program memory", i.e. flash memory.

Using Flash To Store Variables

In Chapter 8, we saw how we can store variables in EEPROM using a special GCC attribute. It's quite natural to expect that a similar thing should be possible for flash memory. Only those variables that have lifetime of "program" can be stored in flash memory. This means the variables that continue to exist till program execution doesn't come to an end. All global variables and static variables fall under this category.

One thing that you must keep in mind is that the flash memory is read-only when application program executes. This causes no issues with your program's instructions, as code is anyway read-only. However, data or your variables in RAM are always read-write. If you store variables in flash memory, the application program cannot change its value. So when you decide to store a variable in flash, you must ensure that it is a read-only variable.

It is important to understand what happens to normal variables in RAM. How do they get there? Are they automatically stored in RAM during In System Programming? It's quite simple really. When your program is compiled, the compiler creates two sections in it, one for code and another for data. When ISP is used to transfer it to MC, entire program is transferred into ATmega32's flash—code + data. When your program execution begins, first thing that happens (even before **main( )** gets called) is some special linker supplied code is used to copy the **data section** of your program into RAM. This is a step that will not be necessary for variables that you plan to store permanently in flash memory. Thus, storing variables in flash memory, whenever possible, helps conserve precious RAM. This is really very important as ATmega32 has 32 KB of flash memory and only 2 KB of RAM.

As an embedded system developer you must think hard about things like strings, arrays variables etc. in your program that can be read-only. If they can be read-only, then they are good candidates for storage in flash memory.

Storing Read-only Variables In Flash

As we saw earlier, ANSI C standard had no provision to specify that a variable be stored in any place other than RAM. As a result, we have to rely on extensions provided by **gcc** compiler to achieve this. For flash memory we use an attribute named **__progmem__**. To instruct the compiler to store a variable in flash (and not to copy it to RAM prior to execution), you must use this attribute as follows:

```
char fch __attribute__( ( __progmem__ ) ) = 'Z' ;
```

Please note that unlike a variable in EEPROM that is read-write, a variable in flash is always read-only. This means that it must be initialized correctly. If not initialized at the program creation time (by assigning a value to it), its value cannot be changed later making it an unassigned variable that contains garbage data. So make sure that you initialize all such variables appropriately.

The Program

Let us now write a program that uses all the concepts that we have learnt in the previous sections. Here is the program...

Header file – flash1.h

```
#ifndef _flash1_h_
#define _flash1_h_

/* Include all system header files here */
# include <avr/io.h>
# include <avr/pgmspace.h>
# include "lcd_io.h"

/* Structures/Classes ... */

/* Extern declarations, prototypes etc. ... */

#endif /* _flash1_h_ */
```

Program file – flash1.c

```
# include "flash1.h"

char ch ='E' ;
char fch __attribute__((__progmem__)) = 'Z' ;

int main ( int argc, char *argv[ ] )
{
   char   rch = pgm_read_byte ( & fch ) ;
   lcd_putc ( rch ) ;
   lcd_putc ( ch ) ;

   return 0 ;
}
```

This simple program illustrates the usage of **__progmem__** attribute. We have declared the variable **fch** as global. We have assigned a value 'Z' to it and marked it with attribute **__progmem__**. Inside **main( )**, we have used **pgm_read_byte( )** function to read this variable from flash memory. We have then displayed the value of the variable on

LCD screen. The approach is very similar to that used for variables in EEPROM. Needless to say, a typical program may contain some variables that are stored in RAM, some in EEPROM and some in flash memory.

The Header File

Note that the header file **avr/pgmspace.h** serves the same purpose for flash memory that **avr/eeprom.h** does for EEPROM memory. It contains useful functions, macros and declarations that help you work with flash memory. It also gives you ability to work with MCs other than ATmega32. For example, ATmega128 MC has more than 64 KB of flash memory. This requires different access mechanism. **avr/pgmspace.h** hides these differences from a programmer, and makes flash memory access uniform.

Some Useful typedefs

PROGMEM is the most commonly used macro from **avr/pgmspace.h**. It is similar to **EEMEM** and marks a variable to be stored in flash memory using gcc attribute. You must write it after the name of the variable which you want to store in flash.

There are some other useful typedefs like **prog_uint16_t**. This declares a new type and can be used instead of **unit16_t** for all the unsigned 16-bit integers that should be stored in flash memory. There are other typedefs like **prog_char**, **prog_uchar**, etc. Some of these typedefs are shown below:

```
#define PROGMEM   __attribute__ ( ( __progmem__ ) )

typedef char PROGMEM prog_char ;
typedef unsigned char PROGMEM prog_uchar ;
```

```
typedef int16_t PROGMEM prog_int16_t ;
typedef uint16_t PROGMEM prog_uint16_t ;
```

We can use these typedefs as shown below:

```
prog_char ch = 'Z' ;
prog_uchar uch = 0x13 ;

prog_int16_t  si = -12 ;
prog_uint16_t  ui = 12 ;
```

Keep in mind that these typedefs are merely for convenience. You can write **PROGMEM** after any of your own variables. This is true for even a structure variable. This will cause the entire structure to be stored in flash memory during execution. Two things that you should keep in mind with all flash variables are:

(a) They must be global or static.
(b) They must be initialized correctly, because these variables are read-only when program executes.

Working With Arrays

Not that we know how to write a character into flash memory and read it back, let us see whether we can do the same thing for an integer of for a character array. Given below is the program that shows how to achieve this.

Header file – flash2.h

```
#ifndef _flash2_h_
#define _flash2_h_
```

```
/* Include all system header files here */
# include <avr/io.h>
# include <avr/pgmspace.h>
# include "lcd_io.h"

/* Structures/Classes ... */

/* Extern declarations, prototypes etc. ... */

#endif /* _flash2_h_ */
```

Program file – flash2.c

```
# include "flash2.h"

/* Global variables */
prog_char message[ ] = { "Hello\n" } ;
int i PROGMEM = 100 ;

/* Function prototypes */
static void myputs ( char *message ) ;

int  main ( int argc, char *argv [ ] )
{
     myputs ( ( char * ) message ) ;
     lcd_puti ( pgm_read_dword ( &i ), 0 ) ;
     return 0 ;
}

static void myputs ( char *pf )
{
     char ch ;
     while ( ( ch = pgm_read_byte ( pf++ ) ) )
           lcd_putc ( ch ) ;
}
```

Here we have called **pgm_read_byte( )** repeatedly to read the character array from flash memory byte by byte. Every character that is read is displayed on the LCD display using the function **lcd_putc( )**. Similarly we have used the function **pgm_read_dword( )** to read a 4-byte integer, and then displayed it on LCD using the function **lcd_puti ( )**.

More On Arrays

Consider the following program:

Header file – ramarrays.h

```
#ifndef _ramarrays_h_
#define _ramarrays_h_

/* Include all system header files here */
# include <avr/io.h>
# include "lcd_io.h"

/* Structures/Classes ... */

/* Extern declarations, prototypes etc. ... */

#endif /* _ramarrays_h_ */
```

Program file – ramarrays.c

```
# include "ramarrays.h"

char hw1[ ] = { "Hello\n" } ;
char *hw2 = "World" ;

int main ( int argc, char *argv[ ] )
{
```

```
    lcd_puts ( hw1 ) ;
    lcd_puts ( hw2 ) ;
    return 0 ;
}
```

This is a simple program that contains two global variables—**hw1** and **hw2**. **hw1** is an array of characters and **hw2** is pointer to a constant string. This difference is important. Most people think that these two are identical—they are not. **hw2** is simply a pointer not an array. To display these variables on LCD screen we have used the **lcd_puts( )** library function. If you observe the program carefully, you will notice that **hw1** and **hw2** are never modified during program execution. They are perfect candidates for being stored in read-only flash memory. The following program shows how this can be done.

Program file – flasharrays.h

```
#ifndef _flasharrays_h_
#define _flasharrays_h_

/* Include all system header files here */
# include <avr/io.h>
# include "lcd_io.h"
# include <avr/pgmspace.h>

/* Structures/Classes ... */

/* Extern declarations, prototypes etc. ... */

#endif /* _flasharrays_h_ */
```

Program file – flasharrays.c

```
# include "flasharrays.h"

prog_char hw1[ ] = { "Hello\n" } ;
prog_char *hw2 PROGMEM = "World" ;

int main ( int argc, char *argv [ ] )
{
    lcd_puts_p ( hw1 ) ;
    lcd_putc ( ':' );
    lcd_puts_p ( hw2 ) ;
    return 0 ;
}
```

In this program we have simply changed the type **char** to **prog_char** for both **hw1** and **hw2**. Inside **main( )**, we have changed **lcd_puts( )** to **lcd_puts_p( )**. The **lcd_puts_p( )** function takes an address of string stored in flash memory, reads it character by character and displays it on LCD screen. You would expect that output of this program is same as the carlier program. When you build burn and execute this program on KSET ES board, the string **Hello** is indeed displayed on LCD. However, the second string doesn't get displayed correctly.

Understanding why the program didn't work as per our expectations is important. For this you must understand difference between **hw1** and **hw2**. **hw1** is a constant pointer to string that is initialized to **Hello\n**. This value is called string literal. As against this, **hw2** is pointer to a constant string–**World**. As far as C language is concerned, **hw1** cannot be changed but **hw2** can be. The attribute **PROGMEM** in first case is applied to entire array and hence to the string which it is initialized to. In case of **hw2**, the attribute is not applied to the string **World**. It gets applied to the pointer **hw2**. Hence, only pointer **hw2** gets stored in flash. This is not what we wanted. We must change the program to make it work as shown below:

Header file – flasharrays2.h

```
#ifndef _flasharrays2_h_
#define _flasharrays2_h_

/* Include all system header files here */
# include <avr/io.h>
# include "lcd_io.h"
# include <avr/pgmspace.h>

/* Structures/Classes ... */

/* Extern declarations, prototypes etc. ... */

#endif /* _flasharrays2_h_ */
```

Program file – flasharrays2.c

```
# include "flasharrays2.h"

prog_char hw1[ ] = { "Hello\n" } ;
prog_char hw2a[ ] = { "World" } ;
char *hw2 = ( char * ) &hw2a[ 0 ] ;

int main ( int argc, char *argv [ ] )
{
    lcd_puts_p ( hw1 ) ;
    lcd_puts_p ( hw2 ) ;
    return 0 ;
}
```

We have kept the **hw1** declaration as is it. We have changed **hw2** to **hw2a** which is an array and initialized it to **World**. We have then declared **hw2** which is a character pointer and stored the base address of array **hw2a** in it. Now we can use **hw1** and **hw2** uniformly—passing them as arguments to **lcd_puts_p( )**. On running the program, both strings get displayed correctly on LCD display. Make sure that you keep this in mind while storing any array in flash memory—not just strings but array of integers, shorts, structures, etc. as well.

What Are Fuses?

Fuses provide a mechanism to control operation and settings of AVR microcontrollers. Types of settings that can be controlled using fuses are:

(a) Clock frequency
(b) Clock source - internal /external
(c) Size of application / boot flash

Each fuse bit can be either ON or OFF. If set to **0**, it is said to be **programmed**. If set to 1, it is said to be **unprogrammed**. Once these fuses are set, they are persistent. They will retain their current value even in absence of electrical power. ATMega32 has two fuse bytes, i.e. a total of 16 fuse bits which can be 0/1. Next two sections will explore both fuse bytes (high and low) in detail. These fuse bits can only be changed when MC enters **programming** mode i.e. when new program is being transferred into it using ISP process. They cannot be changed programmatically.

Fuse - High Byte

Some of the important bits in high fuse byte and their meaning are as follows:

OCDEN (bit 7) - Enables on-chip debugging. This allows low-level debugging using JTAG debugger. This setting may be enabled during development for finding problems in your program.

JTAG (bit 6) - Enable debugging using a semiconductor industry standard called as boundary scan description language (BSDL) files. This is generally used for testing the chip and not used by a programmer in small embedded system.

SPIEN (bit 4) - Enable serial programming and downloading using Serial Peripheral Interface (SPI). SPI is a high speed serial data transfer interface.

EESAVE (bit 3) - Save EEPROM contents during chip erase.

BOOTSZ1..0 (bits 2,1) - Selects boot section size. This allows 32 KB of flash memory to be divided between application and boot section with boot section size in range of 512 byte – 4KB.

BOOTRST (bit 0) - If programmed, jumps to the start of boot-loader section instead of application section.

Fuse - Low Byte

Some of the important bits in low fuse byte and their meaning are as follows:

CKSEL3...0 (bits 3, 2, 1, 0) - Select clock source. Allows external and internal clock selection. If internal clock source is selected for operation, operating frequencies of 1 - 8 MHz can be selected using these bits.

For KSET ES board, these 4 clock selection bits have values **0100**. This causes internal clock of 8MHz to be selected. How do we know this? For this you have to start reading ATmega32 datasheets. For specific information like this, datasheet is the best reference. Reading datasheets is essential stepping stone towards becoming a good embedded systems developer.

ATmega32 Flash Memory

ATmega32 has 32 KB of flash memory. Flash memory is divided in two sections—application section and boot section. Depending on fuse settings **BOOTSZ1..0** in fuse high byte the size of these sections is determined. These two bits in fuse high byte can have four possible values. Figure 9.1 shows their possible values and respective sizes of application and boot flash sections.

BOOTSZ1	BOOTSZ0	App. Sec. Size	Boot Sec. Size
1	1	31.5 KB	512 bytes
1	0	31 KB	1 KB
0	1	30 KB	2 KB
0	0	28 KB	4 KB

Figure 9.1: AtMega32 Fuse settings

Each section (application and boot) is divided into multiple pages. Page size is 128 bytes (64 words). Flash memory is erased and written one page at a time.

Finding Our Fuse Settings

You must be wondering—how do we find out the fuse settings? It's really easy. **avrdude** can read the fuse settings when we transfer the program to KSET ES board. It can also write the fuse bits. Don't do it just yet. It's very risky. If you mess the fuse bits, it would be difficult to restore back these settings. To read the fuse bits, just type following command:

```
avrdude -p atmega32 -P lpt1 -c pony-stk200 -u -U hfuse:r:"high.txt":r -U
lfuse:r:"low.txt":r
```

This will transfer the fuse high and low bytes in two files—**high.txt** and **low.txt** in current directory. We can use the utilities **xxd**— hexadecimal dump and **sed**— Stream Editor to print out these bits in binary format. For KSET ES board, these settings are as follows:

```
$ xxd -b high.txt | sed -ne 's;^.*: ;;gp'
11011001

$ xxd -b low.txt  | sed -ne 's;^.*: ;;gp'
11100100
```

High fuse byte settings indicate that on reset, execution begins from application flash. EEPROM contents are saved during chip erase and size of boot section is 4 KB.

Low fuse byte settings indicate that clock source internal and operating frequency is 8 MHz. Brown out (i.e. low supply-voltage) detection is enabled.

Exercise

[A] Answer the following:

(a) What is the difference between NOR flash and NAND flash?

(b) On what basis do you decide whether the variables should be stored in EEPROM or flash memory?

(c) Write a program to store the following information in flash memory and then read it and display it on LCD display.

Company name

Date on which the embedded system is installed

Version number of the embedded system.

[B] State whether the following statements are True or False:

(a) ATMega32 flash does not support e**X**ecute **I**n-**P**lace.

(b) NAND flash allows random-access to any cell in memory for read operation.

(c) Each block in NOR flash has endurance of 10,000 - 100,000 erase + write cycles.

(d) NOR flash cells can be accessed sequentially like a hard-disk.

(e) KSET AVR board permits in system programming.

(f) **__progmem__** attribute is available in ANSI C.

(g) Fuses are used to control operation and settings of AVR microcontrollers.

(h) Fuses can be used to set the sizes of application and boot flash sections of AVR microcontroller.

(i) Current fuse settings can be found out using the avrdude utility.

[C] Pick up the correct alternative for each of the following questions:

[1] Which of the following statements are correct?

(i) NAND flash has longer erase and write times than NOR flash.
(ii) Each block in the NOR flash has endurance of 10,000 – 100,000 erase + write cycles.

(a) Only (i) is correct.
(b) Only (ii) is correct.
(c) Both (i) and (ii) are correct.
(d) Both (i) and (ii) are incorrect.

[2] Which of the following statements are correct?

(i) I/O interface of NAND flash allows random access for read operations.
(ii) NAND flash provides sequential access for read operations.

(a) Only (i) is correct.
(b) Only (ii) is correct.
(c) Both (i) and (ii) are correct.
(d) Both (i) and (ii) are incorrect.

[3] Which of the following statements are correct?

(i) Cells in the NOR flash can be accessed at random.
(ii) Cells in the NAND flash can be accessed sequentially.

(a) Only (i) is correct.
(b) Only (ii) is correct.
(c) Both (i) and (ii) are correct.
(d) Both (i) and (ii) are incorrect.

[4] Which of the following are the correct ways to do In System Programming?

(i) Parallel Transfer
(ii) Serial Transfer

(a) Only i
(b) Only ii
(c) Both (i) and (ii)
(d) Neither (i) nor ii

[5] In which of the following ISP method all 8 pins of port B are used to transfer data and all port D pins are used for controlling the ISP process?

(i) Parallel Transfer
(ii) Serial Transfer

(a) Only (i)
(b) Only ii
(c) Both (i) and ii
(d) Neither (i) nor ii

[6] Which of the following statements are correct about flash variables?

(i) They must be global or static.
(ii) They must be initialized correctly as they are read-only when program executes.

(a) Only (i) is correct.
(b) Only (ii) is correct.
(c) Both (i) and (ii) are correct.
(d) Both (i) and (ii) are incorrect.

[7] Which of the following statement is correct about the OCDEN bit in the high fuse byte?

(i) It enables on-chip debugging.
(ii) It saves EEPROM contents during chip erase.

(a) Only (i) is correct.
(b) Only (ii) is correct.
(c) Both (i) and (ii) are correct.
(d) Both (i) and (ii) are incorrect.

[8] Which of the following statement is correct about the BOOTRST bit in the high fuse byte?

(i) It enables serial programming and downloading using Serial Peripheral Interface.
(ii) If programmed, it jumps to the start of boot-loader section instead of application section.

(a) Only (i) is correct.
(b) Only (ii) is correct.
(c) Both (i) and (ii) are correct.
(d) Both (i) and (ii) are incorrect.

[9] Which of the following statements are correct?

(i) The SPIEN bit in the high fuse byte enables serial programming and downloading using SPI.
(ii) SPI is a high speed serial data transfer interface.

(a) Only (i) is correct.
(b) Only (ii) is correct.
(c) Both (i) and (ii) are correct.
(d) Both (i) and (ii) are incorrect.

[10] Which of the following statements are correct?

(i) Bits CKSEL3...0 in the low fuse byte are used to select clock source.
(ii) Bits CKSEL3...0 in the low fuse byte allow external and internal clock selection.

(a) Only (i) is correct.
(b) Only (ii) is correct.
(c) Both (i) and (ii) are correct.
(d) Both (i) and (ii) are incorrect.

10 Programming With Sensors

Most embedded systems need to interact with the external world and be aware of their surrounding conditions like temperature, moisture, light etc. Microcontrollers themselves do no possess the ability to measure there inputs. Hence sensors are used for this purpose. Today, a wide variety of sensors are available. These sensors are designed to measure a specific input condition like temperature, wind speed etc. and make the information available to the microcontroller. Most of these sensors generate differing electrical voltage in response to changes in environment. This difference in electrical voltage makes it possible for us—embedded system programmers to develop interesting systems. This is what we intend to learn in this chapter.

What Is An ADC?

Microcontrollers are designed to work with digital quantities. They work with discrete values that can be represented using binary number system. Some sensors produce output electrical voltage that can take any values between 0 - 5 volts. This value is called analog value (continuously changing value). This creates a problem. The problem is that if you connect these sensors to MC directly, it will treat all voltages between 0 - 2.5 V as binary 0 and > 2.5 V as binary 1. This would be unacceptable. How do we convert the output of sensors (analog values) to a format suitable for MC (digital values)? This is where an **A**nalog to **D**igital **C**onverter helps us out.

To understand how an analog voltage gets converted to a digital value, consider a simple scale. Our voltage scale measures 0 - 5V with markings at every 1V intervals. Suppose on the other side of the scale we write corresponding digital numbers with 3 bit values. On binary side of our scale, we have 8 markings. The smallest voltage on scale (0V) is represented using number 000 and highest (5V) is represented using binary 111. As we move on the scale from left to right, each marking on digital side represents 5 / 2^3 = 0.624V. One thing is very clear. On analog side of the scale we can represent fractional voltage like 1.23V. However, on digital side of the scale there are only 8 values 000 001, 010, 011, 100, 101, 110, 111. Fixed values on digital side of the scale are called discrete values. Hence we can use the approximation scheme shown in Figure 10.1 to represent different ranges of voltages.

Analog Voltage	Digital Value
0 - 0.624	000
0.625 - 1.249	001
1.25 - 1.874	010
1.875 - 2.499	011
2.5 – 3.124	100
3.125 - 3.749	101
3.75 - 4.374	110
4.375 - 5.0	111

Figure 10.1: Analog to digital conversion table

This process of conversion analog values to discrete digital data is called Analog to Digital Conversion. In practice this process is carried out using a special electronic circuit called ADC. Let us now understand most important characteristics of ADCs.

ADCs - Some facts

ADCs produce a digital word (group of bits) for input analog voltage. The resolution of ADC is number of words in digital output. More the bits in output, better the resolution. In the example discussed in last section, if we had 8 bits in output then we could have 256 possible values for corresponding analog voltages. Each bit can then represent

$5V/2^8 = 0.01953V = 19.53\ mV$

Another important factor in design of ADCs is conversion time. It is the time the ADC takes to generate digital word. Faster the ADC, better it is. In general, more the resolution (number of bits in digital output), more the conversion time. Different types of ADCs are available. Most important types are:

(a) Parallel comparator ADC
(b) Successive approximation ADC
(c) Dual-slope ADC

Next section describes the fastest of these i.e. the parallel comparator ADC.

Parallel comparator ADC

Fundamental unit in such ADCs is a comparator. A comparator consists of two analog inputs. Its output is either 5V or 0V (i.e. binary 1 or 0). If voltage at its + input is greater than voltage at its - input, output is 5V. Otherwise it is 0V.

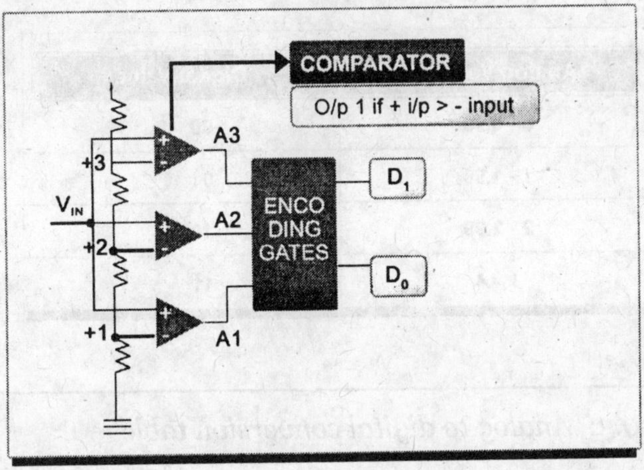

Figure 10.2: Parallel Comparator ADC

Figure 10.2 shows three such comparators. From top to bottom, the - input of comparators are given 3V, 2V and 1V respectively. This is called as reference voltage. + input of each comparator in connected to analog input voltage VIN. Outputs of comparators have been named A3, A2 and A1 respectively. These outputs must be converted to correct digital values. To do that, we need some more digital circuitry—encoding gates. These gates take 3 digital inputs (A3, A2, A1) and produce output word D1, D0. It means that with 3 comparators we can build 2-bit parallel comparator ADC. Our expected input-output table will look as shown in Figure 10.3

Analog Voltage	Digital Value
0 - 0.99	00
1 - 1.99	01
2 - 2.99	10
3 – 4	11

Figure 10.3: Analog to digital conversion table

Consider that input voltage is 2.5V. Output A3 is 0 (+ input < 3V), A2 is 1 (+ input > 2V) and A1 is 1 (+ input > 1V). This must be converted to digital value 10. The logic for this must be written to satisfy the truth table shown in Figure 10.4.

A3	A2	A1	D1	D0
0	0	0	0	0
0	0	1	0	1
0	1	0	1	0
0	1	1	1	0
1	0	0	1	1
1	0	1	1	1
1	1	0	1	1
1	1	1	1	1

Figure 10.4: Encoding gates truth table

Parallel comparator ADC performs the conversion very fast as all comparisons are done in parallel. Only problem is the number of comparators required. For 2-bit resolution we need 3 comparators. For 8-bits 255 comparators will be needed! As a result, it is very expensive. ATmega32 uses successive approximation ADC which is a derivative of this approach. Its conversion time is much higher than ~ 20 nsec, which is the conversion time of parallel comparator ADC.

ATmega32 ADC

ATmega32 contains a 10-bit resolution internal ADC. Its conversion time is ~ 60 µsec. It allows selecting of any one of the eight possible inputs for conversion to digital value. Internally this ADC uses an electronic circuit called multiplexer which selects one of the many inputs (depending on your choice). These 8 inputs are called as channels. These pins are shared with PORTA pins. When ADC is enabled, port A cannot be used for input/output. Of the 8 channels, only one is chosen for conversion. Reference voltage for conversion need not be 5V. In fact internal reference voltage of 2.56V is used most commonly in practice. This ADC uses the Successive Approximation method for converting analog data to digital values. Conversion time is 60 - 260 µsec.

AVR ADC - Sampling

Analog to Digital converters have to deal with input signals that are constantly changing. In fact there is a possibility that input signal changes from the time conversion starts to the time conversion is complete. To deal with this, ADCs provide a sample and hold (S&H) circuit at the input. The input signal at the start of conversion is latched in and even if the real input signal changes, ADC sees the original analog signal. This solves the problem.

There is another issue that an ES developer must deal with—tracking all the changes in input fast enough. Consider an input signal that follows mathematical sine function. To track all the ups and downs in input signal fast enough, how often do we convert to digital value? It depends on time for conversion. We cannot start next conversion until previous one is complete. The rate of conversion is also called sampling interval. If we sample too often we are wasting precious power—which is at a premium in battery powered embedded systems.

The minimum sampling rate was found by scientist Harry Nyquist. It is called Nyquist rate. It says that minimum sampling rate must be twice the rate of changes in input. Thus for signal with **F** cycles/second, sampling rate must be **2F**.

AVR ADC - Registers

In order to use ATmega32 ADC, we must know important registers associated with it. These registers allow us to do following:

(a) Select input channel
(b) Start the conversion
(c) Read the result after end of conversion

In addition to this, we have to select reference voltage—Stable voltage which denotes the maximum value of input analog voltage. For the temperature sensor that we have connected to ADC on the KSET ES board, the reference voltage of 5V is adequate. In practice, depending on range of input voltage, different reference voltage may have to be chosen. Reference voltage and input channel are selected using **ADMUX** (ADC Multiplexer) register. Lower 4 bits are used for channel number and higher two bits (7, 6) are used to select reference voltage.

ADCSR (ADC Control and Status Register) is used to control the ADC and check if conversion is complete. To enable ADC, bit 7 (**ADEN**) in this register must be set to 1. This also ensures that Port-A functionality of ADC channel pins is disabled (ADC channels and Port-A pins are shared. Only one of them can be used at any time). Bit 6 (**ADSC**) is set to 1 to start the conversion for selected input channel. ADC unit will set bit 4 (**ADIF**) to 1, automatically at the end of conversion process. Conversion takes 60 - 260 μsec.

The result of conversion is a 10-bit value which is available in ADC data register (**ADCH**, **ADCL**). Top 6 bits in high-byte of data register (**ADCH**) are reserved. They are always 0.

Measuring temperature

Before we see the program, let us understand the objective and decide the approach. The objective is to measure room-temperature. For this we need to use a temperature sensor. KSET ES board has this sensor—LM35. This sensor produces 10 mV/°C of change in input voltage. For example, if temperature increases by 10 °C, the output voltage of this sensor increases by 100 mV. This sensor is connected to channel 0 (**ADC0**) input on KSET ES board.

We will use 5V as reference voltage. ATmega32 ADC has 10-bit resolution. It means that one bit in output represents

$5V / 2^{10} = 5V / 1024 = 4.88$ mV

Our goal is to display the temperature on LCD screen. The digital output is voltage and not the temperature. How do we get back the temperature?

Temp = Digital Value / (Sensor V/ °C)

= ADC_OUT * 4.88 / 10 = ADC_OUT * 0.488

To get the temperature value, we must multiply the ADC output by 0.488. ATmega32 doesn't support floating point arithmetic. So we can multiple by 49 and display a decimal point with two digits to its right.

The program

Let us now take a look at the program to read ambient temperature. Here it is...

Header file – temperature.h

```
#ifndef _temperature_h_
#define _temperature_h_

#include <avr/io.h>
#include <avr/pgmspace.h>
#include "lcd_io.h"

void delay ( void ) ;
void read_temperature ( void ) ;

#endif  /* _temperature_h_ */
```

Program file – temperature.c

```
#include "temperature.h"

int main ( void )
{
    read_temperature( ) ;
    return 0 ;
}

void read_temperature ( void )
{
    uint16_t    temp ;

    lcd_clrscr( ) ;

    /* Temp. sensor LM35 is connected to ADC0/PA0 pin of ATmega32 */
    ADMUX = 0x40 + 0  ;

    for( ; ; )
    {
        /* control word and SOC command */
        ADCSRA = 0xC0 ;

        /* wait for EOC or while ( ADIF == 0 ) */
```

```
        loop_until_bit_is_set ( ADCSRA, ADIF ) ;

        temp = ADCW * 49 ;

        /* go to top left-hand corner of LCD display */
        lcd_gotoxy ( 0, 0 ) ;

        lcd_puts_p ( PSTR ( "Temperature\n" ) ) ;
        lcd_put_i ( temp, 2, 5 ) ;
        lcd_putc ( ' ' ) ;

        /* display a 'degree' (small circle as superscript) sign */
        lcd_putc ( 0xDF ) ;
        lcd_putc ( 'C' ) ;

        /* wait for some time before we start next conversion */
        delay( ) ;
    }
}

void delay ( )
{
    unsigned char i, j, k ;

    for ( i = 0 ; i < 255 ; i++ )
        for ( j = 0; j < 255 ; j++ )
            for ( k = 0; k < 246 ; k++ )
                ;

    return ;
}
```

Let us now understand the program. At the top we have included **avr/io.h**. This gives us all the prototypes and macros for dealing with I/O registers for ADC. **lcd_io.h** is included for using the LCD library. From **main( )** we have called the function **read_temperature( )** to measure and display the temperature. Inside **read_temperature( )**, we have first cleared the LCD screen. **ADMUX** I/O register for ADC is used to select channel number (0 in this case) and select the reference voltage of 5V. Once this is done, it uses an endless **for** loop to measure temperature continuously. To start temperature conversion, **ADCSR** is set to **oxCo**. This enables ADC and starts the conversion. We must wait till conversion is complete. Time for conversion is ~ 60-260 μsec. The next line **loop_until_bit_is_set** is a macro which loops until bit **ADIF** in **ADCSR** is set to 1. When conversion is complete, this **while** loop breaks and result of conversion is available in ADC data register which is named **ADC**. This is a 16-bit I/O register that contains result of conversion. We multiply it by 49 to get the temperature value. The value is then displayed on LCD uses **lcd_put_i( )**, with decimal point after two digits.

Now the program delays itself by 1 second (**delay( )** function). The **delay( )** function from earlier programs as is unchanged. Since this program has no other job than measuring temperature, it again measures temperature. In practice, since room temperature changes very slowly taking measurements at much lower rate (sampling rate) would be sufficient. In industrial applications the sampling rate has to be adjusted depending on the environment.

Exercise

[A] Answer the following:

(a) What is an ADC and why is it used in embedded systems?

(b) How is the resolution of an ADC determined?

[B] What are the different types of ADCs available?

[C] Pick up the correct alternative for each of the following questions:

[1] For reference voltage of 3 Volts, 8-bit ADC represents

(a) 0.15 V/bit
(b) 11.7 mV/bit
(c) 14 mV/bit
(d) 375 mV/bit

[2] Number of channels in AVR ATmega32 ADC is:

(a) 4
(b) 10
(c) 2
(d) 8

[3] Resolution of AVR ATmega32 ADC is:

(a) 10 bit
(b) 8 bit
(c) 12 bit
(d) 4 bit

[4] Which of the following statements are correct?

(i) ADCs produce a digital word for input analog voltage.
(ii) The resolution of ADC is number of words in digital output.

(a) Only (i) is correct.
(b) Only (ii) is correct.
(c) Both (i) and (ii) are correct.
(d) Both (i) and (ii) are incorrect.

[5] Which of the following statements are correct?

(i) A comparator in Parallel comparator ADC consists of two analog inputs.
(ii) The output of the comparator in Parallel comparator ADC is always 0V.

(a) Only (i) is correct.
(b) Only (ii) is correct.
(c) Both (i) and (ii) are correct.
(d) Both (i) and (ii) are incorrect.

[6] Which of the following statements are correct?

(i) With 3 comparators we can build 2-bit parallel comparator ADC.
(ii) Parallel comparator ADC performs the conversion very fast as all comparisons are done in parallel.

(a) Only (i) is correct.
(b) Only (ii) is correct.
(c) Both (i) and (ii) are correct.
(d) Both (i) and (ii) are incorrect.

[7] How many comparators are needed for 8-bit resolution?

(a) 8
(b) 9
(c) 128
(d) 255

[8] Which of the following functionalities do the registers associated with ATmega32 ADC allow to perform?

(i) Select input channel
(ii) Start the conversion

(iii) Read the result after end of conversion

(a) Only (i) and (ii)
(b) Only (i) and (iii)
(c) Only (ii) and (iii)
(d) (i), (ii) and (iii)

[9] Which of the following statements are correct?

(i) In AVR ADC registers, lower 4 bits are used to select reference voltage.
(ii) In AVR ADC registers, higher two bits (7 and 6) are used for channel number.

(a) Only (i) is correct.
(b) Only (ii) is correct.
(c) Both (i) and (ii) are correct.
(d) Both (i) and (ii) are incorrect.

[10] Which of the following statements are correct?

i. To enable ADC, bit 7 in ADCSR register must be set to 1.
ii. Top 6 bits in high-byte of data register are always 1.

(a) Only (i) is correct.
(b) Only (ii) is correct.
(c) Both (i) and (ii) are correct.
(d) Both (i) and (ii) are incorrect.

11 Interrupts And Timers

We now have the basics of embedded systems under our belt. We have done topics like LCDs, LEDs, EEPROM, Flash and ADC. It is now time to migrate to something more interesting. This includes topics like Interrupts, Timers, UART, I²C, etc. In this chapter, we would study Interrupts and Timers. Rest of the topics will be discussed in chapters to follow. Let us begin with Interrupts.

What Are Interrupts

An interrupt is one of the most important concepts when working with embedded systems. It is best illustrated with an example. Consider that a teacher is conducting a lecture. He wants to make sure that at all times everyone understands what he is explaining. He has two choices to ensure this:

(a) Ask every student in the class if he/she has understood the concept.
(b) Any student raises his/her hand and asks him when he/she has a doubt.
(c)

The first of these two alternatives is called polling, whereas the second is called interrupt. Which one is better? In a large classroom, first approach is certainly very time consuming and inefficient. Secondly, if teacher is required to do this after every concept, he will waste a lot of his creative energy confirming something that may already be true—most students have already understood. Interruption from student who hasn't understood a topic is much better approach as it gives the necessary feedback to the teacher.

How is all this relevant to embedded system programming? In most embedded systems, a microcontroller has numerous tasks to carry out—interacting with external sensors, carrying out serial communication, interacting with I/O ports, performing

11 Interrupts And Timers

We now have the basics of embedded systems under our belt. We have done topics like LCDs, LEDs, EEPROM, Flash and ADC. It is now time to migrate to something more interesting. This includes topics like Interrupts, Timers, UART, I^2C, etc. In this chapter, we would study Interrupts and Timers. Rest of the topics will be discussed in chapters to follow. Let us begin with Interrupts.

What Are Interrupts

An interrupt is one of the most important concepts when working with embedded systems. It is best illustrated with an example. Consider that a teacher is conducting a lecture. He wants to make sure that at all times everyone understands what he is explaining. He has two choices to ensure this:

(a) Ask every student in the class if he/she has understood the concept.
(b) Any student raises his/her hand and asks him when he/she has a doubt.
(c)

The first of these two alternatives is called polling, whereas the second is called interrupt. Which one is better? In a large classroom, first approach is certainly very time consuming and inefficient. Secondly, if teacher is required to do this after every concept, he will waste a lot of his creative energy confirming something that may already be true—most students have already understood. Interruption from student who hasn't understood a topic is much better approach as it gives the necessary feedback to the teacher.

How is all this relevant to embedded system programming? In most embedded systems, a microcontroller has numerous tasks to carry out—interacting with external sensors, carrying out serial communication, interacting with I/O ports, performing

ADC conversion etc. In all the programs we have seen so far, we have used polling approach. For example, in the last chapter, the program that used ADC to read temperature, our program simply waited for conversion to digital value to be complete (**loop_until_bit_is_set**). In practical embedded systems, this waste of time would be unacceptable. In cases likes these, better approach would be to do something else until ADC conversion is complete. On completion of conversion, ADC generates an electronic signal (called interrupt) which is used as a trigger for further action. Interrupts are events that can happen at any time—depending on when activity like ADC conversion is complete. Here, ADC in an internal source of interrupt. Interrupts may be generated by external sources as well. Given below are some examples of interrupts generated through external sources:

(a) Boiler temperature exceeded the limit
(b) Communication timeout has happened
(c) Data transfer was successfully completed
(d) Motion sensor detected movement in a room

ATmega32 microcontroller supports interrupts from external as well as internal devices. Internal interrupts may be generated by EEPROM, USART, Timers, ADC etc. External interrupts can be generated by any device/sensor which is connected to the MC.

Interrupt Service Routine

Before we embark on the interesting journey of interrupts, we must understand fundamentals of interrupts. Interrupts are electronic signals. Their purpose is to stop MC from what it is doing—and execute a special function called Interrupt Service Routine (ISR). Who writes the ISR? We, who else? As a developer, if you plan to use interrupts, you must write an ISR.

ISR for each interrupt is different. How does the microcontroller known which of these ISRs to call? This is done using two things—an interrupt number and a table called Interrupt Vector Table (IVT). Each interrupt is assigned a unique number by designers of ATmega32 microcontroller. Addresses of all ISRs are stored in the IVT. These addresses must be stored in the IVT before the program starts.

Thus IVT is similar to an array of function pointers. Interrupt number is used as an index in the array of these function pointers. When an interrupt occurs, corresponding ISR gets called. When the ISR is called, normal program execution is suspended (stopped). When control returns from the ISR, normal program execution resumes— as if nothing has ever happened. This approach to programming is known as asynchronous programming.

Note that initializing an IVT is the programmer's responsibility, whereas detecting external and internal interrupts is the responsibility of the MC.

Interrupt Priorities And More

In practice, a microcontroller handles numerous interrupts. Not all interrupts are equally important. For example, Timer and EEPROM interrupt may not be equally important. What happens if both the interrupts are received almost at the same time? Which one is serviced first? To deal with cases like these, microcontroller assigns priorities to interrupts. Higher priority interrupts are serviced before lower priority interrupts.

Another situation would be—an interrupt occurs while ISR for previous interrupt is still executing. Is the current ISR completed, before next interrupt is serviced? This depends on the microcontroller and programmer using the system. This scenario is called 'nested' interrupt scenario. Most modern microcontrollers support them. As a programmer, you may allow it or disallow it.

Keeping interrupts enabled during critical operations in a normal program can cause certain problems. It leads to the so called "race conditions" in a program. This is because interrupts suspend the flow of normal execution, though temporarily. We will discuss this topic in more detail in Chapter 13. Until then, hold your breath. As a result, most microcontrollers allow a programmer to disable interrupts. You should keep in mind that keeping interrupts disabled for long time affects system responsiveness adversely.

ATmega32 Interrupt Architecture

Now that we have a general understanding of interrupts and how they work, let us get to the specifics of interrupt architecture of ATmega32 microcontroller.

ATmega32 has a very powerful and flexible interrupt processing unit. It has its own control register and uses Interrupt Vector Table to service interrupt requests. It can service internal and external interrupts. The chip has 3 interrupt pins to which any interrupt signals of external devices can be connected. These are commonly called INT0, INT1 and INT2. In addition to these, ATmega32 has 18 internal interrupt sources. These include ADC Conversion Complete, EEPROM Ready, USART Receive Complete, USART Transmit Complete, Timer0 Overflow, Timer1 Overflow etc. To service these 21 interrupts, there are 21 entries in IVT (Interrupt Vector Table).

As we saw in the previous section, each interrupt has a number assigned to it. Priority of an interrupt depends on this number. Smaller the number higher is the priority.

Related with interrupts, ATmega32 provides two registers—SREG and GICR. Of these SREG is the Status Register that is used to enable/disable interrupts globally. GICR is a General Interrupt Control Register. It is used to enable/disable 3 external interrupts. It also selects the address where execution begins, when MC is reset. Note that after interrupts are enabled globally, each interrupt has to be enabled individually for it to be used in your program.

Interrupt Vector Table

For ATmega32 MC, IVT is not a table of function pointers. Each entry in the table contains an instruction to jump to the address of ISR for that interrupt. The ISR function has to be supplied by us. But, how do we write an ISR? Is it like a normal function? How the address of ISR gets inserted at correct place in IVT? These questions will be answered shortly. So hold your breath! At this stage, it suffices to say that we need help from compiler i.e. GCC to do this. GCC also supplies a default Interrupt Vector Table. When you provide your entry, it gives priority to your entry and replaces default entry with jump to your ISR.

Memory Layout

Before we start using interrupts it is important for us to understand where IVT is located. Once we know this we will also know the layout of our program in ATMega32's flash memory. ATmega32 MC expects that you supply an IVT with 21 entries (21 * 4 = 84 bytes) at the start of application flash section. From Figure 11.1 you can see that each entry contains a jump instruction to address of ISR. Where is the ISR? It is inside our program's code section. Our program has two sections—code and data. Of these, data section is placed adjacent to the IVT. Code section begins wherever data section ends. In order to organize the memory layout as shown above,

we certainly need some help from GCC compiler and the GNU linker that is part of the tool-chain. The mystery will unfold in the next section.

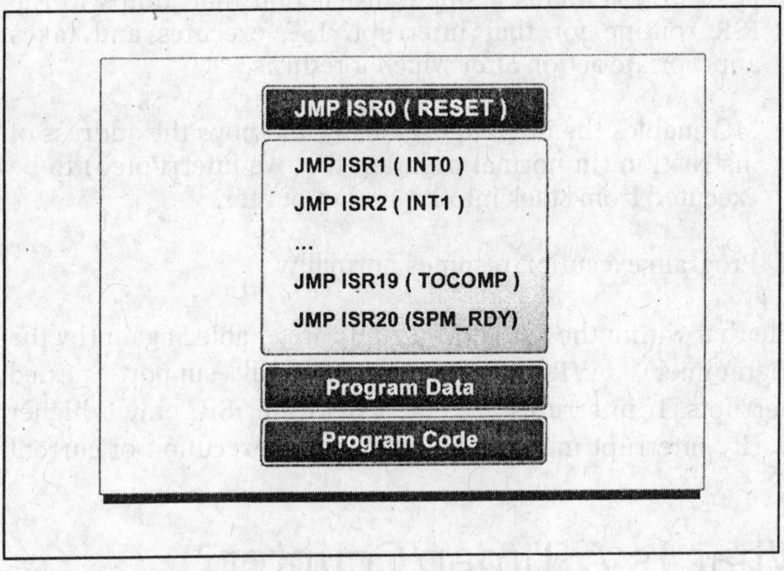

Figure 11.1: ATmega32 Interrupt Vector Table

Interrupt Handling Steps

Let us now understand the steps involved in ATmega32 interrupt processing. They are as follows:

(a) External or internal device/source generates an interrupt signal.

(b) MC completes the execution of current instruction.

(c) It stores the address of next instruction to be executed, on stack and disables interrupts globally.

(d) It checks the interrupt number and loads the address of corresponding IVT entry for execution into Program Counter.

(e) IVT entry contains a single instruction that jumps to the ISR routine for that interrupt. ISR executes and takes appropriate action after which it returns.

(f) MC enables the interrupts globally and pops the address of instruction (in normal program that we interrupted) to be executed from stack into Program Counter.

(g) Program execution resumes normally.

Note that within the ISR, if interrupts are enabled again (by the programmer), AVR ATmega32 MC will support nested interrupts. If interrupts are enabled within ISR, only a higher priority interrupt may come and suspend execution of current ISR.

What Is A Timer/Counter?

Timer or Counter is an electronic circuit that counts. It counts the number of clock cycles. Counter has an internal data register. Value in this register is incremented (or decremented) by 1 every clock cycle. Counters are used to keep an accurate measure of time. They are also used to generate an interrupt when a specified number of cycles have been counted. The clock used with timer unit need not be same as MC clock (8MHz for KSET ES Board).

The size of data register for a timer can be 8/16 bits. After the count reaches maximum value (255 or 65535), counting begins from 0 once again. This is known as wrap-around.

Some of you may be thinking—why not count directly using your own program's instructions? Though this is possible, your program will waste precious CPU time in doing repetitive activity like counting. In a typical ES, counting is best done using a specialized timer unit. ATmega32 supports 3 such timers. This shows that timers form a very import element in design of embedded systems.

ATmega32 Timers

ATmega32 MC has three built-in timers. They are called Timer0, Timer1 and Timer2 respectively. Timer0 and Timer2 are 8-bit timers. Timer1 is a 16-bit timer. Each timer supports dividing the clock frequency by 8, 64, 256 and 1024 respectively. This enables counting to be done at a reduced clock speed. Each timer provides 'Output Compare' functionality. This means the timer's count can be compared against a value in the Output Compare Register. Timers are capable of generating an interrupt when count reaches a specified value. Timers are also capable of generating interrupt when count overflows (reaches maximum value). They support a wide variety of operational modes that we will explore through our programs in the next section.

Fundamental use of a timer is to perform timed operations. For example, we can take sample of an analog input like temperature at regular intervals. Timers can also be used to generate a pulse to control DC motor or stepper motor that may be connected externally to the KSET ES board.

Displaying Time In Seconds

Let's begin with a simple objective—display time in seconds. The value on LCD screen must be incremented by 1 every one second. Ideally we need that MC should be interrupted once every second.

We will use Timer0 for counting. Timer0 will need to count $8*10^6$ cycles for 1 second to elapse. Rather than counting at CPU clock speed, we will scale down (divide) the input clock to Timer0 by 1024. So Timer0 needs to count only $8*10^6 / 1024 \sim 7812$ of its input clock cycles. However, Timer0 has a range of 0 - 255 before generating an 'overflow' interrupt.

So the simplest way to measure one second would be to count the number of Timer0 overflow interrupts and multiply it by 256. For counting 7812 cycles, we need to count 7812 / 256 ~ 31 interrupts. So we can conclude that by the time 31 overflow interrupts occur, 1 second has elapsed.

ATmega32 Timer0

Before we write a program to use Timer0, we must understand I/O registers associated with Timer0. These are as follows:

TCNT0 – This is the data register for Timer0. It contains the current value of count for Timer0. Maximum count can be 0xFF (255). After reaching maximum value, the counter wraps around and starts counting from 0 in next cycle.

TCCR0 – This is the control register for Timer0. It is used to control the mode of operation of timer and to specify its input clock selection and frequency scaling (division) factor.

TIMSK – This is Timer Interrupt Mask Register. It is used to enable overflow interrupt for Timer0. Some bits in this registers are shared by Timer1 and Timer2 units.

Timer0 Control Register

Lowest 3 bits in **TCCR0** are used to decide the clock source for Timer0. These bits are set to binary **101** to for scaling down CPU clock of 8MHz by a factor 1024.

Program

Let us now write the program for displaying time using Timer0. Here is the program...

Header file – timer_int.h

```
# ifndef _timer_int_h_
# define _timer_int_h_

/* Include all system header files here */
# include <avr/io.h>
# include "lcd_io.h"
# include <avr/interrupt.h>

/* Structures / Classes ... */

/* Extern declarations, prototypes etc. ... */
extern void init_avr ( void ) ;
extern void start_timer ( void ) ;

# endif /* _timer_int_h_ */
```

Program file – timer_int.c

```
# include "timer_int.h"

unsigned char sig_count ;
unsigned short stop_watch ;

int main ( void )
{
    init_avr( ) ;
    start_timer( ) ;
    return 0 ;
}
```

```
void init_avr ( void )
{
    lcd_init( ) ;
    sei( ) ;
}

/*
 * Starts 8 bit timer in interrupt mode
 *
 * Frequency = 8 * 10^6
 * Prescalar = 1024 ==> Freq. scaled down to 7812.5
 * Counter goes from 0 to 255. At 1/125000 sec/cycles,
 * 256 * 1/7812.5 = .032768 sec = 32.768 msec
 * For 1 second we need ~ 31 interrupts
 */

void start_timer ( void )
{
    lcd_gotoxy ( 0, 0 ) ;
    lcd_puts ( "Seconds\n" ) ;

    TCNT0 = 0x00 ;
    TCCR0 = 0x05 ;
    TIMSK = 0x01 ;
}

/* Timer 0 overflow interrupt */
SIGNAL ( SIG_OVERFLOW0 )
{
    sig_count++ ;

    if ( sig_count == 31 )
    {
        stop_watch++ ;
        lcd_gotoxy ( 0, 1 ) ;
        lcd_puts ( "  " ) ;
        lcd_gotoxy ( 0, 1 ) ;
        lcd_puti ( stop_watch, 0 ) ;
```

```
        stop_watch = stop_watch % 100 ;
    }
    sig_count = sig_count % 31 ;
}
```

In the header file (**timer_int.h**), we have made prototype declarations for **init_avr( )** and **start_timer( )**. Standard header files **avr/io.h** and **lcd_io.h** are also included in it. One more header file **avr/interrupt.h** also needs to be included for working with interrupts. It contains **sei( )** and **cli( )** functions and a **SIGNAL** macro. In addition it provides macros for interrupt numbers used with AVR MCs.

In **timer_int.c**, we have included the header file **timer_int.h**. **main( )** calls **init_avr( )** to initialize the LCD and enable interrupts globally. **sei( )** call does this. Unless interrupts are globally enabled, all individual interrupts remain masked. After this, **main( )** calls **start_timer( )**. This function goes to the beginning of LCD, and displays string **Seconds** on the LCD screen. Initially, the count value is set to 0. **TCCR0** is set to **0x05** to scale in internal clock by 1024. Finally, bit 0 in **TIMSK** register has been set to 1 for enabling Timer0's overflow interrupt. Now the counting would start and 31 interrupts would get generated every second. To count these interrupts, we have used a global variable **sig_count**. Another global variable **seconds** is used to keep track of number of seconds.

Most important step now is to create an ISR for Timer0 Overflow Interrupt (**TOIE0**). This is achieved via use of **SIGNAL** macro. This macro takes interrupt number **SIG_OVERFLOW0** as an argument. It gets called whenever Timer0's count (**TCNT0**) reaches 255. We increment interrupt count **sig_count** by 1; when it reaches 31, **seconds** counter is incremented by 1. The number of seconds is now displayed at the beginning of second line on LCD screen. To start counting next 31 interrupts, we have used the modulus operator (%). **sig_count** gets reset to 0 whenever it reaches 31.

Build and run this program. You will see the **seconds** value incrementing every one second. Let us now try to understand how exactly the ISR's address gets inserted in the right slot in the IVT.

The SIGNAL Macro

avr/interrupt.h provides interrupt related macros. If you look inside this file, you will find the **SIGNAL** macro defined as:

```
# define SIGNAL( signame  ) \
    void signame ( void ) __attribute__( ( signal ) ) ; \
    void signame ( void )
```

As you can see in this macro the prototype of a new function called **signame( )** is declared. Immediately following that is the first line of definition for function **signame( )**. The attribute **signal** is attached to the function declaration. This is what makes it an Interrupt Service Routine. Now remains the question—how does it get associated with correct interrupt number? If you look carefully, you will find that **SIG_OVERFLOW0** expands to **_VECTOR (9)**. **_VECTOR** further expands to **__vector_**. So finally the ISR looks as follows:

```
void __vector_9 ( void ) __attribute__( ( signal ) ) ; \
void __vector_9 ( void )
```

Other ISRs are named **__vector_1**, **__vector_2**, ... etc. The linker adds 84-byte IVT table at the top. Depending on the name of the ISR, it stores the address of ISR in the IVT. It knows this by looking at the name of the ISR.

You will realize that this is not ANSI C compliant. As mentioned earlier, ANSI C was not designed with the special requirements of today's embedded systems in mind. AVR GCC toolchain helps us by providing necessary magic to make all things work. In absence of such a modern tool-chain programmers generally had to use assembly language for writing ISRs.

Working With Temperature Sensor Using Interrupts

The temperature measurement program that we studied earlier used the polling mechanism. It waited for ADC conversion to be complete (bit **ADIF** in register **ADCSRA** to be set to 1). In practical ES applications this approach results in waste of precious CPU time. Hence we will now use an interrupt-based approach rather than polling to measure temperature.

AVR ADC Registers

Let us quickly revise the important ADC registers and their use. Reference voltage and input channel are selected using **ADMUX** register. Lower 4 bits are used for channel number and top two bits (7, 6) are used to select reference voltage.

ADCSRA (ADC Control and Status Register) is used to control the ADC and check if conversion is complete. To enable ADC, bit 7 (**ADEN**) in this register must be set to 1. This also ensures that Port-A functionality of ADC channel pins is disabled (ADC channels and Port-A pins are shared. Only one of them can be used at any time). Bit 6 (**ADSC**) is set to 1 to start the conversion for selected input channel. The result of conversion

—a 10-bit value—is available in ADC data register (**ADCH**, **ADCL**). Top 6 bits in high-byte of data register (**ADCH**) are reserved. They are always 0.

Measuring Temperature

Temperature measurement and display is the objective of our program. For that, we must convert analog voltage generated by temperature sensor using ATmega32 ADC. Each bit in output of ADC represents 5V / 1024 ~ 4.88 mVolts. Sample and hold is a special circuit used by ADC to hold the input voltage steady during conversion process. To get the temperature from digital output, we use following formula:

```
Temp = Digital Value / (Sensor V/°C)
= ADC_OUT * 4.88 / 10
= ADC_OUT * 0.488
```

The Program

Before we write a program to use Timer0, we must understand I/O registers associated with Timer0. Lowest 3 bits in Timer0 Control Register (**TCCR0**) are used to decide the clock source for Timer0. These bits are set to binary **101** to use a scaling factor of 1024 with CPU clock of 8MHz.

Header file – temperature.h

```
# ifndef _temperature_h_
# define _temperature_h_

/* Measuring temperature using Interrupt driven approach */
# include <avr/io.h>
# include <avr/pgmspace.h>
```

```
# include <avr/interrupt.h>
# include "lcd_io.h"

extern void start_temp_conv ( void ) ;
extern void display_temp ( void ) ;

# endif   /* _temperature_h_ */
```

Program file – temperature.c

```
# include <temperature.h>

uint16_t count ;

int main( void )
{
    lcd_init ( ) ;
    lcd_puts_p ( PSTR ( "Temperature\n" ) ) ;

    sei( ) ;
    start_temp_conv( ) ;
    return 0 ;
}

void start_temp_conv ( void )
{
    /* Temp sensor LM35 is connected to ADC0/PA0 pin of ATmega32 */
    ADMUX = 0x40 ;
    /* Enable ADC, Start Conversion, Enable Interrupt */
    ADCSRA = 0xC8 ;
}

SIGNAL ( SIG_ADC )
{
    display_temp( ) ;
    count++ ;
```

```
    start_temp_conv( ) ;
}

void display_temp ( void )
{
    /* Temperature display format is <DD.FF> */
    lcd_gotoxy ( 0, 1 ) ;
    lcd_put_i ( ADC * 49 , 2, 5 ) ;
    lcd_putc ( ' ' ) ;

    /* Displays a 'degree' (small circle as superscript) sign */
    lcd_putc ( 0xDF ) ;
    lcd_putc ( 'C' ) ;
    lcd_puts ( " - " ) ;
    lcd_puti ( count, 0 ) ;
}
```

Most of the program logic remains same as the earlier program. To begin with **main( )** initializes LCD and displays a string **Temperature** on first line. It calls **sei( )** to enable interrupts globally. Finally, it calls **start_temp_conv ( )** to begin temperature measurement process. **start_temp_conv( )** sets **ADMUX** to **0x40** to select the reference voltage 5V and input channel 0 for conversion. **ADCSRA** is used to enable ADC, start the conversion and enable generation of interrupt at the end of conversion (EOC). **SIGNAL (SIG_ADC)** is the ISR for **ADC** conversion complete interrupt. It calls **display_temp( )** to display the temperature value on second line of LCD screen. It then begins next measurement by calling **start_temp_conv( )**. You can see that we are no longer waiting for **ADIF** bit in **ADCSRA** to be set. As a result, our program no longer uses polling.

This is our second program using interrupts. We are sure you must be comfortable with the interrupt mechanism by now. We will see many more programs involving interrupts in later chapters. So fasten your seat belts.

Understanding TIMER1 In ATmega32

In all timer applications, so far we have used TIMER0. Atmega32 microcontroller supports two other timers—TIMER1 and TIMER2. TIMER2 is another 8-bit timer and supports same features as TIMER0. As a result, we can use it as an alternative when TIMER0 is already occupied. TIMER1 however is different in many ways. It's a 16-bit timer. Since the counter register wraps around after 2^{16} cycles, it can run at much higher input frequency. As a result, it can be used to measure time accurately. It supports output compare mode making it ideal for measuring time for internal and external events.

Using TIMER1 To Display Time In Seconds

In order to understand important registers for TIMER1, let's write a program to display time in seconds. Earlier we implemented this program using TIMER0. TIMER0's count overflows every 32.77 msec—even if we scale its input frequency by 1024. As a result we had to count 31 interrupts for measuring 1 second.

Now let's consider TIMER1 for same time measurement role. ATmega32 MCU runs at 8 MHz clock frequency. TIMER1's input frequency is scaled down by 1024. So it is 7.8125 kHz. This means that if we count 7812.5 cycles of TIMER1, one second would elapse. It's easy to see that we don't need to count 31 interrupts anymore. However, we cannot use "overflow interrupt" for this purpose. We have to use "Output compare" interrupt. In Output Compare mode, TIMER1 will count from 0 to a maximum value specified by programmer in OCR1A – Output Compare Register 1A. Once there is a match, interrupt will be generated and count value would be reset to zero. This feature of clearing the count on compare match is called CTC – Clear Timer on Compare.

Important registers for TIMER1 are as follows:

TCNT1 – Timer1's counter register. This stores the 16-bit count for this timer

TCCR1B – Used to divide timer input clock by 1024 and enable CTC mode

TIMSK – This register is used to enable Output compare interrupt for Timer1

For detailed understanding of these registers, please refer to pages 107-108 of ATmega16/32 MC's datasheet.

Program file – timer1.c

```
# include <avr/io.h>
# include <avr/interrupt.h>
# include "lcd_io.h"

unsigned short seconds ;
void start_timer ( void ) ;

int main ( void )
{
    lcd_init ( ) ;
    sei ( ) ;
    start_timer ( ) ;
    return 0 ;
}
```

```
void start_timer ( void )
{
    lcd_gotoxy ( 5, 0 ) ;
    lcd_puts ( "Seconds\n" ) ;
    TCNT1 = 0 ;
    TCCR1B = 0x0D ;   /* Divide clock by 1024 = 7.812 kHz, Clear counter
                         on output compare match */
    OCR1A = 7813 ;  /* Count these many cycles */
    TIMSK = 0x10 ;  /* Enable output compare interrupt */
}

SIGNAL ( SIG_OUTPUT_COMPARE1A )
{
    seconds ++ ;
    lcd_gotoxy ( 0, 0 ) ;
    lcd_puti ( seconds, 0 ) ;
}
```

Using ADC With Interrupts

To understand time measurement capabilities for TIMER1, consider a program that measures time it takes for ATmega32's ADC unit to convert voltage from temperature sensor to digital representation. The steps for doing this measurement are as follows:

(a) Start TIMER1 from count of 0.

(b) Start ADC conversion process.

(c) Wait for ADC conversion to complete – use EOC (End Of Conversion) interrupt.

(d) Read **TCNT1** inside interrupt handler. This gives us number of timer cycles it took for conversion.

(e) Calculate time for ADC conversion by multiplying the count value with input frequency for TIMER1.

Program Organization

We will use TIMER1 for measuring time for numerous other events. To do this well, we need to separate timing related code in different files–timer.h and timer.c. It exports the following functions:

(f) **timer_init( )** - Initializes timer. It must be called by programmer once to initialize TIMER1 registers.

(g) **timer_start( )** – Resets **TCNT1**. It should be called by programmer whenever he wants to start new timing measurement cycle.

(h) **timer_read_usec( )** – Returns the time elapsed since the measurement began. The value of time is in micro-seconds.

Please note that we will run TIMER1 at same frequency as MCU. So the maximum time that we can measure without wrapping around **TCNT1** is $2^{16} / 8 * 10^6 = 8.192$ milli-seconds.

Header file – timer.h

Contents of the header file (timer.h) are given below:

```
# ifndef _timer_h_
# define _timer_h_

# include <avr/io.h>

extern void timer_init ( void ) ;
extern void timer_start ( void ) ;
```

```
extern uint16_t timer_read_usec ( void ) ;

#endif   /* _timer_h_ */
```

Implementation – timer.c

Timer API is implemented as follows:

```
# include "timer.h"

void timer_init ( void )
{
      TCCR1B = 0x01 ;  /* No scaling. Run at 8MHz Frequency */
}

void timer_start ( void )
{
      TCNT1 = 0 ;
}

/* Displays conversion time in microseconds
   count / (8M) = count/8 usec i.e. count >> 3 usec  */
uint16_t  timer_read_usec ( void )
{
      return TCNT1 >> 3 ;
}
```

timer_read_usec( ) shifts the count value 3 bits to the right. This divides the number by 8. This directly gives us time in microseconds as it runs at 8MHz frequency.

Measuring Temperature Conversion Time

This program is similar to temperature measurement program in Chapter 10. Temperature sensor LM35 is connected to ADC0 input of ATmega32 (Channel 0). In that program we used polling approach (wait for **ADIF** bit in **ADCSRA** to be set). In the current program, we will show you how to use interrupts with ADC. We use timer APIs developed in previous section to find the time for measurement. The program to do this is shown below:

Implementation – adctime.c

```
# include <avr/io.h>
# include <avr/pgmspace.h>
# include <avr/interrupt.h>
# include <util/delay.h>
# include "lcd_io.h"
# include "timer.h"

void avr_init ( void ) ;
void display_temp ( void ) ;
void read_temp ( void ) ;

int main ( void )
{
    avr_init ( ) ;
    lcd_puts_p ( PSTR ( "Temp: " ) ) ;
    read_temp( ) ;
    return 0 ;
}

void avr_init ( void )
{
    lcd_init ( ) ;
    timer_init( ) ;
    sei ( ) ;

    /* Turn off pull-ups */
```

```
    DDRA = 0 ;
    PORTA = 0 ;
}

void read_temp ( void )
{
    ADMUX = 0x40 ;
    ADCSRA = 0xC8 ;   /* Enable ADC, Start Conversion,
                         Enable ADC EOC Interrupt */
}

SIGNAL ( SIG_ADC )
{
    display_temp( ) ;
    timer_start( ) ;
    read_temp( ) ;
}

void display_temp ( void )
{
    uint16_t   count = timer_read_usec( ) ;

    lcd_gotoxy ( 6, 0 ) ;
    lcd_put_i ( ADC * 49 , 2, 5 ) ;
    lcd_putc ( 0xDF ) ;
    lcd_putc ( 'C' ) ;

    lcd_clrline ( 1 ) ;
    lcd_gotoxy ( 0, 1 ) ;
    lcd_puti ( count, 0 ) ;
    lcd_gotoxy ( 3, 1 ) ;
    lcd_puts_p ( PSTR ( "usec" ) ) ;
    _delay_ms ( 300 ) ;
}
```

Let's understand the initialization steps. We first initialize timer and LCD libraries. Interrupts are enabled globally using

sei( ). Since ADC uses same external pins as PORTA, we must turn-off internal pull-up resistors. For this we mark 8 pins of **PORTA** as input (by writing 0 to **DDRA**). We then write 0 **PORTA** turn-off internal pull-up resistors at these pins. Before starting the temperature measurement, we must initialize ADC. **ADMUX** register is used to select Channel 0 as source. **ADCSRA** is used to enable ADC unit, enable conversion complete interrupt and begin the conversion process. Please note, that timer has already started counting as we have initialized it (**timer_init**) just before starting the temperature conversion.

ADC Conversion complete interrupt handler calls **timer_read_usec( )** to find the conversion time in micro-seconds. It displays temperature value on first line and conversion time on second line of LCD screen. **lcd_clrline( )** is used to clear second line (NOTE: Line numbering begins with 0). **_delay_ms( )** is used to delay execution by 300 msec. After this delay another round of temperature measurement is started by **ADC** interrupt handler by calling **timer_init( )** followed by **read_temp( )**. It's important not to forget to call **timer_start( )** before every measurement.

This approach for timing measurement can be used for other event measurement activities when working with Embedded Systems.

Exercise

[A] Answer the following:

(a) Write a program to display time in the format hh:mm:ss For example, after 1 minute in over, second line on LCD screen should have 00:01:00. After 1 hour, the LCD should display 01:00:00, etc.

(b) Using AVR ATmega32 Timer/Counter0, display a stop-watch with 10th of a second accuracy on LCD screen. The time displayed should increment after every 100 mili-seconds. For example:

0.0, 0.1, ... , 1.0, ... , 2.1, 2.2, 2.3, ... , 3.0

[B] Pick up the correct alternative for each of the following questions:

[1] How many bits does AVR ATmega32 Timer/Counter0 have?

(a) 8
(b) 16
(c) 4
(d) 32

[2] Which register is used to select frequency scaling factor to Timer/Counter0?

(a) TCCR0
(b) TCNT0
(c) TIMSK
(d) TCCR2

[3] Which of the following is correct way of writing interrupt service routine for Timer/Counter0 overflow interrupt?

(a) SIGNAL (SIG_ADC)
(b) SIG_OVERFLOW (SIGNAL)
(c) SIGNAL (SIG_OVERFLOW0)
(d) SIGNAL (int SIG_OVERFLOW0)

[4] How many external interrupt pins does AVR ATmega32 have?

(a) 10
(b) 2
(c) 3
(d) 4

[5] How many entries does AVR ATmega32 IVT have?

(a) 21
(b) 18
(c) 3
(d) 22

[6] Which of the following is true about AVR ATmega32 IVT?

(a) It's an array of pointers.
(b) It's an array of interrupt service routines corresponding to all internal and external interrupts.
(c) It's a structure of functions.
(d) It's a pointer to single function.

[7] Which of the following register is used to enable/disable interrupts globally?

(a) SREG
(b) StatusRegister
(c) EDINTRREG
(d) InterruptREG

[8] Which of the following register is used to enable/disable 3 external interrupts?

(a) GICR
(b) InterruptREG
(c) EDIntrReg

(d) ED3ExtrReg

[9] When the count reaches maximum value 255 or 65535 counting begins from 0 once again, it is known as ________________.

(a) Wrap-around
(b) Restart
(c) Start again
(d) Begin count once again

[10] Which of the following timers are 8-bit timers?

(i) Timer0

(ii) Timer1

(iii) Timer2

(a) Only (i) and ii)
(b) Only (i) and (iii)
(c) Only (ii) and iii)
(d) (i), (ii) and (iii)

[11] Which of the following registers are associated with Timer0?

(i) Data Register for Timer0 (TCNT0)

(ii) Control Register for Timer0 (TCCR0)

(iii) Timer Interrupt Mask Register (TIMSK)

(a) Only (i) and ii)
(b) Only (i) and (iii)
(c) Only (ii) and iii)
(d) (i), (ii) and (iii)

[12] Which of the following statements are correct?

(i) Timer or Counter counts the number of clock cycles.

(ii) The value of the internal data register present in the Counter is incremented or decremented by 1 in every clock cycle.

(a) Only (i) is correct.
(b) Only (ii) is correct.
(c) Both (i) and (ii) are correct.
(d) Both (i) and (ii) are incorrect.

[13] Which of the following statements are correct?

(i) The size of the data register for a timer can be 8/16 bits.

(ii) Timer0 is a 16-bit timer.

(a) Only (i) is correct.
(b) Only (ii) is correct.
(c) Both (i) and (ii) are correct.
(d) Both (i) and (ii) are incorrect.

[14] Which of the following statements are correct?

(i) The Data Register for Timer0 contains the current value of count for Timer0.

(ii) The Control Register for Timer0 is used to control the mode of operation of timer and specify input clock selection and scaling factor.

(a) Only (i) is correct.
(b) Only (ii) is correct.

(c) Both (i) and (ii) are correct.
(d) Both (i) and (ii) are incorrect.

[15] Which of the following statements are correct?

(i) The Timer Interrupt Mask Register is used to enable overflow interrupt for Timer0.

(ii) Bits in the Timer Interrupt Mask Register are used by Timer1 and Timer2.

(a) Only (i) is correct.
(b) Only (ii) is correct.
(c) Both (i) and (ii) are correct.
(d) Both (i) and (ii) are incorrect.

[16] Which of the following statements are correct?

(i) Lower 3 bits in TCCR0 are used to decide the clock source for Timer0.

(ii) Lower 3 bits in TCCR0 are set to binary 010 to use a scaling factor of 1024 with CPU clock of 8MHz.

(a) Only (i) is correct.
(b) Only (ii) is correct.
(c) Both (i) and (ii) are correct.
(d) Both (i) and (ii) are incorrect.

12 Serial Communication

Man is a social animal. Humans have created societies from the earliest days of civilization. Most humans have strong desire for communication. Embedded Systems are quite similar to this. Most embedded systems can't live in isolation. They need to communicate with the operator or other Embedded Systems present around them. This chapter will explore how this communication can be done.

Data Communication

Means and forms of communication have evolved over the years; yet the oldest and simplest remains to be the serial communication. It is in widespread use even today. In serial communication, information is transferred bit-by-bit. As a result, it is slower than many other forms of communication. The biggest advantage is simplest possible wiring as you can see from Figure 12.1.

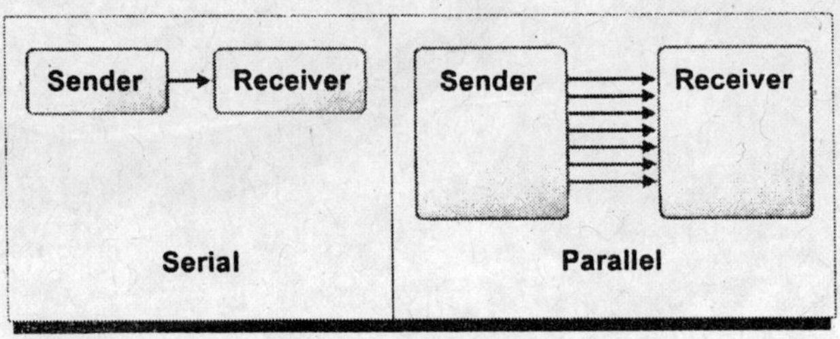

Figure 12.1: Serial and Parallel Communication

Parallel communication involves transfer of more than 1-bit of information between sender and receiver simultaneously, hence the name—parallel communication. It is faster than serial communication in most cases. The disadvantage is higher cost and more complicated wiring.

Serial Data Transmission Types

There are three types/modes of serial communication commonly used in practice depending on direction of transfer. They are:

Simplex mode - In this mode, transmission can happen in only one direction. Such communication is typical in case of sensors. For example, earthquake sensors that take seismic reading and transmit them to the monitoring station operate in simplex mode. Monitoring station needs no communication back to the sensor. As a result, one way communication is ok.

Half-Duplex mode - In this mode, transmission happens in only one direction at any time. Direction of data transfer can be changed, after which sender becomes receiver and receiver becomes the sender. This mode is commonly used by police radios. One person talks whereas the other listens. Once he stops talking, other person can start talking.

Full-duplex mode - In this mode, transmission can happen in both the directions simultaneously. Our normal telephone communication uses this mode. This is the most flexible mode and allows double the speed of data transfer compared to half-duplex mode.

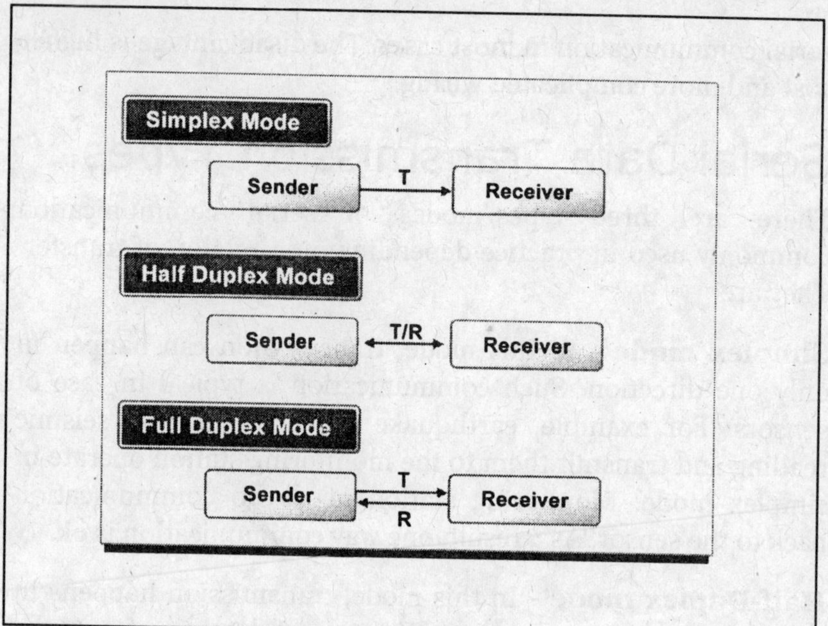

Figure 12.2: Serial communication types

Parallel To Serial, Serial To Parallel

Internally, MC maintains the data in registers. ATmega32 uses 8-bit registers. For serial communication, data is sent (transmitted) bit-by-bit. To convert data into serial format, we need parallel-in serial-out shift register (also called barrel shifter). The data received bit-by-bit must be loaded into 8-bit registers. This requires a serial-in, parallel-out shift register. In addition, some handshaking between communicating systems is necessary to ensure that start and end of communication can be done correctly. Details of this will be explained in next section. When data is to be transmitted over large distances, serial communication is used in conjunction with normal telephone lines using a Modem (Modulator-Demodulator).

Modem performs Digital to Analog conversion on sending side and Analog to Digital on receiving side.

Modems ushered in the era of networking. Even today, most internet users rely on modems to connect to data networks (internet) using conventional telephone lines.

Serial Communication Transmission Modes

There are two commonly used modes in serial communication:

(a) Synchronous
(b) Asynchronous

A clock is an electronic signal that is used to synchronize (coordinate) the actions of two or more circuits. A clock signal oscillates between a high (typically +5V) and a low voltage (typically 0V), normally with a 50% duty cycle, and is usually a square wave. In synchronous serial communication, sender and receiver must share the clock signal. This becomes a challenge over even few meters of distance. However, advantage of this approach is better communication speed in most cases.

Asynchronous communication doesn't require a shared clock between sender and receiver, and provides much better error detection mechanism. As a result, asynchronous serial communication is more commonly used in practice.

Asynchronous serial communication transmits 5 - 8 data. Order of transmission is from least significant to most significant bits. Start bit is used at the beginning to indicate that data bits will follow. After all the data bits have been transmitted, 1 or more stop bits are used to indicate end of data word. Parity bit may be used to provide error detection capability.

What is parity? It is best illustrated with an example. Consider that data word size is 8 bits and we transmit a data word - 0110 0011. Total number of 1's in this bit pattern is 4. Parity is an extra bit that is added to the data to make the total number of 1's in it an odd or even number. Thus, if we are using even parity, then an extra bit should be added if number of 1's in the number is odd. Likewise, if we are using odd parity, then extra bit should be added to make the number of 1's is even. In case of 0110 0011, if we are using even parity the parity bit must be set to 0, as number of 1's in this pattern is already even (4). If we are using odd parity, we need to set the parity bit to 1.

How does parity help us detect errors? It's really simple. If we always transmit even parity, i.e. even number of 1's, receiver can count number of 1's in the bits received. If this count turns out to be odd, it means there was an error in the transmission. Thus parity can help us detect single-bit errors reliably. Only disadvantage of using parity bit is the overhead of transmitting an extra bit. For every 8-bit data word, one extra bit is transmitted. This is 12.5% overhead. All the bits inclusive of start and stop-bits together constitute a frame.

Asynchronous Serial Transfer

Now that we have understood the fundamentals of asynchronous serial communication, let's take a closer look at it. Normally serial communication line/wire is in high signal state. This is also called as marking state. To start the transmission, sender takes the line to a low signal state for 1-bit time interval. Exact duration depends on the rate of serial transmission (also known as baud rate). This is the start-bit. After start bit, sender starts transmitting data bits D0, D1, ... , etc. Finally, an optional parity bit is transmitted. In the end, one or two stop bits are transmitted by taking the signal to a high state for those many 1-bit intervals.

How can we measure the speed of serial communication? Using bit-rate (no. of bits transmitted per second) would be wrong because we are also transferring parity, start and stop bits. Hence Baud rate is used as a measure of data transfer rate over a serial communication link. Baud rate simply indicates number of changes of communication signal per second. It is named after French inventor Emile Baudot, who was a pioneer in communication field. In 1874, she created the Baudot code used in telegraphs. Typical values of baud rates are 2400, 9600, 19200, 57600 etc. Bit rate or number of bits transmitted per second (BPS) is calculated as

BPS = Bits transmitted per baud x Bauds per sec

If number of bits transmitted per baud (bits/baud) is one, then baud rate is identical to bits/second rate.

Serial communication parameters are described using a simple convention: **3400 8-N-1** — indicates a 3400 bits/sec speed with 8 data bits no parity and 1 stop bit. Typical values that we will use with KSET ES board are: **9600 8-N-1**.

Maximum data rates available in asynchronous serial communication are 115.2 kbps in most cases. Distance between communicating systems also influences this rate.

RS232 Cable With KSET ES Board

RS-232C is a standard created by Electronic Industries Association (EIA) for cable that connects two systems for serial communication. Original standard defines a 25-pin standard. We have used a 9-pin cable because other pins are unused in most cases. This 9-pin cable connector has two ends—male and female. The female end will fit in your PC's serial port. Other end will fit in serial port for KSET ES board. Out of 9-pins only three wires have meaning:

Tx - Transmit
Rx - Receive
Gnd - Ground

We recommend using a Null-modem serial cable. In this cable, the Rx pin of first system (PC) is connected to Tx pin of second system (KSET ES Board). Similarly, Tx pin of first system is connected to the Rx pin of second system. This ensures that whatever one system sends reaches another directly.

AVR ATmega32 - USART Facts

ATmega32 provides a very powerful and flexible serial communication unit. It is capable of synchronous as well as asynchronous serial communication modes. USART stands for **U**niversal **S**ynchronous **A**synchronous **R**eceiver **T**ransmitter. It supports Full-duplex operation and contains a baud-rate generator that is capable of various bit-rates. Frames with 5-9 bits of data word are supported. Parity calculation for transmission and verification for reception is also done by this unit. It supports 1 or 2 stop bits depending on programmer's choice. We will study use of this USART in the section to follow.

Sending & Receiving Characters

Our first program using USART (Universal Synchronous Asynchronous Receiver Transmitter) involves sending receiving characters between PC and KSET ES board. To do this, we must set matching communication parameters on PC and our program executing inside ATmega32 present in the KSET ES board. USART has many I/O registers associated with it. So hold take a deep breath and get ready!

To set the baud rate, we have to use **UBRR**—USART Baud Rate Register. The value in this 16-bit register must be set to **f_{AVR} / (16 * Baud) - 1**. f_{AVR} is the clock frequency at which ATmega32 runs. For KSET ES board it is 8MHz. After this, we must select frame format to indicate how many data bits and stop bits are used. **UCSRB** and **UCSRC** (USART Control and Status Registers B & C) are used for this purpose. **UCSRA** the third control and status register is used to keep track of received and transmitted characters' status. The data to be transmitted has to be first written in **UDR**—USART Data Register. The received data becomes available in the **UDR** under same name. Internally, USART has two data registers—one for transmit and another for receive. Then why only one is exposed to the programmers? It was a design decision of those who created ATmega32 processor. If you read from **UDR** you get the received word from Rx (receive) register. If you write to it, the data to be transmitted gets written to Tx (transmit) register inside USART.

Most important thing to keep in mind during transmission is that unless **UDRE** (USART Data Register Empty) bit is set, you should not write a new value for transmission into **UDR**.

The Program

With this much background we can now write a program that can send a string "Hello World" from the KSET ES board to the PC. Here is the program...

Header file – uart1.h

```
#ifndef _uart1_h_
#define _uart1_h_
```

```
# include <avr/pgmspace.h>
# include <avr/io.h>
# include "lcd_io.h"

# define UART_BAUD_SELECT   ( F_CPU / ( baud * 16l ) - 1 )

/* Global variables */

/* Function prototypes */
extern void uart_init ( unsigned int baud ) ;
extern void uart_tx_char ( unsigned char s ) ;
extern unsigned char uart_rx_char ( void ) ;

#endif /* _uart1_h_ */
```

Program file – uart1.c

```
#include "uart1.h"

int main ( void )
{
    char *h = "Hello World\n" ;

    uart_init ( 9600 ) ;
    lcd_init( ) ;

    while ( *h )
    {
    l   cd_putc ( *h ) ;
        uart_tx_char ( *h++ ) ;
    }

    while ( 1 )
    {
        unsigned char uch = uart_rx_char( ) ;
        /* Backspace and delete keys are ignored */
        if ( uch != 0x8 && uch != 0x7F )
```

```
        lcd_putc ( uch ) ;
    }

    return 0 ;
}

void uart_init ( unsigned int baud )
{
    UBRRH = UART_BAUD_SELECT >> 8 ;
    UBRRL = ( uint8_t ) UART_BAUD_SELECT ;

    /* Enable 8-bit receiver and transmitter */
    UCSRB = _BV( RXEN ) | _BV ( TXEN ) ;
    UCSRC = _BV ( URSEL ) | _BV ( UCSZ1 ) | _BV ( UCSZ0 ) ;
}

void uart_tx_char ( unsigned char s )
{
    /* Wait for data register to be empty */
    loop_until_bit_is_set ( UCSRA , UDRE ) ;
    UDR = s ;
}

unsigned char uart_rx_char ( void )
{
    /* wait for data data word to be received */
    loop_until_bit_is_set ( UCSRA , RXC ) ;
    if ( UCSRA & ( _BV ( PE ) | _BV ( DOR ) | _BV ( FE ) ) )
        return ( unsigned char ) - 1 ;

    return UDR ;
}
```

The program is quite simple. **main( )** calls **uart_init( )** to initialize UART to use baud rate of 9600 with 1 stop-bit and no parity. LCD is initialized with **lcd_init( )**. It then transmits all the characters in the string **Hello World\n** to the PC. After this, it enters an endless while loop which prints every character received from the PC to the LCD display on the KSET ES board. Two special characters— **Delete** and **Backspace** are skipped as they are not printable characters.

Let us now try to understand the details of this program.

UART Initialization

All programs that use serial communication functionality must initialize the serial port correctly. We will use USART inside ATmega32 for asynchronous communication—hence the name UART. **uart_init( )** takes only one parameter—baud rate.

First step is to set the value is **UBRRH**, **UBRRL** the high and low bytes of USART Baud Rate Register to correct values. When you build the program, you can see compiler flag

```
-D F_CPU=8000000
```

So rather than hard-coding the MC frequency we will use this macro in defining value for **UBRR**. It is equal to

```
F_CPU / (16L * baud ) – 1
```

Top 8 bits of this expression are written to **UBRRH** and lower 8 bits are written to **UBRRL**. Next two statements set the frame format. **UCSRB** is used to enable full-duplex communication (Tx and Rx). **UCSRC** is used to enable 8-bit data and 1 stop-bit. Once this is done, we are ready to send and receive characters. **_BV** is a macro that is used to set a particular bit in a number to 1. It is defined as follows:

```
# define _BV( bit )     (1 << bit )
```

For example, expression **_BV(TXEN)** gets reduced to **_BV(3)** which implies **1** << **3**. This macro allows us to set a bit number in a register conveniently.

All our serial communication programs, will use this routine. Make sure that you understand this function well.

UART Send And Receive

Once UART is initialized, we are ready to send and receive data. **uart_tx_char( )** function takes byte to be transmitted as a parameter. It waits till **UDRE** (UART Data Register Empty) bit in **UCSRA** is set. We are using polling approach here. Later in this book, we will also use interrupt-based transmit/receive during serial communication. After data register is empty we write the byte to be transmitted to **UDR**. Serial transmission now begins. If we call this function again while previous transmission is still in progress, **UDRE** will be 0, preventing an accidental overwrite of **UDR** (transmit) register.

uart_rx_char( ) waits until **RXC** (Receive Complete) bit in **UCSRA** is set. Thereafter, we check any of the bits—**PE** (Parity Error), **DOR** (Data Overrun) or **FE** (Frame Error) are set. Any of them being set indicates an error. Otherwise, we return **UDR** (Receive Register) contents to the caller.

Configuring Hyperterminal

Before we can build and execute this program, we must use a serial communication application on the PC. We propose to use the Hyperterminal program that comes ready-made with all Windows XP systems, for this. We need to configure PC's serial port using this program. For this, start the Hyperterminal program from **Start** | **Programs** | **Accessories** | **Communication** | **Hyperterminal**. Open the Hyperterminal application and choose **serial9600** as the name of connection. In **Connect To** dialog, select **COM1** which is first serial port on your PC and click OK. COM properties dialog will open up. Make sure that you select **9600** as baud rate and **Parity** as **None**. **Flow Control** must be set to **None**. On clicking OK, Hyperterminal connects to serial port and you can now execute your program on KSET ES board.

Using PC keyboard To Interact With ES

Let us now write a program that uses serial communication to make the PC keyboard act as a keyboard for KSET ES board. Most embedded systems including KSET ES board do not have a keyboard of their own. So this technique will be quite useful. Using this technique, we can design an interactive application that seek input from user and display messages to the user directly on the serial port. As we did earlier, we will initialize USART for asynchronous mode with 9600 baud, no parity, 8 data bits and 1 stop bits. Given below is the source code of the program:

Header file – uart2.h

```
# ifndef _uart2_h_
# define _uart2_h_

# include <avr/pgmspace.h>
# include "lcd_io.h"
# include "uart1.h"

# define FIRST_LINE   0
# define SECOND_LINE   1

# define FIRST_POSITION   0
# define LAST_POSITION    LCD_CHARS_PER_LINE
```

```
# define FRAME_ERROR     11
# define DATA_OVERRUN_ERROR  22
# define PARITY_ERROR     33

# define ENTER_KEY    0x0D
# define BACKSPACE_KEY    0x7F
# define DELETE_KEY   0x08

# define BAUD_RATE   9600

# endif /* _uart2_h_ */
```

Program file – uart2.c

```
# include "uart2.h"

void uart_tx_string ( uint8_t *s )
{
      while ( *s )
            uart_tx_char ( *s++ ) ;
}

int main ( void )
{
      uint8_t rc ;
      int c_pos = FIRST_POSITION ;
      int c_line = FIRST_LINE ;

      uart_init ( BAUD_RATE ) ;
      uart_tx_string ( "Enter input: " ) ;
      lcd_clrscr( ) ;

      for ( ; ; )
      {
            /* cursor */
```

```
lcd_gotoxy ( c_pos , c_line ) ;
lcd_putc ( '_' ) ;

rc = uart_rx_char( ) ;

switch ( rc )
{
    case FRAME_ERROR :
    case DATA_OVERRUN_ERROR :
    case PARITY_ERROR :
        lcd_puts_p ( PSTR ( "ERR" ) ) ;
        break ;

    case BACKSPACE_KEY :
    case DELETE_KEY :
        lcd_gotoxy ( c_pos, c_line ) ;
        lcd_putc ( ' ' ) ;

        // if cursor is in second line and first position
        if ( c_line == SECOND_LINE &&
            c_pos == FIRST_POSITION )
        {
            c_line = FIRST_LINE ;
            c_pos  = LAST_POSITION ;
        }

        if ( c_pos != FIRST_POSITION )
        {
            // move to character that has to be deleted
            c_pos-- ;
            lcd_gotoxy ( c_pos , c_line ) ;

            // Delete the character
            lcd_putc ( ' ' ) ;
        }

        lcd_gotoxy ( c_pos , c_line ) ;
        uart_tx_char ( '\b' ) ;
```

```
            break ;

        case ENTER_KEY :

            if ( c_line == FIRST_LINE )
            {
                lcd_gotoxy ( c_pos , c_line ) ;
                lcd_putc ( ' ' ) ;

                c_line = SECOND_LINE ;
                c_pos = FIRST_POSITION ;
            }

            uart_tx_char ( '\r' ) ;
            break ;

        default :

            lcd_gotoxy ( c_pos , c_line ) ;
            if ( rc == '\r' )
                rc = '\n' ;
            else if ( rc == '\t' )
                rc = ' ' ;
            lcd_putc ( rc ) ;

            // Increment x if LAST_POSITION (End of line)
            if ( c_pos != LAST_POSITION )
                c_pos ++ ;

            if ( c_pos == LAST_POSITION &&
                c_line == FIRST_LINE )
            {
                // find if reach the end of first line if so
                // move to first position of the second line
                c_line = SECOND_LINE ;
                c_pos = FIRST_POSITION ;
            }
            break ;
```

```
        }
    }
    return 0 ;
}
```

Program Structure

The program consists of two files—**uart2.h** and **uart2.c**. Please copy **uart1.h** and **uart1.c** from previous program in the directory of the current program and delete **main( )** function from **uart1.c**. The current program uses the functions present in these files. In **uart2.h**, ENTER and BACKSPACE keys are #defined using macros **ENTER_KEY** and **BACKSPACE_KEY**. **BAUD_RATE** is also #defined as 9600. It also contains macros and prototypes for working with keyboard input from PC. Macros **FIRST_LINE** and **LAST_LINE** indicate the line numbers on LCD display. Macros **FIRST_POS** and **LAST_POS** are used to track first character and last character on a line on LCD display.

uart2.c #includes **uart2.h**. It defines the **uart_tx_string( )** function at the beginning. Function **main( )** initializes LCD and UART. It receives one character at a time in an endless **while** loop using **uart_rx_char( )**. Special handling of certain characters is required as explained in the following sections.

Handling 'ENTER' Key

To start with, we have initialized local variables **c_pos** and **c_line**. They point to first character on first line. We have also set the **err_cnt** to 0. On detecting **Enter** key, we have called **clear_error( )** routine to check and clear previous error condition if any. If current line is first one on LCD display, we go to the beginning of second line by setting **c_pos** to 0

(**FIRST_POS**) and setting **c_line** to **LAST_LINE**. It also sends the character **\r** — carriage return back to the PC so that cursor goes to next line in Hyperterminal window.

Handling Delete & Backspace Keys

Delete and backspace keys are handled in identical manner. We must deal with two important cases:

(a) Cursor is at the first character on second line
(b) Cursor is somewhere in the middle of first or last line

In the first case, we must adjust **c_pos** and **c_line** to go back to the last character on first line. In second case we simply have to create an effect of erasing the previous character. For this, we simply decrement **c_pos** and display a space character. Finally, we transmit **\b** back to the PC so that previous character in Hyperterminal window is also erased.

Error Handling

If **uart_rx_char( )** encounters an error it returns **0xFF** to the caller. We have handled that as a special case by clearing the LCD screen and displaying the string **ERROR** on the screen. **c_pos** and **c_line** are reset to 0. **err_cnt** is incremented by 1 as it is the error counter. **clear_error( )** function is called in each case to see if the character reception has resumed in an error free manner. If so, the LCD starts displaying characters entered in the PC's Hyperterminal window once again.

Normal Character Processing

The **default** case handles all normal characters. Here first step is to check and clear previous error condition, if any. Then we must ensure that cursor doesn't go beyond the last character on second line. Received character is then displayed on LCD screen. Same character is sent back to PC for display in Hyperterminal window. If we reach the end of first line, the cursor is moved to first character on next line.

A helper function **uart_tx_string( )** is also used in this program. It transmits all characters in a string (except \0) one by one.

Exercise

[A] Answer the following:

(a) Modify the program discussed in this chapter. Change the baud rate to 38,400. (Hint: You will have to use correct value for UBRR calculation. PC's Hyperterminal's settings should continue to use the same settings).

(b) Write a program to read all characters typed from PC in Hyperterminal window until "ENTER" key is hit and display them on LCD screen of KSET ES board.

[B] Pick up the correct alternative for each of the following questions:

[1] Which of the following types/modes of serial communication are used depending on the direction of transfer?

(i) Simplex mode
(ii) Half-Duplex mode
(iii) Full-duplex mode

(a) Only (i) and (ii) are correct
(b) Only (i) and (iii) are correct

(c) Only (ii) and (iii) are correct
(d) (i), (ii) and (iii) are correct

[2] Which of the following type of serial communication is used in telephone system?

(a) Simplex mode
(b) Half-Duplex mode
(c) Full-duplex mode
(d) Simple as well as Half-Duplex mode

[3] Which of the following modes in serial communication are commonly used?

(i) Synchronous
(ii) Asynchronous

(a) Only (i)
(b) Only (ii)
(c) Both (i) and (ii)
(d) Neither (i) nor (ii)

[4] Which of the following statements are correct?

(i) To convert data into serial format, parallel in-serial-out shift register is needed.

(ii) The parallel in-serial-out shift register is called as barrel shifter.

(a) Only (i) is correct.
(b) Only (ii) is correct.
(c) Both (i) and (ii) are correct.
(d) Both (i) and (ii) are incorrect.

[5] Which of the following statements are correct?

(i) Modem performs Digital to Analog conversion on receiving side.
(ii) Modem performs Analog to Digital conversion on sending side.

(a) Only (i) is correct.
(b) Only (ii) is correct.
(c) Both (i) and (ii) are correct.
(d) Both (i) and (ii) are incorrect.

[6] Which of the following statements are correct?

(i) In synchronous serial communication, sender and receiver must share the clock signal.

(ii) Asynchronous serial communication transmits 5 – 8 data bits and transmits from least significant to most significant bits.

(a) Only (i) is correct.
(b) Only (ii) is correct.
(c) Both (i) and (ii) are correct.
(d) Both (i) and (ii) are incorrect.

[7] Which of the following are the high and low bytes of USART Baud rate Register?

(a) UBRRHigh and UBRRLow respectively
(b) UBRRH and UBRRL respectively
(c) USARTH and USARTL respectively
(d) USARTBRRH and USARTBRRL respectively

[8] Which of the following statements are correct?

(i) The UCSRC is used to enable full-duplex communication.
(ii) The UCSRB is used to enable 8-bit data and 1 stop-bit.

(a) Only (i) is correct.
(b) Only (ii) is correct.
(c) Both (i) and (ii) are correct.
(d) Both (i) and (ii) are incorrect.

[9] Which of the following statements are correct?

(i) Parallel communication involves transfer of more than 1-bit of information between sender and receiver simultaneously.

(ii) In serial communication, information is transferred bit-by-bit.

(a) Only (i) is correct.
(b) Only (ii) is correct.
(c) Both (i) and (ii) are correct.
(d) Both (i) and (ii) are incorrect.

[10] Which of the following statements are correct?

(i) Baud rate is used as a measure of data transfer rate over serial communication link.
(ii) All the bits exclusive of start and stop-bits constitute a frame.

(a) Only (i) is correct.
(b) Only (ii) is correct.
(c) Both (i) and (ii) are correct.
(d) Both (i) and (ii) are incorrect.

13 Serial Communication Using Interrupts

In the last chapter we saw how serial communication is done using polling. While this approach is simpler, it's not practical to use polling in all the cases. For example, when hundreds of bytes are to be transmitted, we cannot block caller by waiting for all the bytes to be transmitted. In most cases, caller wants to submit all the bytes for transmission in one shot and do some other operation while the USART transmits these characters one by one. Since USART unit has only one transmit register, this cannot be done in hardware. We can certainly implement this by combining interrupt driven serial communication approach with some changes in our serial communication software implementation. In this chapter we will explore in detail the interrupt-based asynchronous serial communication.

Why Use USART Interrupts?

ATmega32's USART is capable of generating interrupts during transmission as well as reception of data. We have already seen its operation using 'polling'. Before starting a new transmission we wait in a while loop till "Data Register is Empty" bit is set to 1. In large Embedded System applications, this is certainly a problem. It prevents CPU from doing other useful operations while previous transmission is still in progress. For typical baud rate of 9600, sending 1 byte data (and 1 start + 1 stop bit) takes 1042 μsecs. In the same time period 1042 / .125 = 8333 instructions could have been executed on the CPU. If we use interrupts this 'busy waiting' can be avoided.

USART Interrupts

ATmega32 can generate three USART interrupts. These are:

- Transmit Data Register Empty

- Transmit Complete

- Receive Complete

First two interrupts are generated during transmission. What is the need for having two transmission interrupts? This is explained below in detail.

Transmit Data Register Empty Interrupt

If enabled, this interrupt is generated every time **UDR** (Transmit Data Register) is empty. This doesn't mean that the entire frame has been transmitted. Optional parity bit and one or more stop bits are yet to be transmitted when this interrupt is generated. It gives us opportunity to write the next byte in **UDR** as early as possible. In cases where you have lot of data to be transmitted, this may improve the response time.

This interrupt is quite special. Normally an interrupt triggers its ISR (Interrupt Service Routine) to be invoked. After returning from ISR, that interrupt is marked as 'cleared' by the hardware automatically. Unlike other interrupts this is not always the case with **UDRE** (USART Data Register Empty) interrupt. If you don't write a new value to the **UDR** (transmit) register before returning from its ISR, it is not cleared. In fact this results in yet another call to the same ISR. This continues to happen until one of the following events happens:

- New value is written by programmer to **UDR**.
- Programmer disables **UDRE**.

This peculiar behavior makes this interrupt hard to use in situations where new byte to be transmitted is not immediately available. Hence most programmers prefer the second USART transmit interrupt–TXC (Transmission Complete) interrupt.

Tx Complete Interrupt

This interrupt is generated by USART hardware as soon as the complete frame–start bit, data bits, parity and stop bit(s) have been transmitted. Unlike **UDRE** this interrupt is automatically cleared by hardware as soon as its ISR returns. It is not required that programmer supplies the next byte to be transmitted immediately. Next byte can be transmitted at a later time.

Rx Complete Interrupt

This interrupt is as interesting as the UDRE interrupt. It is generated by USART hardware to indicate that entire frame has been received and the received data is available in **UDR** (USART Receive Data Register). Inside interrupt handler (ISR) caller must read the **UDR**. If caller doesn't read the received data, this interrupt remains raised and will result in another call to same ISR. Therefore, it's important to read **UDR** value inside its ISR.

Transmitting Using Interrupts

Let us see a program that uses interrupts to transmit data using USART. For this, we have to copy **uart1.c** and **uart1.h** files from Chapter 12 into the project directory for the program that we intend to write here. The function **uart_init( )** in these files will have to be changed to enable Tx Complete interrupt. We also need to provide an ISR for the Tx Complete interrupt. TxC interrupt uses **SIG_UART_TRANS** macro from system header ·file **avr/iom32.h**. Finally, we will need to copy **timer.h** and **timer.c** from Chapter 11 into the current project directory. Using functions in it, we will measure time taken to transmit one frame at 9600 baud.

Header file - uarti.h

```
# ifndef _uarti_h_
# define _uarti_h_

# include <avr/io.h>
# include "uart1.h"
# include "timer.h"
# include <avr/interrupt.h>
# include "lcd_io.h"

# endif /* _uarti_h_ */
```

Implementation file – uarti.c

```
# include "uarti.h"

int main ( void )
{
    timer_init( ) ;
    lcd_init( ) ;
    uart_init ( 9600 ) ;
    sei( ) ;
    uart_tx_char ( 'H' ) ;
    return 0 ;
}
```

Here **timer_init( )** is used to initialize the timer to doing measurements. **uart_init( )** is used to enable USART Rx and Tx and enable TxC interrupt. **uart1.c** copied from earlier chapter will have to be modified to do transmission using this interrupt. The modified **uart1.c** is shown below.

New Implementation file – uart1.c

```
#include "uart1.h"
#include "lcd_io.h"
#include "timer.h"

volatile uint8_t    tx_ready ;

void uart_init ( unsigned int baud )
{
     UBRRH = UART_BAUD_SELECT >> 8 ;
     UBRRL = ( uint8_t ) UART_BAUD_SELECT ;

     /* Enable 8-bit receiver and transmitter */
     UCSRB = _BV( RXEN ) | _BV ( TXEN ) | _BV( TXCIE ) ;
     UCSRC = _BV ( URSEL ) | _BV ( UCSZ1 ) | _BV ( UCSZ0 ) ;
     tx_ready = 1 ;
}

void uart_tx_char (unsigned char s )
{
     timer_start( ) ;
     while ( !tx_ready )
          ;


     tx_ready = 0 ;
     UDR = s ;
     lcd_putc ( s ) ;
}

SIGNAL ( SIG_UART_TRANS )
{
     uint16_t    t = timer_read_usec ( ) ;
```

```
    lcd_clrscr ( ) ;
    lcd_puts( "Time: " ) ;
    lcd_puti( t, 0 ) ;
    tx_ready = 1 ;
}
```

uart_init( ) has now been changed. It enables **TXCIE** bit in **UCSRB** to enable TxC interrupt. Other initialization steps are unchanged. Global boolean variable **tx_ready** is used to decide if transmission can happen immediately. When set to 1, UDR can be written and next transmission can begin immediately. When TxC interrupt is generated, it is set to 1 to indicate that next transmission can being now. It is set to 1 before returning from **uart_init( )**.

uart_tx_char( ) begins time measurement with call to **timer_start( )**. It then waits until **tx_ready** becomes 1. This may take time if previous transmission hasn't been finished yet. Once out of the **while** loop, **tx_ready** is set to 0 once gain and the byte to be transmitted is written to **UDR**.

After every frame is transmitted, TxC interrupt is generated. First step in interrupt handler is to get the time in microseconds for transmission of 1 frame. The ISR clears LCD screen, displays time and sets **tx_ready** to 1. Next transmission which may be pending can now begin.

Verifying The Baud Rate

If you try this program on KSET ES board, it will display value 1054. Is this what we expected? Let's find out:

1 Frame = 10 bits, Baud rate = 9600

Time for 10 bits = 10 / 9600 = 1042 μsec

Why is our value higher? This is because at the start of ISR compiler adds instructions to save all CPU registers on stack. This adds 30-40 extra instructions before we are able to call **timer_read_usec( )** to read the time for transmission.

What Is Concurrency?

While working with embedded systems, it is important to understand the element of concurrency. Concurrency exists in any program which works with interrupts. Interrupts can occur any time in the middle of program execution. The occurrence of an interrupt results in a call to its corresponding ISR. This independent context of execution is known as interrupt context.

An example of this is doing USART data transmission using interrupts. Your main program calls **uart_tx_char( )** to transmit a byte. It returns as soon as transmission is started. The transmission complete interrupt (TxC) occurs after every frame has been transmitted. This activity is called 'interrupt context' and it shares some global variables with main program (main execution context).

Race Conditions

To understand race conditions, consider following program:

```
# include <avr/io.h>

uint8_t count ;
uint8_t total ;

int main ( void )
{
    uart_init ( 9600 ) ;
    sei ( ) ;
    uart_tx_char ( 'h' ) ;
```

```
    count = count + 1 ;
    total = count + 1 ;

    return 0;
}

SIGNAL ( SIG_UART_TRANS )
{
    count -- ;
    total -- ;
}
```

The main program initializes USART, enables interrupts and updates two global variables **count** and **total**. Inside Tx Complete interrupt handler, value of **count** and **total** is changed. If interrupt occurs after first statement **count = count + 1** has been executed, then final value of **total** will be different. As you can see, it's a race between two contexts– main context and interrupt context. This shows that unless we are able to execute two statements inside **main( )** 'together' (or atomically), results are not predictable.

Dealing With Race Conditions

Race conditions always exist in a system with multiple contexts. How do you avoid them? In order to avoid them, we must disable interrupts for the duration of Critical Section. Critical Section is a set of instructions which should execute together without being interrupted. This concept is of great significance in working with multi-tasking and interrupt-driven systems where CPU time is shared between different contexts.

Generalized USART Library

In all our USART programs so far, we have copied **uart1.h** and **uart1.c** to our project directory and made changes in them.

Rather than making changes to these files for every variation of USART programming, what we will now do is create a generalized library to implement common part of the USART interface. Specific changes, as needed, can be implemented in a separate file. Let us see how we can make this library truly general-purpose. Given below are the header file and the implementation files of this library.

Header file - uart.h

```
# ifndef _uart_h_
# define _uart_h_

# include <avr/io.h>
# include <avr/interrupt.h>
# include <inttypes.h>

typedef void ( *INITFUNC_T ) ( void ) ;
typedef void ( *RXFUNC_T ) ( unsigned char ) ;
typedef void ( *TXFUNC_T ) ( unsigned char ) ;

extern void uart_init ( unsigned int baud, uint8_t enable_ints ) ;
extern void uart_tx_char ( unsigned char s ) ;

extern void uart_set_initfunc ( INITFUNC_T ) ;
extern void uart_set_rxfunc ( RXFUNC_T ) ;
extern void uart_set_txfunc ( TXFUNC_T ) ;

# endif /* _uart_h_ */
```

Here, at the top system header files have been included. **INITFUNC_T** is a **typedef** for function pointer which takes no arguments and returns nothing. **RXFUNCT_T** and **TXFUNC_T** are **typedef**s for function pointers that take

unsigned char as argument and return nothing. We have used function pointers here to allow for different implementations of UART transmit and receive.

This file exports following API functions:

uart_init( ) – It initializes the UART. First parameter is the baud rate and second parameter is a boolean which is set to 1 by caller to enable TxC and RxC interrupts during initialization. If set to 0, no UART interrupts are enabled.

uart_tx_char( ) – It is called to transmit a single character.

uart_set_initfunc( ) – It sets the address of caller specific initialization routine to specified parameter. UART library users who want to initialize their own internal data structures at the end of **uart_init( )** would use this API to pass their initialization function address to UART library.

uart_set_rxfunc( ) – It sets the address to Rx function. UART library will invoke function specified by this parameter whenever a character has been received in interrupt mode.

uart_set_txfunc – Sets the address to Tx function. UART library will invoke function specified by this parameter whenever current frame has been transmitted completely. It is also called by **uart_tx_char( )** to transmit next character.

Implementation file – uarti.c

```
# include "uart.h"

# define UART_BAUD_SELECT   ( F_CPU / ( baud * 16l ) - 1 )

volatile    static INITFUNC_T uart_InitFunc ;
```

```
volatile   static RXFUNC_T uart_RxFunc ;
volatile   static TXFUNC_T uart_TxFunc ;

void uart_init ( unsigned int baud, uint8_t enable_ints )
{
    UBRRH = UART_BAUD_SELECT >> 8 ;
    UBRRL = ( uint8_t ) UART_BAUD_SELECT ;

    if ( enable_ints )
        UCSRB = _BV( RXEN ) | _BV ( TXEN ) | _BV( RXCIE ) |
                _BV( TXCIE ) ;
    else
        UCSRB = _BV( RXEN ) | _BV ( TXEN ) ;

    UCSRC = _BV ( URSEL ) | _BV ( UCSZ1 ) | _BV ( UCSZ0 ) ;

    if ( uart_InitFunc )
        uart_InitFunc( ) ;
}

void uart_set_initfunc ( INITFUNC_T init_func )
{
    uart_InitFunc = init_func ;
}

void uart_set_rxfunc ( RXFUNC_T rx_func )
{
    uart_RxFunc = rx_func ;
}

void uart_set_txfunc ( TXFUNC_T tx_func )
{
    uart_TxFunc = tx_func ;
}

void uart_tx_char ( unsigned char ch )
{
    if ( uart_TxFunc )
```

```
        uart_TxFunc ( ch ) ;
}

SIGNAL ( SIG_UART_RECV )
{
    uint8_t c = UDR ;
    if ( uart_RxFunc )
        uart_RxFunc ( c ) ;
}

SIGNAL ( SIG_UART_TRANS )
{
    if ( uart_TxFunc )
        uart_TxFunc ( 0xff ) ;
}
```

As you can see, **uart_init( )** enables **RXCIE** and **TXCIE** if **enable_ints** parameter is true. It enables bi-directional communication for USART hardware in asynchronous mode with baud rate passed by user deciding the **UBRR** contents. In the end it calls the function whose address is stored in function pointer **uart_InitFunc**. This address is specified by the caller before calling **uart_init( )**.

Interrupt handlers for **Tx** and **Rx** complete call the functions **uart_TxFunc( )** and **uart_RxFunc( )** respectively. Note that **uart_TxFunc( )** is also called by **uart_tx_char( )** to actually transmit the character. To distinguish between two calls, **ISR** calls **uart_TxFunc( )** with parameter **oxff**. This is simply to let the called function know that if it has a queue of pending characters, it can now transmit the next character as previous one has been successfully transmitted.

To understand how exactly Generalized USART library is used to create a specific implementation we will study a complete example of buffered transmission in the next section.

Two Approaches For Doing I/O

In embedded systems Input/Output can be implementing using one of the two approaches:

- Synchronous or blocking
- Asynchronous or non-blocking

For the time being consider the case of USART to transmit characters. If we have more than one character to transmit, how do we transmit them knowing that only one character can be transmitted at a time. In blocking approach, we wait for previous character to be transmitted without doing anything else in the meantime. This process is continued until every character has been transmitted.

Problems With Blocking I/O

In non-blocking approach, we submit the character for transmission and do some other activity until that character has been transmitted. When that character is fully transmitted, we transmit the next character—but not wait until it is transmitted. The advantage of non-blocking approach is clear. We don't waste time waiting for time consuming I/O operation—utilizing that time to do other useful tasks in the embedded systems application. This approach is also known as asynchronous I/O.

Implementing blocking I/O is trivial and involves polling (we have already seen this approach earlier in Chapter 10). One of the approaches to asynchronous I/O is Producer-Consumer approach.

Implementing Non-blocking I/O – Producer-Consumer Approach

Producer-consumer algorithm uses a simple technique to implement asynchronous I/O operation. It is best illustrated using Figure 13.1 shown below. A queue of pending requests in maintained in a buffer. Three variables–**n_input**, **n_output** and **n_pending** are used to track the requests in buffer. To start with, all of them are initialized to zero.

When a request is created (character is to be transmitted) by Producer it is placed at index **n_input** in the buffer, provided that the buffer is not already full. **n_input** is then incremented by 1. **n_pending** is incremented by 1 to indicate that one more request is pending.

When Consumer (Tx Complete ISR) is ready to consume the request (transmit the character), it does the following:

- It checks if **n_pending** is greater than 0. If not, it does nothing.
- If there are pending requests, **n_output** is used to extract request (character) from buffer and service (transmit) it.
- **n_output** is incremented by 1.
- **n_pending** is decrement by 1 to indicate that one less request is pending.

In real-world systems, buffer is limited in capacity. As a result , we should use **Bounded-buffer Producer-Consumer** algorithm. It needs to handle wrap-around of **n_input** and **n_output** index variables. This is illustrated in the program given below.

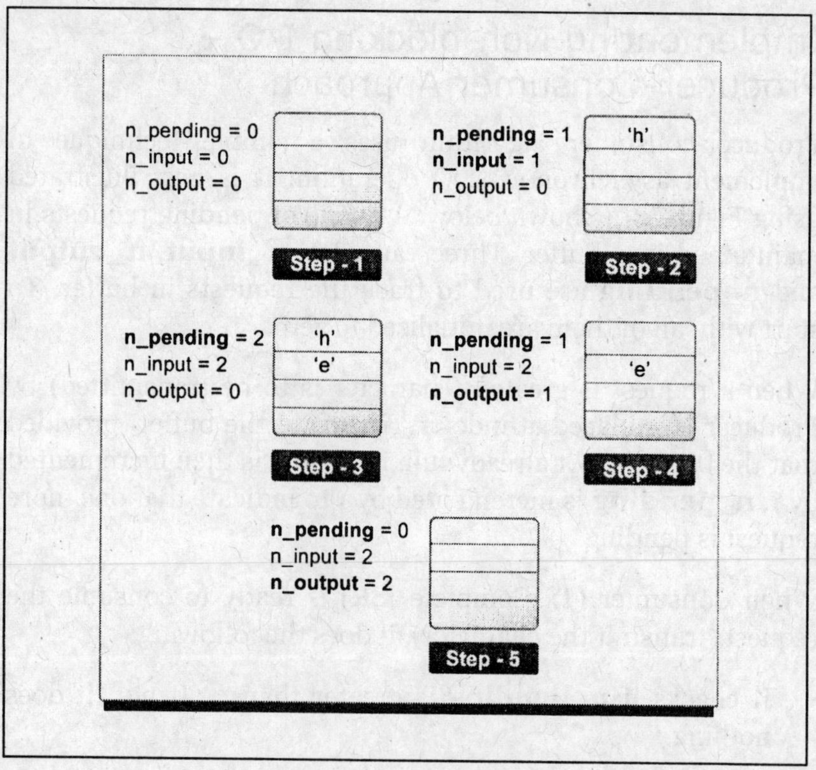

Figure 13.1: Producer Consumer Algorithm

Here is the header file for asynchronous UART transmit using bounded buffer producer-consumer approach. It uses generalized USART library developed earlier:

Header file – buftx.h

```
# ifndef _buftx_h_
# define _buftx_h_

# include "uart.h"

# define TX_BUFSIZE 16
```

```
typedef struct TxBuf
{
     uint8_t   buf [ TX_BUFSIZE ] ;
     uint8_t   n_input ;    /* Offset of next input character. */
     uint8_t   n_output ;   /* Offset of next character to be transmitted. */
     uint8_t   n_pending ;  /* Number of characters currently pending */
} TxBuf_t ;

extern void buf_initfunc ( void ) ;
extern void buf_txfunc ( unsigned char ch ) ;

# endif  /* _buftx_h_ */
```

TxBut_t is used to hold together the pending requests buffer and three variables used in producer-consumer algorithm. The API **buf_initfunc( )** is used to initialize producer-consumer implementation. Address of this function is passed to generalized USART library by call to **uart_set_initfunc( )**. **buf_txfunc( )** is the transmit function which will be called by generalized UART library. It's address is passed to it using **uart_set_txfunc( )**.

Here is the implementation for asynchronous UART transmit using producer-consumer approach:

Implementation file – buftx.c

```
# include "buftx.h"

/* Global variables */
volatile   uint8_t   tx_ready ;
volatile   TxBuf_t   sendBuf ;

static void bufInit ( volatile TxBuf_t * ) ;
```

```
static void bufPut ( volatile TxBuf_t *, uint8_t ch ) ;
static void tx_now ( unsigned char ch ) ;

void buf_initfunc ( void )
{
    bufInit ( &sendBuf ) ;
    tx_ready = 1 ;
}

static void bufInit ( volatile TxBuf_t *p )
{
    p->n_pending = 0 ;
    p->n_input = 0 ;
    p->n_output = 0 ;
}

static void tx_now ( unsigned char ch )
{
    tx_ready = 0 ;
    UDR = ch ;
    return ;
}

static void bufPut ( volatile TxBuf_t *p, uint8_t ch )
{
    if ( tx_ready )
    {
        tx_now ( ch ) ;
        return ;
    }

    while ( p->n_pending >= TX_BUFSIZE )
        ;

    cli ( ) ;

    p->buf [ p->n_input ] = ch ;
    p->n_input ++ ;
```

```
    p->n_input   %=  TX_BUFSIZE ;
    p->n_pending ++ ;

    sei ( ) ;
}

/* If called from interrupt context, ch is passed in as 0xff. In that case we must
set tx_ready = 1 */
void buf_txfunc ( unsigned char ch )
{
    if ( ch == 0xff )
    {
        tx_ready = 1 ;
        if ( sendBuf.n_pending > 0 )
        {
            tx_now ( sendBuf.buf [ sendBuf.n_output ] ) ;
            sendBuf.n_output ++ ;
            sendBuf.n_output %= TX_BUFSIZE ;
            sendBuf.n_pending -- ;
        }
    }
    else
        bufPut ( &sendBuf, ch ) ;
}
```

It's a somewhat large program. So let us try to understand it one step at a time.

sendBuf and **tx_ready** are global variables. First one is used as producer-consumer buffer. **tx_ready** is set to 1 whenever transmission is no longer is progress. Tx Complete ISR clears this flag and consumes next pending character in **sendBuf**, if any.

bufInit( ) and **bufPut( )** are functions used within this file hence their prototypes are tagged as **static**. **bufInit( )** initializes producer-consumer fields in **sendBuf** appropriately.

buf_initfunc( ) calls **bufInit( )** to initialize **sendBuf** and set **tx_ready** to a value 1. It is called by **uart_init( )** present in generalized USART library to initialize producer-consumer transmission buffer. We will soon see a complete example that demonstrates its usage.

tx_now( ) is a function that must be called only if **tx_ready** is 1. It resets **tx_ready** to 0 to and writes the input character to **UDR** (transmit data register).

buf_txfunc( ) is called by generalized USART library routine with parameter **0xff**, to transmit next pending character. It may be called by from main program via **uart_tx_char( )**.

In first case, it executes in interrupt context. It sets **tx_ready** to 1 and calls **tx_now( )** to start transmitting next pending character, if any. After transmitting the pending character, it updates **n_output** field in **sendBuf** and uses modulo (%) operator to make sure that it wraps around correctly when its value reaches **TX_BUFSIZE**. **n_pending** is decremented by 1.

In case of normal invocation via **uart_tx_char( )** it calls **bufPut( )** to add the character to the buffer/queue of pending requests. **bufPut( )** checks if **tx_ready** is 1. If so, it begins transmitting the character immediately after which it returns to the caller. If **tx_ready** is 0, it knows that previous character is still being transmitted. It has to consider two possibilities at this stage:

Check if the buffer is already full i.e. **n_pending** is >= **TX_BUFSIZE**. In that case the **while** loop forces the caller to wait. When previous transmission is complete, TxC ISR will call **buf_txfunc( )** which decrements **n_pending** and allows current character to be written to the buffer.

Once it is determined that the buffer is not full, we must write our character to it and update **n_pending** and **n_input**. Here is the classic race condition. It exists because **n_pending** is also changed inside Tx Complete ISR. To avoid this race condition we have used Critical Section. The statements that change **sendBuf** fields, have been put inside calls to **cli( )** and **sei( )** to ensure that they are executed un-interrupted. If interrupt was to occur in the same time period it will remain blocked until **sei( )** re-enables the masked interrupts.

Using Buffered USART Transmit

Here is the program that shows how to use buffered transmit implementation along with generalized USART library. Make sure that **uart.h** and **uart.c** from previous chapter and **buftx.h** and **buftx.h** are in same directory where this program is created:

Implementation file - uart3.c

```
# include <avr/io.h>
# include "buftx.h"
# include "lcd_io.h"

static void rx ( uint8_t ) ;

int  main ( void )
{
    int i = 0 ;

    lcd_init( ) ;

    uart_set_initfunc ( buf_initfunc ) ;
    uart_set_txfunc ( buf_txfunc ) ;
```

```
    uart_set_rxfunc ( rx ) ;
    uart_init ( 9600, 1 ) ;

    for ( i = 0 ; i < 100 ; i ++ )
        uart_tx_char ( '0' + ( i % 10 ) ) ;

    return 0 ;
}

void rx ( uint8_t ch )
{
    lcd_putc ( ch ) ;
    uart_tx_char ( ch ) ;
}
```

Exercise

[A] Answer the following:

(a) What are the advantages of using interrupts while sending data using ATmega32 USART?

(b) What are the advantages of buffering during interrupt driven transmit for ATmega32 USART?

(c) What is producer-consumer problem? What is its significance in asynchronous communication systems?

14 Building Interactive Embedded Systems

Most computing systems would be quite boring if they didn't have any interactive element in them, Your CD player, TV, Apple iPOD, mobile phone are all interactive in nature. Most ES do not have a complete keyboard. For example, a mobile phone has multiple characters assigned to each key. With practice most users get accustomed to these limited input capabilities. Even the display in such systems is quite small. Colored displays are not present due to cost constraints in many embedded systems. This chapter explores how to build interactive embedded systems.

Interacting With Users

Two fundamental features of most interactive system are:

(a) Input device - typically a keyboard or buttons
(b) Output device - LCD display, touch-screen, CRT screen etc.

Embedded Systems present unique set of challenges for user-interface designers. This forces you to think creatively and make user interfaces intuitive, easy to use and exciting.

Some embedded devices may not have any input or output devices connected to them. A good example would be your home ADSL modem that is used for internet connection. We need to use serial port or remote network connection with embedded web server to interact with such devices.

Interaction In KSET ES Board

KSET ES board has four numbered keys near its bottom left corner. They are labeled as KEY2 (DOWN), KEY3 (UP), KEY4 (OK) and KEY5 (CANCEL) respectively. These are push-button style keys. When released, they return to their normal "un-pressed" state automatically. All four keys are connected to two pins each of ports C and D. When pressed, the MC pins to which the keys are connected have 0V. On releasing them, the pins will have 5V.

Due to mechanical nature of these and many other keys found in various embedded systems, they bounce—for however small period of time on releasing. This causes the voltage at the MC pins to fluctuate for that period. We will study how to work bouncy keys later in this chapter.

One important criterion in interactive applications is responsiveness. Our application should be able to respond quickly to user actions. To achieve this with buttons, we must check the state of buttons frequently enough. Button state can be found by reading corresponding PIN voltages.

Keys & Microprocessor Connection

Let us now see how the 4 keys are connected to MC. Each key has two terminals. One is connected to PORT C or D of ATmega32 MC while other is connected to ground. If the key is pressed, the circuit gets completed and current flows in it. To prevent excess current flows from damaging the key as well as delicate MC circuitry, we must add a resistor between power-supply and ground terminal of the keys. One option is to connect it externally. This is not required because ATmega32 ports have an internal "pull-up" resistor that can be enabled by a programmer.

The keys are connected to MC as follows:

KEY2 - PINC7, KEY3 - PINC6

KEY4 - PID2, KEY5 - PIND3

Detecting Input Using Keys

To find out which MC port pins are used for keys, you should check the board "Connector Map" document. Every ES board manufacturer will provide one such document to the system designers. In addition to this, we must know how to enable the internal "pull-up" resistor at each of these pins. To achieve this we simply have to set that bit in **PORTC** or **PORTD** register This is done by calling the set bit in register function **sbi( ) as shown below:**

```
sbi ( PORTC, PINC7 ) ;
```

For checking the key states regularly we will use Timero.

Bouncy keys Issue

As discussed earlier, we must device a strategy to deal with bouncy keys. If we don't, user inputs will be ambiguous at times and may yield unexpected results. Our objective is to read the keys' state only after it settles down in final position. In addition, we must let the programmer handle the keystroke. To achieve this, we will use a simple state-machine. Any key can be in one of the following states:

- NOT PRESSED
- PRESSED
- RELEASED

Initially a key is in NOT PRESSED state. When user presses it, it enters PRESSED state and remains there until the user releases his/her finger. There is no "bounce" issue so far. When he/she releases the key, it bounces until it reaches a steady state. To avoid an ambiguity about it's value during this time period, we will keep the key in RELEASED state until programmer handles it explicitly and acknowledges it. After this, the key goes back to NOTPRESSED state.

With this scheme we no longer have the issue of key "bouncing" after it is released as we always let the programmer deal with the key being PRESSSED before we consider that it is NOT PRESSED.

Let us now study a program that demonstrates the use of keys. We will first develop the buttons library (**buttons.h** and **buttons.c**). This way we will be able to use the library in all future programs where keys are used.

Buttons Library

As usual, we will keep the #includes and declarations of this library in the header file (buttons.h) and the implementation of these functions in the program file (buttons.c). The contents of the header file are given below:

Header file – buttons.h

```
# ifndef _BUTTONS_H_
# define _BUTTONS_H_

# include <compat/deprecated.h>
# include <avr/io.h>

extern uint8_t key2_state ;
extern uint8_t key3_state ;
extern uint8_t key4_state ;
extern uint8_t key5_state ;

/* button states */
# define NOTPRESSED    0x00
```

```
# define PRESSED          0x10
# define RELEASED         0x01

/* AVR Buttons pin connections */
# define KEY2    PINC7   /* Port C pin */
# define KEY3    PINC6   /* Port C pin */
# define KEY4    PIND2   /* Port D pin */
# define KEY5    PIND3   /* Port D pin */

# define KEY_NOT_PRESSED( addr, b )  bit_is_set(_MMIO_BYTE(addr), b)
# define KEY_PRESSED( addr, b )      bit_is_clear( _MMIO_BYTE(addr), b)
# define RESET_KEY_STATE( k )        (k) = NOTPRESSED

/* Function prototypes */
extern void  buttons_init ( void ) ;
extern int  buttons_check ( void ) ;

# endif /*_BUTTONS_H_*/
```

This header file includes the system header files. **compat/deprecated.h** is included as it contains **sbi** macro used in setting the pull-up resistor at PORT C & D pins. It also contains extern declarations for variables **key2_state**, **key3_state**, **key4_state** and **key5_state** which are used to track the three state of respective buttons—NOTPRESSSED, PRESSED, RELEASED.

Important helper macros and their purpose are as follows:

KEY_NOT_PRESSED - Used internally by buttons library to check if a key is not pressed.

KEY_PRESSED - Called internally by buttons library to check if a key is pressed.

RESET_KEY_STATE - Called by users of buttons library to reset the state of key from RELEASED to NOTPRESSED state.

Only two other functions are exposed by buttons library:

buttons_init( ) - Called by users of buttons library to initialize the state of buttons

buttons_check( ) - Called regularly by users of buttons library to do state transitions for buttons if required.

Macro **_MMIO_BYTE** from **avr/io.h** return value gives us access to a memory mapped I/O register.

Implementation

This file implements the "buttons" API (Application Programmers Interface). API is a set of functions from buttons library that can be called by its users.

Impementation file – buttons.c

```
# include "buttons.h"

/* Globals */
uint8_t key2_state ;
uint8_t key3_state ;
uint8_t key4_state ;
uint8_t key5_state ;

int check_button ( uint8_t *pstate, uint16_t port_addr, uint8_t pin ) ;

/* Enable Pull-up resistor's for port's Pins */
void buttons_init( )
{
     sbi ( PORTC, KEY3 ) ;
     sbi ( PORTC, KEY2 ) ;
     sbi ( PORTD, KEY4 ) ;
     sbi ( PORTD, KEY5 ) ;
```

```
}

int check_button ( uint8_t *pstate, uint16_t port_addr, uint8_t pin )
{
    switch (*pstate)
    {
        case NOTPRESSED :
            if ( KEY_PRESSED ( port_addr, pin ) )
            {
                *pstate = PRESSED ;
            }
            break ;

        case PRESSED :
            if ( KEY_NOT_PRESSED ( port_addr, pin ) )
            {
                *pstate = RELEASED ;
                return 1 ;
            }
            break ;
    }
    return 0 ;
}

int  buttons_check( )
{
    int released = 0 ;

    released |= check_button ( &key2_state,  _SFR_ADDR(PINC), KEY2  ) ;
    released |= check_button ( &key3_state,  _SFR_ADDR(PINC), KEY3 ) ;
    released |= check_button ( &key4_state,  _SFR_ADDR(PIND), KEY4 ) ;
    released |= check_button ( &key5_state, _SFR_ADDR(PIND), KEY5 ) ;

    return released ;
}
```

At the top it contains definitions of variables **key2_state**, **key3_state**, **key4_state** and **key5_state**. **read_button( )**

function that is used internally in this file to read and change the state of a button is also declared here. **buttons_init( )** initializes pull-up resistors at pins 6 & 7 of PORTC and pins 2 & 3 of PORTD using the function **sbi( )** (set bit in register). All users of buttons library must call this function during their initialization.

read_button( ) function takes three parameters. First one is address of state variable associated with a key, second one contains the address of I/O port to which key is connected and third one is the pin number of that port where the key is connected. It checks if the state of specified key and takes following actions:

If the key is currently in **NOTPRESSED** state and user has pressed the key, it changes its state to **PRESSED**.

(a) If key is in **PRESSED** state and it is released, then it will change the state to **RELEASED**.

(b) If the key is in **RELEASED** state, it does nothing.

(c) If the key has transitioned to **RELEASED** state, it returns 1, otherwise it returns 0. It keeps the key in **RELEASED** state until user resets the key back to **NOTPRESSED** by calling **RESET_KEY_STATE** macro. This avoids the key "bouncing" issue as explained earlier.

Finally, **buttons_check( )** is the public API function implemented in **buttons.c**. It reads the state of all four buttons and returns **true** if any of the keys was released. Otherwise, it returns 0.

Macro **_SFR_ADDR** gives us the address of an I/O register that is used as an argument. In this case, we use **PINC** and **PIND** as arguments.

Menu Library

Most interactive systems today use menu driven approach. For example - PC based programs like MS Word, Excel, Internet Explorer, Mozilla Firefox etc. use menu driven approach extensively. In embedded systems it is even more relevant because entering a choice manually is difficult due to limited keyboard capabilities. You may have seen many embedded systems like DVD players, Televisions remotes, electronic wristwatches etc. that use menus for managing configuration settings and presenting a simple interface to the end users. Only ingredient for success in this is creativity, so start thinking!

For the KSET ES board we are going to build a "menu library". It allows you to create menu based programs quickly. The library has two files—**menu.h** and **menu.c**. Of these, the code of **menu.h** is given below:

Header file - menu.h

```
# ifndef _MENU_H_
# define _MENU_H_

# include <avr/io.h>
# include <avr/interrupt.h>
# include "lcd_io.h"
# include "avrlibtypes.h"
# include "buttons.h"
# include <avr/pgmspace.h>
```

```
# define UP          KEY3
# define DOWN        KEY2
# define OK          KEY4
# define CANCEL      KEY5

struct menu_item
{
    char name[ 16 ] ;
    void ( *func )( void ) ;
};

/* Function prototypes */
void display_menu ( struct menu_item *, uint8_t num_items ) ;

# endif  /* _MENU_H_ */
```

The header file includes standard header files and #defines for 4 keys—UP, DOWN, OK and CANCEL. Keys 2 & 3 will be used to navigate between the menu items— up or down. KEY4 will be used to select an item and KEY5 to go back to return from the menu based system to the caller.

How does the user of this library known when a given menu item is selected? For that we associate a "callback function" or a function pointer with each menu item. User of menu library will supply a function pointer with each menu item. Menu library will call the function for the selected menu item. Programmer performs action relevant to that selection after which the function returns. **menu_item** structure encapsulates one entry in the choice of items presented to the user.

display_menu( ) is the only function exposed by menu library. It takes two arguments—first argument is the base address array of menu items. Second argument is the number menu items in that array.

Given below is the implementation code for the menu library.

Implementation file - menu.c

```
#include "menu.h"

void delay( void ) ;

void delay ( void )
{
    uint8_t i, j, k ;
    for ( i = 0; i < 255; i++ )
    {
        for ( j = 0 ; j < 255 ; j++ )
        {
            for ( k = 0 ; k < 4 ; k++ )
                ;
        }
    }
    return ;
}

void display_menu ( struct menu_item *m, uint8_t nitems )
{
    uint8_t citem = 0 ;

    while ( 1 )
    {
        lcd_clrscr( ) ;

        lcd_puts ( m[ citem ].name ) ;
        if  ( ( nitems – citem ) > 1 )
        {
            lcd_putc ( '\n' ) ;
            lcd_puts ( m[ citem + 1 ].name ) ;
        }
```

```
        lcd_gotoxy ( 0, 0 ) ;
        lcd_command ( LCD_DISP_ON_BLINK ) ;

        if  ( key4_state == RELEASED )
        {
            lcd_command ( LCD_DISP_ON ) ; /* turn off blinking character*/
            RESET_KEY_STATE ( key4_state ) ;
            m[ citem ].func( ) ;
        }

        if ( key5_state == RELEASED )
        {
            RESET_KEY_STATE ( key5_state ) ;
            /* turn off blinking character */
            lcd_command ( LCD_DISP_ON ) ;
            return ;
        }

        if ( key3_state == RELEASED )
        {
            RESET_KEY_STATE ( key3_state ) ;
            If ( citem > 0 )
                citem-- ;
            else
                citem = nitems – 1 ;
        }

        if ( key2_state == RELEASED )
        {
            RESET_KEY_STATE ( key2_state ) ;
            if ( ( nitems – citem ) > 1 )
                citem++ ;
            else
                citem = 0 ;

        delay( ) ;
    }
```

}

display_menu( ) gets the array of menu items from the caller. Each entry in this array contains:

- Menu String
- Function to be called if this menu item is selected by the caller

It uses a local variable **c_item** to track current item being displayed on the screen. Inside the **while** loop, the LCD screen is first cleared. Two menu items can be displayed on the screen simultaneously—one per row. Menu items at index **c_item** and **c_item + 1** are displayed on lines 1 and 2 respectively of the LCD display. After this, the cursor is taken back to the beginning of first line. Blinking cursor is used to make the user aware of current item. The user can now press any of the four keys. Let's see how they are handled.

KEY4 is the OK key. If user presses it, we must turn-off the blinking cursor on LCD, reset the KEY4 state and call **m[citem].func( )**. This invokes the function corresponding to that selection. Only after this function returns, further keystroke processing can happen.

KEY5 is the CANCEL key. If user presses it we return to the caller of **display_menu( )** immediately and stop the menu display on screen. Before returning, we clear the state of KEY5.

KEY3 is the UP key. We first reset its state and if current item is not the first one in array, we decrement **c_item**. Otherwise, we wrap around **c_item** and set it to **nitems - 1**. In the next iteration of the while loop LCD gets cleared and user gets the correct effect by seeing appropriate entries displayed on the screen.

KEY2 is the DOWN key. We first reset its state and if current item is not the last one in array, we increment **c_item**. Otherwise we wrap around **c_item** and set it to **0**. In the next iteration of the while loop, LCD gets cleared and user gets the correct effect by seeing appropriate entries displayed on the screen.

Finally, we have added a small delay between consecutive iterations of the loop. If we don't add the delay, user will see the menu items change too fast when he presses UP/DOWN keys.

Demo Application

Let us now write a program that demonstrates how to use the button and the menu library. Here is the program...

Impelementation file – menu_demo.c

```
# include "menu.h"

void init  avr ( void ) ;
void start_timer ( void ) ;
void print_option1  (void ) ;
void print_option2 ( void ) ;
void print_option3 ( void ) ;
void wait_for_ok ( void ) ;

int main( void )
{
     struct menu_item main_menu[ ] =
     {
          { " OPTION 1", print_option1 },
          { " OPTION 2", print_option2 },
          { " OPTION 3", print_option3 }
     };
```

```
    init_avr( ) ;
    display_menu ( main_menu,
                    sizeof ( main_menu ) / sizeof ( main_menu[ 0 ] ) ) ;

    return 0 ;
}

void init_avr ( void )
{
    lcd_init( ) ;
    buttons_init( ) ;
    start_timer( ) ;
    sei( ) ;
}

void start_timer( )
{
    TCNT0 = 0x00 ;
    TCCR0 = 0x05 ;
    TIMSK = 0x01 ;
}

SIGNAL ( SIG_OVERFLOW0 )
{
    buttons_check( ) ;
}

void print_option1 ( void )
{
    lcd_clrscr( ) ;
    lcd_puts ( "OPTION 1 SELECTED" ) ;
    wait_for_ok( ) ;
}

void print_option2 ( void )
{
    lcd_clrscr( ) ;
    lcd_puts ( "OPTION 2 SELECTED" ) ;
```

```
    wait_for_ok( ) ;
}

void print_option3 ( void )
{
    lcd_clrscr( ) ;
    lcd_puts ( "OPTION 3 SELECTED" ) ;
    wait_for_ok( ) ;
}

void wait_for_ok( )
{
    while ( key4_state != RELEASED )
        ;
    RESET_KEY_STATE ( key4_state ) ;
}
```

Now a brief explanation about the program...

Inside **main( )** we have declared an array **main_menu[ ]** that contains 3 entries—Option 1, 2 & 3. Each entry has a function **print_option1( )**, **print_option2( )** and **print_option3( )** respectively. These functions handle respective menu items being selected. First character in each menu string is a blank. It ensures that blinking cursor doesn't overlap with the menu item.

In this program, **main( )** initializes LCD and buttons (**buttons_init( )**). It starts TIMER0 with a frequency scaling of 1024 and enables TIMER0's overflow interrupt. So the buttons state will be checked 31 times every second. This is good enough to ensure that any user actions will be "sampled" regularly and our application is responsive enough. Finally, it uses **sei( )** to enable interrupts globally.

ISR for **SIG_OVERFLOW0** checks the keys and takes appropriate action. It first uses **buttons_check( )** to transition the buttons to correct state. If any of the buttons were released, **display_menu( )** clears the LCD screen. Then it checks if the keys 2 - 5 are in **RELEASED** state, and displays a message on the screen indicating key-press that was detected. After handling a key it calls **RESET_KEY_STATE (keyX_state)** where "X" is 2, 3, 4 or 5 to reset the key back to **NOTPRESSSED** state.

Once the initialization is over, next step is to call **display_menu( )** with **main_menu[ ]** array as the first argument and number of items in it as the second argument. This function will display options 1, 2 & 3 on the screen and navigate between them.

If option1 is selected, **print_option1( )** will be called. This function will clear the LCD and displays a string "OPTION 1 SELECTED" on the screen. It waits for **OK** button to be pressed before returning back to the **display_menu( )** function.

print_option2( ) and **print_option3( )** are identical except for the message that they display. Helper functions **init_avr( )** and **start_timer( )** have already been explained in previous chapter. ISR for Timer0 simply calls **buttons_check( )** to poll the state of buttons.

Ensure that when you create a new project **menu_demo** you copy the files **buttons.h, buttons.c, menu.h** and **menu.c** to the **menu_demo** directory.

This application simply showed how easy it is for us to detect a key being pressed by a user and take appropriate action based on that. In real-life you can build very interesting user interfaces using these four little buttons. We will demonstrate to you how to build an alpha-numeric pager interface in the following sections.

What Is A Pager?

Pager is a small electronic device used for sending and receiving short text messages. These devices were quite popular before mobile phones replaced them all over the world. Then why are we creating a pager interface? Let's understand how pagers worked. Pagers were quite ingenious. Most pagers had a small two-line LCD display and no keyboard. They had four keys – LEFT, RIGHT, SELECT and SEND. So how did users type anything on these pagers? When sending messages, a pager displayed characters A-Z and digits 0-9 on second line. Users used left-right keys to move the cursor between characters. When cursor displays the character of choice, user presses SELECT key, character under cursor would be displayed on first line of the screen. One by one all characters would be selected and entire message would appear on first line. Once the message is composed SEND key was used to transmit the message to another pager device.

Most embedded systems have very few keys and hardly ever contain a complete keyboard. In this program we show you how to build creative interfaces in interactive Embedded System applications. We hope that it will ignite your imagination.

Proposed Solution Using KSET ES Board

KSET ES board has four keys and 2-line LCD display. Using these, we can create a nice pager interface. We will use second line of LCD to display A-Z characters (26) and 0-9 digits (10) i.e. a total of 36 characters. Width of our LCD screen is only 16 characters. So how will this work? To make it work, we must implement horizontal scrolling on second-line of LCD screen.

Here is the header file:

Header file - pager.h

```
#ifndef _pager_h_
#define _pager_h_

#include <avr/io.h>
#include <avr/interrupt.h>
#include <avr/pgmspace.h>
#include <string.h>
#include "lcd_io.h"
#include "buttons.h"

#define LEFT_KEY        KEY2
#define RIGHT_KEY       KEY3
#define SELECT_KEY      KEY4

#define left_state      key2_state
#define right_state     key3_state
#define select_state    key4_state

struct keypad {
   PGM_P      keys ;
   uint8_t    num_keys ;
   uint8_t    k_pos ;
   uint8_t    x_coord ;
   uint8_t    out_cur ;
};
#endif /* _pager_h_ */
```

At the top, we have included necessary system header files. **lcd_io.h** is included to work with LCD display and **buttons.h** for working with buttons. We need only 3 keys in our application – KEY2, KEY3 and KEY4. To make it easier for us to work with these keys, we have redefined these macros as LEFT_KEY, RIGHT_KEY and SELECT_KEY respectively. Working with keys requires us to work with "state variables" for each of these buttons. So we have re-defined these state variables as left_state, right_state and select_state for keys 2, 3 and 4 respectively. This ensures that we don't make silly mistakes (typos) while working with these variables in our implementation.

The **keypad** structure is used to capture information about:

(a) Values and number of characters displayed on second line (A-Z and 0-9). These characters are stored in flash memory to save precious RAM during program execution. Its type **PGM_P** expands to **const prog_char *** - Pointer to constant string in program memory.

(b) Cursor position on the second line.

(c) Index of character within character array for character under the cursor.

(d) Next position on the first line where selected character will be displayed.

Our implementation will use a global variable of this structure and update it when user navigates through the keypad using LEFT, RIGHT and SELECT keys.

Implementation

Pager implementation uses buttons library. So copy **button.c** and **buttons.h** created earlier in the same directory where

pager.h and **pager.c** are created. **init_avr** and **start_timer** are used to initialize microcontroller and TIMER0 respectively. Tagging the function prototype as **static** ensures that function is visible only within the same file. Functions for handling keypad activity are as follows:

kp_init – Initializes the keypad variable.

kp_display – Displays correct 16 characters from keys array.

kp_left – Called when user presses LEFT key.

kp_right – Called when user presses RIGHT key.

kp_show_line1 – Displays selected character at correct position on first line of LCD display.

Each function receives **volatile struct keypad *kp** as an argument. What is the reason for making this variable volatile? Here is the explanation. This argument will be passed the address of a global variable. Some of these functions are invoked from **TIMER0** interrupt handler. They may be called from **main** as well. Most compilers including **gcc** may optimize access to these variables by caching their values in CPU registers – R0-R31. This causes a problem in situation when function called from **main** is executing and interrupt occurs. Program's execution will be suspended and interrupt handler is invoked. If some field in this structure variable was changed in that function already, interrupt handler must use the most up-to-date value of that field. If function that was interrupted never got a chance to update that value in memory, value inside the interrupt handler will be stale. This almost certainly leads to problem in your application. Once a variable is marked as volatile, compiler follows the rule of load-modify-store (read-modify-write) to when working with such variables. As a result the updated values are reflected in the memory immediately.

Here is the pager implementation:

Implementation file – pager.c

```
#include "pager.h"

static void init_avr ( void ) ;
static void start_timer ( void ) ;

static void kp_init ( volatile struct keypad *kp ) ;
static void kp_display ( volatile struct keypad *kp ) ;
static void kp_left ( volatile struct keypad *kp ) ;
static void kp_right ( volatile struct keypad *kp ) ;
static void kp_show_line1 ( volatile struct keypad *kp ) ;

volatile struct keypad *active_kp ;
volatile struct keypad ascii_kp ;

int main ( void )
{
    PGM_P   alphabets =
        PSTR ( "abcdefghijklmnopqrstuvwxyz0123456789" ) ;

    init_avr( ) ;
    kp_init ( &ascii_kp ) ;

    ascii_kp.keys = alphabets ;
    ascii_kp.num_keys = strlen_P ( alphabets ) ;

    active_kp = &ascii_kp ;
    kp_display ( active_kp ) ;
    return 0 ;
}

void init_avr ( void )
{
```

```
    lcd_init( ) ;
    buttons_init( ) ;
    start_timer( ) ;
    lcd_command ( LCD_DISP_ON_BLINK ) ;
    sei( ) ;
}

void start_timer ( void )
{
    TCNT0 = 0x00 ; /* Overflow after 32.768 msec */
    TCCR0 = 0x05 ; /* Divide by 1024 */
    TIMSK = 0x01 ; /* Enable TOV0 */
}

SIGNAL ( SIG_OVERFLOW0 )
{
    buttons_check( ) ;
    if ( left_state == RELEASED )
    {
        RESET_KEY_STATE ( left_state ) ;
        kp_left ( active_kp ) ;
    }
    else if ( right_state == RELEASED )
    {
        RESET_KEY_STATE ( right_state ) ;
        kp_right ( active_kp ) ;
    }
    else if ( select_state == RELEASED )
    {
        RESET_KEY_STATE ( select_state ) ;
        kp_show_line1 ( active_kp ) ;
    }
}

void kp_init ( volatile struct keypad *kp )
{
    memset( (void *)kp, sizeof ( *kp ), 0 ) ;
}
```

```
void kp_display ( volatile struct keypad *kp )
{
    uint8_t    i ;
    uint8_t    cnt = 0 ;

    lcd_gotoxy ( 0 , 1 ) ;
    for ( i = kp->k_pos ; cnt < LCD_CHARS_PER_LINE ; i ++ )
    {
        lcd_putc ( pgm_read_byte ( & kp->keys [ i % kp->num_keys ] ) ) ;
        cnt ++ ;
    }

    kp->x_coord = 0 ;
    lcd_gotoxy ( kp->x_coord , 1 ) ;
}

void kp_left ( volatile struct keypad *kp )
{
    if ( kp->k_pos == 0 )
        kp->k_pos = kp->num_keys - 1 ;
    else
        kp->k_pos -- ;
    if ( kp->x_coord > 0 )
    {
        lcd_gotoxy ( -- kp->x_coord , 1 ) ;
        return ;
    }
    else
        kp_display ( kp ) ;
}

void kp_right ( volatile struct keypad *kp )
{
    if ( kp->x_coord < LCD_CHARS_PER_LINE )
    {
        kp->k_pos ++ ;
        kp->k_pos %= kp->num_keys ;
```

```
        lcd_gotoxy ( ++ kp->x_coord , 1 ) ;
        return ;
    }
    else
        kp_display ( kp ) ;
}

void kp_show_line1 ( volatile struct keypad *kp )
{
    lcd_gotoxy ( kp->out_cur ++ , 0 ) ;
    kp->out_cur %= LCD_CHARS_PER_LINE ;
    lcd_putc ( pgm_read_byte ( & kp->keys [ kp->k_pos ] ) ) ;
    lcd_gotoxy( kp->x_coord , 1 ) ;
}
```

Let us go through the program now. **main** initializes **ascii_kp** variable to use **alphabets** array containing characters a-z and numbers 0-9. It initializes the LCD and starts the timer for polling the state of keys every 33 msecs. Interrupts are enabled globally and cursor blinking is turned on to show the selected character to the user. Finally it calls **kp_display** to display 16 characters from **alphabets** array on the second line of LCD screen. Now program is entirely driven by user input. Depending on the keys pressed by user appropriate action is taken.

TIMER0 overflow interrupt handler is used to check the state of each of the three keys – LEFT, RIGHT and SELECT. If LEFT key is pressed, **kp_left** is called. **kp_left** checks if we are at lowest index in **keys** array. In that case, **k_pos** (current index in **keys** array) is reset to **kp->num_keys – 1**; otherwise it is decremented by 1. Similarly, if **x_coord** on LCD screen is > 0 then cursor is taken one place to the left and **x_coord** is decremented by 1. Otherwise we have to call **kp_display** to re-display appropriate 16 "virtual keyboard" characters on second line. Why is this needed – to ensure that we are able to select from all 32 characters in **keys** array. In **kp_display** we use the modulo operator in C (%) to display 16 characters starting with **k_pos**. Whenever **kp_display** is called **x_coord** is reset to 0 and cursor is taken to 1st character on 2nd line.

If RIGHT key is pressed, **kp_right** is called. If **x_coord** on LCD screen is < 16 then cursor is taken one place to the right and **x_coord** is incremented by 1. Then it increments **k_pos** (current index in **keys** array) by 1 and used modulo (%) operator to wrap it around in case when it reaches **kp->num_keys – 1**. If cursor in at the last character on LCD display, **kp_display** is called to re-display the "virtual keyboard" and reset **x_coord** back to 0.

If SELECT key is pressed, **kp_show_line1** is called. It increments **kp->our_cur** by 1 and does a module operation to ensure that is doesn't go beyond 16. Then it reads the current keypad character from program memory (flash) and displays it. After this the cursor is restored to second line with x coordinate set to **kp->x_coord**.

This program demonstrates that embedded system interfaces can be cleverly created and can easily overcome the limitations like lack of a complete keyboard. We hope this will inspire you to build such interfaces in future.

Exercise

[A] Answer the following:

(a) Write a program to do the following:

- Display string "hello world" on first line of LCD screen

- On second line display "hello KSET".
- Use KEY2, KEY3, KEY4 and KEY5 as left, right, down and up arrows. When you use these keys the "cursor" on LCD should move accordingly.

(b) Write a program to use keys 2, 3, 4 and 5 to provide "scroll-bar" functionality on the LCD display. You should be able to do:

- Horizontal scrolling (left and right). To prove the point display a string longer than 16 characters in a single line and then scroll-right to show characters after first 16 characters.
- Vertical scrolling (up and down). To prove the point display up-to 5 lines and scroll vertically between them using up and down arrow keys. At all times correct lines should be displayed.

15 Working With RTC Using I^2C Bus

Communication systems created over last 20 years rarely exhibit the simplicity and elegance embodied by I²C. The techniques that we have seen so far (e.g. UART) allow only point-to-point communication. In practice, when large number of external devices are to be connected to microcontroller, need to identify them (addressing) and being able to transfer large amount of data over relatively large cable/track lengths is required. I²C (Inter IC Control) is a remarkable example of the principle – necessity is the mother of invention.

I²C (Inter IC Control) is a serial communication standard. It was created for use within consumer electronics appliances like TVs, VCRs, audio equipment which have large number of peripherals connected to the MC. Another requirement in these devices is that internal wiring must be very simple. Research for this was done by Philips. Today, it has become a very popular standard and is accepted by many companies. Intel, Texas Instruments, Maxim, Atmel, ST Micro, Infineon, and Analog Devices are just some of the companies that use I²C for serial communication.

I²C allows large number of external devices to be connected directly to the MC without having to use separate MC pin for each device. Bidirectional communication is possible. Up to 128 devices can be connected on a single 'bus'. It uses only 2 wires– both of them bidirectional. These wires are:

(a) **SDA** – Serial Data Input/Output
(b) **SCL** – Serial Clock

Due to this simplicity, many texts refer to it a TWI – Two Write Interface, as it needs only two wires. The network topology is a shared bus system. Each device on the bus has unique 7-bit address. At any point in time, any two devices on the bus may be communicating. To ensure smooth exchange of information, Master-Slave protocol is used. Master is a device capable of initiating communication, whereas Slave is a device that obeys the commands generated by the master. The reason why it is called Slave is because; it doesn't play an intelligent role in the communication process.

Clock on I²C bus decides the maximum speed of data transfer. It can operate in one of the following three modes:

(a) Standard – 100 kbit/s
(b) Fast – 400 kbit/s
(c) High-speed – 3.4 Mbit/s

All the devices on the bus must use same mode of operation. This normally means that slowest device dictates the speed at which other devices can operate.

Advantages of I²C/TWI

TWI bus allows multiple potential master devices on the bus. Its advantages are as follows:

(a) It uses a simple addressing scheme.
(b) It requires small space to implement in ICs.
(c) It has a low cost.

Because of these advantages, TWI is used in connecting external memories like serial EEPROM, RAM, NVRAM and other chips like RTC (Real Time Clock) to the MC. Most of these peripherals transfer the data in small chunks and do not need very high data-transfer rates. On KSET ES board, TWI bus is used to connect RTC (Real Time Clock) chip to the microcontroller. You must first understand the fundamentals of TWI bus and the protocol before we can show you how to work with this device.

TWI Bus Interconnections And Frame Format

Interconnections on TWI bus are shown in Figure 15:1.

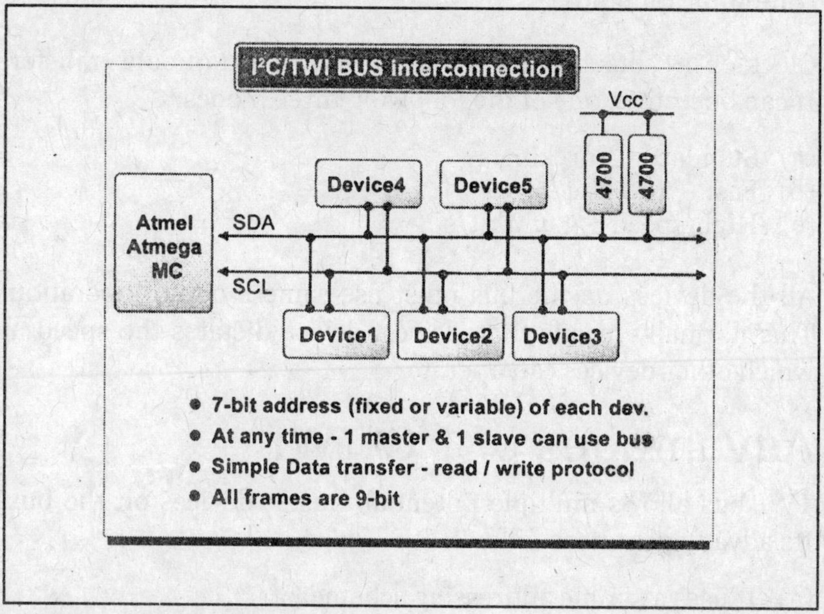

Figure 15.1: I²C/TWI bus topology

From interconnections, it's clear that at any point in time only two devices could be involved in the data transfer. Before data transfer can happen, master must "win" election on the bus. This election process ensures that if more than one device attempts to be the master, one of them will win it. Other one waits for the current master to release the bus. Data on TWI bus is transferred in frames. Each frame is 9-bits in length. This is very similar to USART transmission and reception that we have studied in Chapters 12 and 13. Most important difference between serial communication and TWI is that former is used for point-to-point communication, whereas, TWI is used for connecting multiple devices together.

Details of TWI data transfer protocol for read/write operations are as follows:

(a) One master device wins control of bus using a process called 'bus arbitration'.

(b) Master device transmits **START** Condition **(S)** bit on on SDA line.

(c) Master devices sends Slave Address (SLA - 7 bits) on SDA line. This address is allows other devices on the bus to check if the master wishes to communicate with them.

(d) After this, master sends **R/W** bit on SDA line. This bit indicates the direction of data transfer to the slave device. Slave device now knows whether it's a transmitter or receiver.

(e) The Slave device with matching address in SLA phase, will respond with a positive acknowledgement **ACK**. This tells the master that the Slave device is ready for data transfer. Without receiving an acknowledgement, no data transfer will take place.

(f) What happens thereafter depends on whether Master is a is transmitter or receiver. If master is transmitter:
- It sends first 8-bits of data to the slave.
- Slave returns an **ACK** bit to the master.

If master is a receiver:

- Slave sends first 8-bits data to the master.

– Master will return an **ACK** to the slave.

(g) Previous step will be repeated until all data is transmitted / received between master and the slave device. At any stage, if acknowledgement is not received, data transfer will be aborted by master by sending **STOP** condition (bit) on the bus.

(h) At the end of data transfer, master sends **STOP** Condition **(F)** bit on the bus. This indicates to the slave that no further data transfer will be done.

The essence of these steps is captured in Figure 15.2.

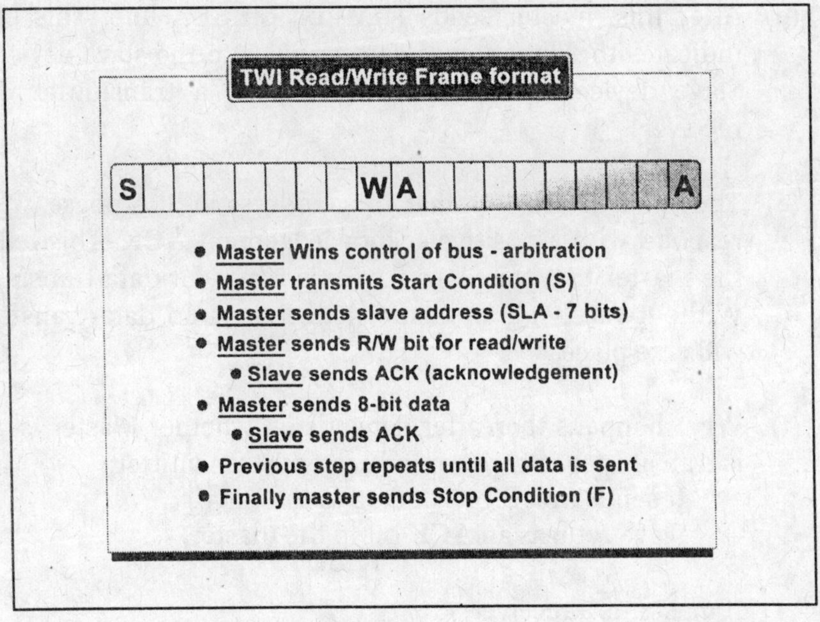

Figure 15.2: TWI frame format

ATmega32 TWI unit supports starting all these operations on TWI bus. Next section describes the support for TWI bus in ATmega32 microcontroller.

ATmega32 TWI support

ATmega32 has extensive support for I²C/TWI protocol. It can operate as a master as well as slave. In either of these roles, it supports bidirectional data transfer. It supports 7-bit addressing mode. When acting as slave it can be programmed to use any 7-bit address value sent by the master i.e. it's "slave address" is configurable. This is very important in practice because many of the smaller TWI devices have hard-coded 7-bit address. Since MC is capable of using a SLA assigned by the programmer, address conflicts can be easily resolved. ATmega32 supports up to 400 kbits/sec data transfer rate i.e. fast mode. TWI support is very easy to use and configure. In addition, this unit also supports noise suppression. I/O registers associated with ATmega32's TWI unit are as follows:

TWAR TWI Address Register. Used to set 7-bit slave address of the MCU when it operates in 'Slave Receiver' mode.

TWBR – TWI Baud Rate Register. It is used to set SCL frequency when MC operates in Master mode.

TWCR – TWI Control Register. Used to control the operation on TWI bus.

TWSR – TWI Status Register. Contains a numeric code indicating the status of previous operation on TWI bus.

TWDR – TWI Data Register. Used to store the data byte to be transmitted when used as Master Transmitter. Also stores the received byte when in Master Receiver or Slave Receiver mode.

All these registers have a role to play during read/write operations on TWI bus. As explained earlier, all devices on the bus must operate at same speed. It is the slowest device which decides the speed of operation. When AVR MC operates in master mode, SCL (Serial Clock) signal is generated by it's TWI unit. In this, **TWBR** register has a similar role as **UBRR** register that is used with USART unit. Its value depends on **F_CPU,** i.e. on microcontroller frequency and the bus frequency.

ATmega32 Control Register – TWCR

This is an I/O register that is used to control the operations on TWI bus. It is also used to control TWI operation i.e. enable/disable it. It initiates following operations on TWI bus:

(a) Send START condition.
(b) Send STOP condition.
(c) Halt the bus while our application programs reads the received data and status registers.
(d) Generates an ACK when MC is operating in receiver mode (as Master Receiver or Slave Receiver).

The Role Of TWINT Bit In TWCR

TWINT bit is set by TWI hardware unit when current job is complete. **SCL** low period is stretched when this is low. Unless SCL line goes to high again, operations on TWI bus are halted. To resume TWI operations, we must clear this flag (by writing "1" to it) through our application. This starts operation of TWI bus once again. Note that once TWI operation has resumed, contents of other TWI registers like **TWDR** and **TWSR** can change. So you must read them before you clear **TWINT** bit. **TWINT** bit is peculiar because it is set to 1 by hardware at the end of current TWI operation. To clear it, i.e. to set it to 0 in 'hardware' we have to write 1 to its bit position in **TWCR**. Readers without background in digital electronics may find this strange, but we will have to accept it as a design decision made by engineers who designed this microcontroller.

TWI Library

As described above, working with TWI unit for ATmega32 requires a programmer to make use of 5 different registers. In addition, you must be aware of several 'conditions' or status of the TWI bus as various operations are carried out on the bus. TWI is a shared bus transport. It's important that each device on a bus obeys the protocols for read / write exactly as described in TWI standard. If you implement this support yourself, it's a considerable effort and would require significant amount of testing to ensure that bus is never left in an inconsistent state. We have developed a simple TWI access library that enables you to access TWI functionality without worrying about the minute details of TWI protocol. In implementing this library, we have also used system header file **util/twi.h** to get access to various flags and bits associated with TWI registers in ATmega32 MC. This header file defines macros for various flags and status values needed for doing TWI operations. Our implementation consists of two files – **twi_driver.h** and **twi_driver.c**. Let us understand the APIs in this library and their implementation details. These are given below. Later on, we will show you how to use these APIs for interacting with **RTC** chip **DS1307**.

Header file – twi_driver.h

```
#ifndef _TWI_DRIVER_H_
```

```
# define _TWI_DRIVER_H_

# include <avr/io.h>
# include <util/twi.h>

extern void twi_init ( void ) ;

extern unsigned char twi_send_start ( void ) ;
extern void twi_send_stop ( void ) ;
extern unsigned char twi_send_slave_address (unsigned char ) ;

extern unsigned char twi_send_byte ( unsigned char ) ;
extern unsigned char twi_receive_byte ( char not_last_byte ) ;

# define SUCCESS        0xFF

# endif       /* !_TWI_DRIVER_H_ */
```

twi_init( ) function is called to initialize TWI unit. **twi_send_start( )** and **twi_send_stop( )** are used to generate and transmit **START** and **STOP** conditions on the TWI bus. **twi_send_slave_address( )** is used to transmit SLA+W (Slave Address + Write bit) or SLA+R (Slave Address + Read bit) on TWI bus. **twi_send_byte( )** sends the byte specified by input parameter. **twi_receive_byte( )** returns one data byte sent by slave to the master on TWI bus.

Implementation file – twi_driver.c

```
# include "twi_driver.h"

/* Address of ATmega32 if it is used as 'Slave Receiver' */
# define OWN_ADDR    0x60

static uint8_t _get_byte ( uint8_t*, char not_last_byte ) ;
```

```
static void twi_wait_int ( void ) ;

void twi_init ( void )
{
    TWAR = OWN_ADDR ;
    TWBR = ( F_CPU / 100000UL – 16 ) / 2 ;
    TWCR = _BV ( TWEN ) ;
    return ;
}

void twi_wait_int ( void )
{
    while ( ! ( TWCR & _BV( TWINT ) ) )
        ;
}


uint8_t twi_send_start ( void )
{
    TWCR = _BV ( TWINT ) | _BV ( TWSTA ) | _BV ( TWEN ) ;

    twi_wait_int( ) ;  // Wait for TWI interrupt flag to be set
    if ( ( TWSR != TW_START ) && ( TWSR != TW_REP_START ) )
        return TWSR ;
    return SUCCESS ;
}

void twi_send_stop ( void )
{
    TWCR = _BV ( TWINT ) | _BV ( TWSTO ) | _BV ( TWEN ) ;
}

uint8_t twi_send_byte ( uint8_t data )
{
    twi_wait_int( ) ;

    TWDR = data ;
    TWCR = _BV ( TWINT ) | _BV ( TWEN ) ;
```

```
    twi_wait_int( ) ;

    if ( TWSR != TW_MT_DATA_ACK )
        return TWSR ;

    return SUCCESS ;
}

/* Send a SLA + W/R to the bus */
uint8_t twi_send_slave_address ( uint8_t adr )
{
    twi_wait_int( ) ;

    TWDR = adr ;
    TWCR = _BV ( TWINT ) | _BV ( TWEN ) ;

    twi_wait_int( ) ;

    if ( TWSR != TW_MT_SLA_ACK && TWSR != TW_MR_SLA_ACK )
        return TWSR ;

    return SUCCESS ;
}

uint8_t  _get_byte ( uint8_t *rx_ptr,char not_last_byte )
{
    twi_wait_int( ) ;

    /* When receiving last byte from slave, it will be sent a NACK.
       This makes the slave stop transmitting. */
    if ( not_last_byte )
        // Clear int flag and enable acknowledge to receive data.
        TWCR = _BV ( TWINT ) | _BV ( TWEN ) | _BV ( TWEA ) ;
    else
        /* Don't enable ACK to tell slave to stop transmitting */
        TWCR = _BV ( TWINT ) | _BV ( TWEN ) ;
```

```
    twi_wait_int( ) ;
    *rx_ptr = TWDR ;        // Received byte from slave

    /* If ACK has been transmitted or this was the last byte & NACK has
       been sent then return SUCCESS */
    if ( ( ( TWSR == TW_MR_DATA_NACK ) && ( not_last_byte == 0 ) ) ||
            ( TWSR == TW_MR_DATA_ACK ) )
        return SUCCESS ;

    return TWSR ;
}

uint8_t twi_receive_byte ( char not_last_byte )
{
    uint8_t  ch ;
    uint8_t  status = _get_byte ( & ch , not_last_byte ) ;
    if ( status == SUCCESS )
        return ch ;
    else
        return 0xff ;
}
```

Let us now understand these functions. At the top, we have defined a macro **OWN_ADDR**. It is used to assign the address to ATmega32 when its MCU mode is Slave. On KSET Embedded Systems board, MCU is the only TWI device capable of being a master. Only other TWI device is RTC chip–which can operate as slave. Unless you connect an external TWI device to this board which can act as master device, this address is not required. However, our library can be used on similar boards where MCU may be used as a slave device.

twi_init( ) – Sets the baud rate on the bus to 100 kbits/sec i.e. normal mode. **TWBR** register is used for this. The formula used here is **((F_CPU / SCL freq.) – 16) / 2**, where **F_CPU** is microcontroller frequency–8,000,000 (8 MHz) and

SCL frequency is 1,00,000 (100 kHz). **TWEN** bit in **TWCR** is set to 1 to enable TWI operation.

twi_wait_int( ) – This function is called after initiating any new operation on TWI bus. It waits until **TWINT** flag in **TWCR** is set. Thereafter, it returns to the caller. We have used polling while working with TWI bus.

twi_send_start( ) – Initiates **START** condition on the bus. It uses bits in **TWCR** to do this. This process involves 'Master election'. If another master device wins the election, then appropriate status value would be set in **TWSR** register by MCU's TWI hardware. In addition, **TWINT** bit in **TWCR** is set by the hardware to indicate end of this phase. This function checks the status of operation using **TWSR** (TWI Status Register). If status register indicates status other than **TW_START** or **TW_REP_START** (Repeated Start), it returns **TWSR** contents to the caller indicating an error. Otherwise, it returns **SUCCESS**. What is 'Repeated Start' condition? It requires some explanation. On TWI bus, once the direction of data transfer from master to slave is decided, by sending SLA+R or SLA+W, it cannot be changed without going through the START → SLA+R/W process once again. This requires master to initiate **START** once again while it is already controls (owns) the TWI bus. If this is second or subsequent **START** condition, status register will indicate that it is repeated start. Irrespective of number of Repeated Start conditions used, only one **STOP** condition must be used to release the bus.

twi_send_slave_address( ) – This function calls **twi_wait_int( )** to wait for earlier operation on TWI bus to finish. It then writes the SLA (Slave Address)–a 7-bit value in top 7 bits of **TWDR** register, with **TW_READ** or **TW_WRITE** bit in least significant position. Once the address has been written to **TWDR**, it clears **TWINT** bit to begin transmitting SLA+R/W on the bus. It then waits for this operation to complete by calling **twi_wait_int( )**. TWI hardware will set the status of operation in **TWSR**. If status is either **TW_MT_SLA_ACK** (TWI Master Transmitter Slave Acknowledgement) or **TW_MR_SLA_ACK** (TWI Master Receiver Slave Acknowledgement), slave has accepted our request. Otherwise, operation is considered to have failed and we must return error to the caller. Please note that success status value in **TWSR** depends on whether ATmega32 is a transmitter or receiver. These status values are defined in system header file **util/twi.h**.

twi_send_stop( ) – This function enables the **TWSTO** bit in **TWCR** to send stop condition on the bus. It then clears **TWINT** in **TWCR** to send STOP condition on the bus. It doesn't wait for the operation to finish.

twi_send_byte( ) – This function calls **twi_wait_int( )** to wait for earlier operation on TWI bus to finish. It then writes the byte to be transmitted in **TWDR**. **TWINT** bit in **TWCR** is cleared to begin transmission. It waits for transmission to complete and an acknowledgement to be received. It does so by calling **twi_wait_int( )**. If the status is **TW_MT_DATA_ACK** (Master Transmitter Data Acknowledgement), it means that byte was received successfully by slave and this function returns **SUCCESS** to the caller.

twi_receive_byte( ) – This function uses a local function **_get_byte( )** to read single data byte sent by a slave device. If **_get_byte( )** returns **SUCCESS**, it returns received character to the caller. Otherwise, it returns **oxff** to indicate an error.

_get_byte( ) – This is the function that reads one byte sent by the slave device, when ATmega32 is operating as master receiver. It uses **twi_wait_int( )** to wait for earlier operation on TWI bus to finish. **not_last_byte** input parameter indicates if this was the last byte expected from slave. If this is the last byte, **TWINT** in **TWCR** cleared. As a result MCU's TWI unit doesn't generate an **ACK**. If this was not the last byte, **TWEA** bit in **TWCR** is set enable generation of **ACK** from the MCU (master). When slave receives this **ACK**, it will send the next byte. In either case, it calls **twi_wait_int( )** once again. Status **TW_MR_DATA_ACK** is treated as success if **not_last_byte** was set. If **not_last_byte** is cleared, status **TW_MR_DATA_NACK** is treated as success. In all other cases, it returns failure. In case of success, received byte is read from **TWDR** register and returned to the caller.

Having understood the building blocks in TWI access library, we will now study how to use this library to read of time/date values from **DS1307** RTC chip.

Purpose Of RTC Chip

In any embedded system, RTC chip is used as a reliable source for keeping track of time. It maintains time even if there is no main power. If main power supply becomes unavailable, it uses a secondary battery, generally CR-2032 (3V, 230mAh) to maintain the time accurately. KSET Embedded Systems Development Board uses this battery and RTC chip DS1307. This RTC chip is designed to consume very little power ensuring long battery life. RTCs are also used in Personal Computers to maintain time.

Basics Of DS1307

KSET ES board uses DS1307 RTC chip is manufactured by Maxim (Dallas Semiconductors). It provides TWI serial interface with 100 kbits/sec data transfer rate. It runs on main power while it is available, and switches to backup power automatically when main power supply is lost. It consumes only 500nA in battery backup mode.

Additional advantage of this RTC chip is extra internal 56 bytes RAM that it has. This RAM can be used for storing any of your program's variables that change frequently and must be maintained persistently. Only other writeable non-volatile memory inside ATmega32 is EEPROM. However, writes to EEPROM are quite slow. In comparison to this, 56 bytes memory inside DS1307 is normal SRAM with battery backup. Such memory is often called as NVRAM (Non-Volatile RAM). On the KSET ES board, DS1307 is connected to ATmega32 microcontroller via SDA and SCL pins. DS1307 maintains two digits for a year - so it can store years between 0 to 99.

DS1307 Initialization And Internal Storage

DS1307 has 64 1-byte registers inside it. Lowest 8 bytes are reserved for storing date and time fields. These special internal registers are called as Timekeeper registers. Their addresses within the chip are 0x00 – 0x07. They can be read and written, allowing us to read the date and time values and change them. Date and time values in these registers are stored in BCD (Binary Coded Decimal) format. BCD format packs one decimal digit each in 4-bits of a byte. This can be best understood with an example, as follows:

Decimal 53 = 0101 0011 BCD

Top 4 bits represent decimal digit 5 and lower 4-bits represent decimal digit 3. This means that after reading the time/date values from DS1307, programmer must convert them to binary representation. Similarly, if we have to write these values to DS1307 registers, they must be converted to BCD format.

DS1307's internal oscillator circuitry must be enabled as a part of our program's initialization sequence. This is achieved by writing a binary **0** at bit number 7 in timekeeper register 0x00. Address of DS1307 on TWI bus is hard-coded. It is 0xD0. We will use this address in our program as slave address to communicate with DS1307 chip. It's obvious by now that we must understand the details of timekeeper registers to start working with it. Next section describes these registers in detail.

Timekeeper Registers

Figure 15.3 shows the timekeeper registers for DS1307. Let's understand them one by one.

Addr.	B7	B6	B5	B4	B3	B2	B1	B0	Function
00H	CH	10's secs.			units secs.				Seconds
01H	0	10's mins.			units mins.				Minutes
02H	0	12 / 24	A/P / 10's	10's	units hours.				Hours
03H	0	0	0	0	0	DAY			Day number.
04H	0	0	10's Date		units Date				Date
05H	0	0	0	10's	units Month				Month
06H	10's year				unit year				Year

Figure 15.3: DS1307 Timekeeper Registers

Address 0x00 – Used to store the number of seconds elapsed. Since largest value of seconds in decimal 59, highest digit in 10's place cannot be more than 0101. As a result, only 7 bits are enough to store seconds in BCD representation. Topmost bit is dedicated for initializing oscillator for DS1307.

Address 0x01 – Used to store the number of minutes elapsed. Since largest value of minutes in decimal 59, highest digit in 10's place cannot be more than 0101. As a result, only 7 bits are enough to store seconds in BCD representation. Topmost bit is always 0.

Address 0x02 – Used to store the number of hours elapsed. DS1307 supports both 12 and 24 hour modes. In both these modes, largest digit in 10's place is Decimal 2 (Binary 0010). To enable 12-hour mode, Bit 6 must be written 1. When operating in 12-hour mode, Bit 5 is used as AM/PM indicator. **1** in this bit means PM and **0** means AM. In 24-hour mode, Bit 5 and Bit 4 are used to store 10's digit in an hour.

Address 0x03 – Used to store the day number in a week. Since largest value of day number is 7, 3 bits are enough to store it in BCD representation. Topmost 5 bits are all zeros.

Address 0x04 – Used to store the date in a month (with leap years handling). Largest date in a month is 31. Only two of the higher 4 bits are enough to represent 10th place decimal digit for a date.

Address 0x05 – Used to store the month number. Largest month number is 12. Only one of the higher 4 bits is enough to represent 10th place digit in a month.

Address 0x06 – Used to store year number from start of a century. Largest year number supported by DS1307 in is 99. As a result, all 8-bits are required to represent 10th and unit's place in a year.

When reading from any of the timekeeper registers, data is always returned in BCD representation.

Read/Write Operation Sequence

The steps for reading and writing date and time values from / to DS1307 chip are as follows:

(a) MC initiates START condition on the bus. Since there is no other master, it wins the election.
(b) MC sends Slave Address (SLA+W) i.e. 0xD0 + W. This tells DS1307 to be ready for data transfer. DS1307 responds with an ACK.
(c) MC sends internal timekeeper register address to DS1307 in the next frame.

What happens now depends on whether you wish to read or write timekeeper registers.

- To read the timekeeper registers, direction of data transfer will have to be changed. We must send a Repeated Start followed by 0xD0 + R (SLA + R) to change the MCU role to Master Receiver. Thereafter, we can read all timekeeper registers one by one.

- To write timekeeper registers, no further action is needed as MCU is already in Master Transmitter role. We can to write the timekeeper registers one by one.

After every read/write from a timekeeper register, DS1307 automatically increments internal address by 1. As a result, we don't have to send timekeeper register address to DS1307 for subsequent read and write operations. This auto-increment is very convenient as most programs read or write timekeeper registers sequentially.

Communicating With RTC Chip

Before DS1307 chip can do timekeeping task, DS1307's internal oscillator circuitry must be enabled. For this, we need to perform operations on TWI bus. We will use the TWI library developed earlier to accomplish this. Create a new project **rtc_twi**. Two files will now be created – **rtc_twi.h** and **rtc_twi.c**. Copy the TWI library files **twi_driver.h** and **twi_driver.c** developed earlier, to this project's directory. The header file and the implementation file source code, is given below:

Header file – rtc_twi.h

```
#ifndef _rtc_twi_h_
#define _rtc_twi_h_

#include <avr/io.h>
#include <stdio.h>
#include <util/delay.h>
#include "twi_driver.h"
#include "lcd_io.h"

typedef struct cTime
{
    uint8_t  sec;
    uint8_t  min;
    uint8_t  hour;
    uint8_t  day;
    uint8_t  date;
    uint8_t  month;
    uint8_t  year;
```

```
} cTime_t;

/* DS1307 Slave Address */
# define DS1307_ADDR    0xD0

static __inline__ uint8_t bcd_to_bin( uint8_t x )
{
    return ( ( ( x & 0xf0 ) >> 4 ) * 10 + ( x & 0x0f ) );
}

static __inline__ uint8_t bin_to_bcd ( uint8_t x )
{
  return ( ( ( x / 10) << 4 ) | ( x % 10 ) );
}

extern void rtc_init ( void );
extern uint8_t rtc_read_time ( cTime_t *tm );
extern void rtc_display_time ( void );

#endif      /* _rtc_twi_h_ */
```

At the top, we have included necessary system headers, TWI driver header and LCD library header files. **struct cTime** is used to represent time and date information. Each field in this structure is 8-bit because none of them exceed 255. **static __inline__** functions are similar to preprocessor macros. We have used them instead of macros, as they are more convenient for passing parameter and allow values to be returned.

bcd_to_bin( ) converts a number from 8-bit BCD to binary representation. It uses bitwise operators to extract top 4-bits i.e. 10's place digit and multiplies it by 10. Lower 4-bits are added to this to give correct binary representation.

bin_to_bcd( ) converts from binary to 8-bit BCD representation. It calculates the 10's place digit by dividing the input argument by 10. Being an integer division fraction part is discarded automatically. Result is shifted 4 places to the left to give us top 4-bits in BCD representation. Lower 4-bits i.e. unit's place bits are obtained by doing module 10 arithmetic.

These conversion functions will be used extensively when reading from and writing to DS1307. The program shown below displays a digital clock on LCD screen and updates it every second.

Implementation – rtc_twi.c

```
#include "rtc_twi.h"

static uint8_t rtc_enable_osc ( void ) ;

uint8_t rtc_enable_osc ( void )
{
   uint8_t     rc ;
   uint8_t     sec = 0;

   rc = twi_send_start ( ) ;
   if ( rc == SUCCESS )
      rc = twi_send_slave_address ( DS1307_ADDR + TW_WRITE ) ;
   if ( rc == SUCCESS )
      rc = twi_send_byte ( 0 ) ;

   if ( rc == SUCCESS )
      rc = twi_send_start ( ) ;
   if ( rc == SUCCESS )
      rc = twi_send_slave_address ( DS1307_ADDR + TW_READ ) ;
   if ( rc == SUCCESS )
      sec = twi_receive_byte( 0 ) & 0x7F ;

   if ( rc == SUCCESS )
      rc = twi_send_start ( ) ;
```

```
    if ( rc == SUCCESS )
      rc = twi_send_slave_address ( DS1307_ADDR + TW_WRITE );
    if ( rc == SUCCESS )
    {
      rc = twi_send_byte ( 0 );
      if ( rc == SUCCESS )
        rc = twi_send_byte ( sec );
      twi_send_stop ( );
    }
    return rc ;
}

uint8_t rtc_read_time ( cTime_t *tm )
{
    uint8_t    rc;

    rc = twi_send_start ( );
    if ( rc == SUCCESS )
      rc = twi_send_slave_address ( DS1307_ADDR + TW_WRITE );
    if ( rc == SUCCESS )
      rc = twi_send_byte ( 0x00 );

    if ( rc == SUCCESS )
      rc = twi_send_start ( );
    if ( rc == SUCCESS )
      rc = twi_send_slave_address( DS1307_ADDR + TW_READ );

    if ( rc == SUCCESS )
    {
      tm->sec = bcd_to_bin ( twi_receive_byte ( 1 ) );
      tm->min = bcd_to_bin ( twi_receive_byte ( 1 ) &0x7f );
      tm->hour = bcd_to_bin ( twi_receive_byte ( 1 ) &0x3f );
      tm->day = bcd_to_bin ( twi_receive_byte ( 1 ) );
      tm->date = bcd_to_bin ( twi_receive_byte ( 1 ) &0x3f );
      tm->month = bcd_to_bin ( twi_receive_byte ( 1 ) & 0x1f );
      tm->year = bcd_to_bin( twi_receive_byte ( 0 ) & 0xFF );

      twi_send_stop ( );
```

```
  }
  return 1 ;
}

void WriteTimeToLCD ( cTime_t *time )
{
  uint8_t          TimeBuffer [ 16 ] ;
  uint8_t          DateBuffer [ 16 ] ;
  static char      *days[ ] = { "Mon", "Tue", "Wed", "Thu", "Fri", "Sat", "Sun" }
;

  sprintf ( TimeBuffer, "%3s %02d:%02d:%02d\n",
          time->day <= 7 ? days [ time->day -1 ] : "",
          time->hour, time->min, time->sec ) ;
  sprintf ( DateBuffer, "    %02d-%02d-%02d", time->date,
          time->month, time->year ) ;

  lcd_puts ( TimeBuffer ) ;
  lcd_puts ( DateBuffer ) ;
}

void rtc_display_time ( void )
{
  cTime_t    TimeStamp ;

  for ( ;; )
  {
    rtc_read_time ( &TimeStamp ) ;
    lcd_gotoxy ( 0, 0 ) ;
    WriteTimeToLCD ( &TimeStamp ) ;
    _delay_ms( 50 ) ;
  }
}

void rtc_init ( void )
{
  twi_init ( ) ;
  rtc_enable_osc ( ) ;
```

```
}

int main ( void )
{
    lcd_init ( ) ;
    rtc_init ( ) ;
    rtc_display_time ( ) ;
    return 0 ;
}
```

Let's understand this implementation one function at a time:

main( ) – It initializes the LCD library. Then it initializes TWI library by calling **rtc_init**. Finally, it calls **rtc_display_time** to read the time and display it on LCD screen.

rtc_enable_osc( ) – This function writes **0** to Bit7 in timekeeper register **0x00**. To do this, it first transmits **START** condition on TWI bus and sends **SLA+W** to let DS1307 know that ATmega32 will be Master Transmitter. After this, it sends value **0x00** on the bus. This is to tell RTC chip what internal timekeeper register address to use. We can't just write single bit in a register without losing contents of remaining bits. To avoid that, we must use **Read-Modify-Write** technique. First we read existing value of timekeeper register 0x00. Bit7 is zeroed off by doing a bitwise **AND** operation with **0x7F**. Now this value must be written back. The MC mode is changed to Master Transmitter by issuing a Repeated **START** followed by **SLA+W**. First, timekeeper register address **0x00** is sent to the RTC chip. Followed by this, the modified value is sent. This will enable internal oscillator circuit if it's not already enabled. To end the initialization process, we transmit **STOP** condition on TWI bus and return to the caller.

rtc_display_time( ) – This function has an infinite **for** loop. Inside the loop, **rtc_read_time** is used to read the time from

RTC chip. This time is then displayed on the LCD screen by calling **WriteTimeToLCD**. Before starting the next iteration of the loop, a delay by 50 milliseconds is used.

rtc_read_time( ) – This function uses TWI library to initiate START condition followed by **SLA+W**. Internal timekeeper register address **0** is then sent to RTC using **twi_send_byte**. To read from RTC, we must change MC mode to Master Receiver by issuing Repeated **START** followed by **SLA+R**. Now we are ready to read time and date fields from the RTC. First three reads give us seconds, hours and minutes. Higher order bits from these values are masked off to ensure than correct 10's place digits are read. All these values are converted to binary representation (**bcd_to_bin**) before storing then in **cTime_t** structure's fields. Four more reads (**twi_receive_byte)** are used to get day of the week, date, month and year from RTC. For final read, **not_last_byte** argument of **twi_receive_byte** is passed as zero to generate **NACK** (Negative Acknowledgement) for RTC. This informs RTC that no further data will be read by the master. Finally MCU releases the TWI bus is by transmitting **STOP** condition.

WriteTimeToLCD( ) – This function writes formatted string for **hh:mm:ss** and **dd-mm-yy** to LCD screen. It uses **sprintf** to generate the strings for display on LCD screen. The day of the week is converted to a three letter string – Mon, Tue, Wed etc. This makes it easier for users to understand the time displayed on LCD screen.

Our next program shows how to build an interactive application to enter values for time and date fields and write those values to DS1307 chip.

Program Organization

Before we can write time/date to DS1307 chip, we need to copy some of the programs and libraries developed earlier to current project directory.

Copy **buttons.c** & **buttons.h**. They are required to build interactive time entry interface using two of the keys on KSET ES board as arrow keys.

Copy **twi_driver.c** & **twi_driver.h**. They are required for using TWI functionality in ATmega32.

Copy **rtc_twi.c** & **rtc_twi.h** from previous section. They contain interfaces to initialize RTC chip and read time from it. From **rtc_twi.c**, delete **main( )** function. Our current project already has it's own **main( )** function.

Now, create a new AVR project **rtc_write**. We will let the user to enter new values for all date and time fields using keys on KSET ES board.

Header file – rtc_write.h

```
#ifndef _rtc_write_h_
#define _rtc_write_h_

#include "rtc_twi.h"
#include <avr/interrupt.h>
#include <avr/pgmspace.h>
#include "buttons.h"

#define up_state        key3_state
#define down_state      key2_state
#define ok_state        key4_state
```

```
#define cancel_state        key5_state

#endif        /* _rtc_write_h_ */
```

We have included necessary system header files. RTC Read API header file is required to use for **cTime_t** structure declared there and prototypes of other useful functions. **buttons.h** declares extern variables for maintaining the state of each button. Since we have assigned specific role to each button, we have created our on macros–**up_state**, **down_state**, **ok_state** and **cancel_state** to represent the state of these keys based on the role they are used for. KEY3 is UP arrow, KEY2 is DOWN arrow, and keys 4 and 5 are OK and CANCEL keys respectively. **avr/pgmspace.h** has been included because we will use the macro **PGM_P** in our implementation.

Implementation – rtc_write.c

```
#include "rtc_write.h"

static uint8_t lcd_prompt ( uint8_t max, uint8_t min,
              PGM_P prompt, uint8_t cur_val ) ;
static void    start_timer ( void ) ;

uint8_t rtc_write_time ( cTime_t *time )
{
  uint8_t    rc ;

  rc = twi_send_start ( ) ;
  if ( rc == SUCCESS )
    rc = twi_send_slave_address ( DS1307_ADDR + TW_WRITE ) ;

  if ( rc == SUCCESS )
    rc = twi_send_byte ( 0x00 ) ;
```

```
    if ( rc == SUCCESS )
    {
        twi_send_byte ( time->sec ) ;
        twi_send_byte ( time->min ) ;
        twi_send_byte ( time->hour ) ;
        twi_send_byte ( time->day ) ;
        twi_send_byte ( time->date ) ;
        twi_send_byte ( time->month ) ;
        twi_send_byte ( time->year ) ;

        twi_send_stop ( ) ;
    }
    return rc ;
}

uint8_t  lcd_prompt ( uint8_t max , uint8_t min , PGM_P prompt , uint8_t cur )
{
    uint8_t val = cur ;

    lcd_clrscr ( ) ;
    while ( 1 ) {
        if (up_state == RELEASED) {
            RESET_KEY_STATE ( up_state ) ;
            if ( val < max )
                val++ ;
            else
                val = min ;
        }
        if (down_state == RELEASED ) {
            RESET_KEY_STATE ( down_state ) ;
            if ( val > min )
                val-- ;
            else
                val = max;
        }
        lcd_gotoxy ( 0 , 0) ;
        lcd_put_i ( val , 0, 2 ) ;
```

```
        lcd_putc ( '\n' ) ;
        lcd_puts_p ( prompt ) ;
        if ( ok_state == RELEASED ) {
            RESET_KEY_STATE( ok_state ) ;
            break ;
        }
        _delay_ms ( 200 ) ;
    }
    val = bin_to_bcd ( val ) ;
    return val ;
}

int main ( void )
{
    cTime_t    tm ;

    buttons_init ( ) ;
    start_timer ( ) ;
    sei ( ) ;
    rtc_init ( ) ;

    rtc_read_time ( &tm ) ;

    tm.sec     = lcd_prompt ( 59, 0, PSTR ("Enter Sec") , tm.sec ) ;
    tm.min     = lcd_prompt ( 59, 0, PSTR ("Enter Min") , tm.min ) ;
    tm.hour    = lcd_prompt ( 23, 0, PSTR ("Enter Hour") , tm.hour ) ;
    tm.day     = lcd_prompt ( 7, 1, PSTR ("Enter Day") , tm.day ) ;
    tm.date    = lcd_prompt ( 31, 1, PSTR ("Enter Date") , tm.date ) ;
    tm.month   = lcd_prompt ( 12, 1, PSTR ("Enter Month") , tm.month ) ;
    tm.year    = lcd_prompt ( 20, 0, PSTR ("Enter Year") , tm.year ) ;

    rtc_write_time ( &tm ) ;

    rtc_display_time( ) ;

    return 0;
}
```

```
void start_timer()
{
    TCNT0 = 0x00 ;
    TCCR0 = 0x05 ;
    TIMSK = 0x01 ;
}

SIGNAL(SIG_OVERFLOW0)
{
   buttons_check();
}
```

Let's understand this one function at a time:

lcd_prompt( ) – This function is used to present an interactive interface for entering numbers. The number to be accepted as input must be in **min** to **max** range. For example – if we seek month number from user, **min** & **max** would be 1 and 12 respectively. **cur** is the current value of input from where the changes should begin. **prompt** is string that appears on second line of LCD screen. Arrows keys **UP** and **DOWN** are used to cycle between **min** and **max**. When **UP** key is pressed, value of **cur** is incremented by 1. It is decremented by 1 every time **DOWN** key is pressed. Wrap-around of values is handled correctly to implement circular data entry interface. When user wishes to accept current value being displayed, he presses **OK** key. This value is then returned to the caller after converting it to BCD representation.

main( ) – It initializes buttons library by calling **buttons_init**. Then it calls **start_timer** to start polling of buttons state. These familiar initialization functions are borrowed from programs we have seen in earlier chapters. It uses **TIMER0** overflow interrupt to check the state of keys at regular intervals. ISR for **SIG_OVERFLOW0** has been used for this purpose. **rtc_init** is used to initialize TWI library and enable DS1307's oscillator. Finally, **rtc_read_time** is used to read current time from DS1307 chip. These time fields will be used as reference values when user is prompted to enter new values for each of the date and time fields. **lcd_prompt** is called with correct **max** & **min** range for seconds, minutes, hours, date, month, and year. Once the user has entered new values for these fields, **rtc_write** is called to write them back to DS1307 RTC chip. Thereafter we simply display current time on LCD screen by calling **rtc_display_time** which repeatedly reads the date/time fields from DS1307 and displays it.

rtc_write( ) – This function sends **START** condition on TWI bus followed by **SLA+W** to let DS1307 know that ATmega32 will be in Master Transmitter role. It first sends value **0x00** to RTC. This is to tell RTC the internal timekeeper address to use. Followed by this, the modified values of time/date fields are written back. **twi_send_byte** is called repeatedly to send all seven date-time fields one by one to DS1307 chip. Finally **STOP** condition is sent on the TWI bus to release it.

This completes our interaction with DS1307 chip. We have shown you how to read and write time using TWI library routines. We hope that they will inspire you to create powerful embedded system projects and applications.

Exercise

[A] Answer the following:

(a) Write a program to do the following:

- Create an interactive interface to allow user to set an alarm using dd/mm/yy hh:mm format.

- Program should display a message on LCD screen when time specified by alarm is reached.

(b) Modify the program written earlier to store the alarm times even if active power to KSET ES board is turned off (Hint: Use the additional 56 bytes of NVRAM inside DS1307 to store alarm time).

16 Build Process Internals

Until now, we have used the development environment for AVR ATmega32 with KSET ES board, quite mechanically. We realize that though your embedded system career has begun with KSET ES board, in future you would come across many more boards and environments. To be able to successfully work with them you need to understand each stage in the development process in detail. In this chapter we will take a detailed look at the different stages of the development process.

Stages In Development Process

The build process involves following stages:

(a) Preprocessing, compilation & assembly
(b) Linking
(c) Conversion to Intel Hex Format
(d) Transfer of flash ihex file to flash memory
(e) Transfer of EEPROM ihex file to EEPROM

Next few sections will discuss these stages in detail. Understanding these concepts is important when you are working with a different microcontroller. If you understand this development environment, you can create a similar development environment for another MC.

Preprocessing, Compilation And Assembly

Each .c/.cpp file is preprocessed, compiled and then assembled. In our build environment, there is a single command visible for these three steps. This command is given below:

```
avr-gcc -c -g –Os  -funsigned-char -funsigned-bitfields -fpack-struct
        -fshort-enums -Wall -Wstrict-prototypes
        -Wa,-ahlms=obj/hello.lst -mmcu=atmega32
        -DAVRGCC_VERSION=345 -DF_CPU=8000000
        -IC:/myavrprograms/topdir/avr/inc -I.
        -MD -MP -MF .dep/hello.o.d hello.c -o obj/hello.o
```

In this case the file **hello.c** is being preprocessed, compiled and assembled. All compiler options begin with a - (hyphen) character. Their meanings are as follows:

- **-c -g -Os** — Compile the file, generate information suitable for use by debugger and optimize the generated code to conserve space.
- **-funsigned-char -funsigned-bitfields -fpack-struct** — Treat all **char** types in a C program as unsigned unlike the default **signed** interpretation. If bit-fields are used inside your structures, they are also treated as unsigned data type. Finally structures declared in the program should not be padded for alignment purposes—this ensures that no padding bytes are added in middle or end of structure.
- **-Wa,-ahlms=obj/hello.lst -mmcu=atmega32** — Pass options to the assembler and product assembly language listing in **obj/hello.lst**. The symbolic information is also included in the assembly listing. The MCU type is ATmega32. For other MC, you will have to make suitable changes.
- **-fshort-enums -Wall -Wstrict-prototypes** — Enum types should be assigned just enough space for number of values in it. Any suspicious syntax should emit warnings, and prototypes of all functions used in a program must be declared.

- **-DAVRGCC_VERSION=345 DF_CPU=8000000** — First constant defines the version of AVR GCC compiler used in the build process and second (**F_CPU**) defines the frequency of operation of ATmega32 MC. This constant is 8 MHz. If your MC uses a different frequency, make sure that you change this constant correctly.

- **-IC:/myavrprograms/topdir/avr/inc -I.** — Include files are searched in current directory and **C:/myavrprograms/topdir/avr/inc**.

- **-MD -MP -MF .dep/hello.o.d hello.c -o obj/hello.o** — Generate dependency list for **hello.c**. The object file generated after compilation is created inside folder **obj**. Name of the object file is **hello.o**.

Linking

At linking stage, one or more object files are combined with libraries to generate an executable file. The command to do this is given below:

```
avr-gcc  obj/hello.o
 -Wl,-Map=obj/hello.map -Wl,--cref
 -mmcu=atmega32  -o obj/hello.elf
```

Here **obj/hello.o** is the object file that is input to the linker. Libraries, if any, will also appear immediately after this option. All linker flags begin with a - (hyphen) character. Their meanings are as follows:

- **-Wl,-Map=obj/hello.map -Wl,--cref** — Writes the linker map which includes the addresses of all the sections in the executable file **obj/hello.elf**, symbols in it along-with addresses and other useful information. This file helps you understand the memory layout of your program. Cross reference table containing a list of object files and symbols imported from them is also appended to the end of this map file.

- **-mmcu=atmega32 -o obj/hello.elf** — MCU is ATmega32 and the output executable file is **obj/hello.elf**.

In addition to object file for our program, some libraries and an object files are automatically linked with every program. These are:

- **libc.a** — Standard C library functions.
- **libgcc.a** — Frequently used extensions used by an ES developer.
- **crtm16.o** — Run-time code that contains an empty IVT (Interrupt Vector Table) and necessary code to be called before **main( )** function and after return from **main( )**.

Understanding Static Libraries

There are two types of libraries used when working with C programs:

(a) Statically linked libraries
(b) Dynamically linked libraries (DLL)

Today, most PC based programs use DLLs. Their biggest advantage is that the library gets loaded in system only once even if more than one program is using it. The implementation/code for functions inside these libraries that our programs uses, never becomes part our executable file. This avoids repetition of same code in different executable files.

However, in most embedded systems (except large ones) DLLs are not supported. Most MC based developments systems cannot support them due to the complex linking and loading procedures involved add to the overhead in these systems.

AVR GCC tool-chain does support static libraries. Most programmers think that static libraries are a bad idea because they increase the size of their executable file. Their contention is that even if they use a single function present in these libraries, the entire library becomes part of the executable file. That would be unacceptable in ES environment as flash space in which an ES resides is limited. Reality is quite different. Let us understand this with an example.

libc.a that we saw earlier are examples of static libraries. It is nothing but an archive (similar to a zip file) that contains object files like **memccpy.o**, **memcpy.o**, **memcmp.o**, **fclose.o**, **fprintf.o**, **fread.o**, etc. Suppose our program uses only two functions— **memcpy( )** and **fclose( )** from C-library. When linking is done, linker will only extract two files **memcmp.o** and **fclose.o** from the archive **libc.a**. These two extracted object files become part of our executable—not entire static library as most people would imagine. To take full advantage of this, designers of Standard Library for AVR GCC environment have created separate .c files for every API like **memcpy( ), fclose( )**, etc. This ensures that a large number of small object files are present inside the static library. Only those object files which we really need become part of **hello.exe**.

Moral? Go ahead, use static libraries without any fear of bloating the size of the executable file—GNU linker is smarter than most people think!

Conversion To Intel Hex Format

The executable file that is created after linking uses a format called ELF (Executable Linking Format). This format divides an executable file in different sections—code section, data section, debug section, strings section, etc. However, ATmega32 flash memory when written must contain only code and data sections. Thus the ELF file format has to be converted into a format that contains only code and data sections. This format is known as Intel Hex (ihex) format. This format was invented by Intel Corporation for transferring programs to flash memory. It is an ASCII, record-oriented format. It contains absolute addresses where code and data is to be written into flash memory. It has become a de-facto standard over the last 20-30 years. Hence we have to convert **obj/hello.elf** from **ELF** to **ihex** format. This is achieved using following command:

```
avr-objcopy -O ihex -R .eeprom obj/hello.elf hello.hex
```

Here the Object copy utility uses **obj/hello.elf** as input and generates an output file **hello.hex**. The format of this file is **ihex**. By default the **.hex** file also contains EEPROM data in the section named **.eeprom**. The **-R** option is used to remove that section. Sections **.text** (code), **.data** (Initialized data), **.bss** (un-initialized data) get written to **hello.hex**.

EEPROM Data File

The data file for EEPROM **(hello.eep)** contains the initial values of EEPROM variables. The format of this file is also **ihex**. The command to extract **.eeprom** section from **obj/hello.elf** is as follows:

```
avr-objcopy -j .eeprom - -set-section-flags=.eeprom="alloc,load"
            - -change-section-lma .eeprom=0 -O ihex obj/hello.elf hello.eep
```

The options and their meanings are given below:

- **-j .eeprom** — Specifies that only **.eeprom** section must be copied from **obj/hello.elf**
- **--set-section-flags=.eeprom="alloc,load"** — Specifies that the section must be loaded during program execution.
- **--change-section-lma .eeprom=0** — Specifies that data addresses in EEPROM must begin with 0. This is required because EEPROM and RAM are independent read/write memories both of which begin from 0.
- **-O ihex obj/hello.elf hello.eep** — Specifies that Intel-hex format should be used and output should be sent to file **hello.eep**.

EEPROM is internal to AVR microcontroller and has to be written to separately. **avrdude** writes flash and EEPROM one after another. Next two sections describe how this is done.

Writing To Flash And EEPROM

When you type **make program** in command window, the **avrdude** utility is invoked with following options:

```
avrdude -p atmega32  -P lpt1  -c pony-stk200
        -U flash:w:hello.hex  -U eeprom:w:hello.eep
```

Let us understand each of the options used here one by one:

- **-p atmega32** — Specifies that the "Part Number" being used is ATmega32 MC. **avrdude** is an application that works with hundreds of different MCs from variety of manufacturers. Part number uniquely identifies the microcontroller that we are using.

- **-P lpt1** — Specifies that PC's parallel port-1 should be used for transferring flash and EEPROM contents.

- **-c pony-stk200** — Specifies that the type of programming dongle that is attached to PC's parallel port is compatible to one that comes with Atmel Corporation's STK200 board.

- **-U flash:w:hello.hex** — Performs write operation on "flash" memory with input from **hello.hex**.

- **-U flash:w:hello.hex** — Performs write operation on "EEPROM" memory with input from **hello.eep**.

Reading From Flash And EEPROM

avrdude is an extremely powerful utility. It also allows you read the current contents of flash and EEPROM memories. When you type **make read**, **avrdude** is invoked with following options:

```
avrdude -p atmega32 -P lpt1 -c pony-stk200 -U flash:r:hello_flash.bin:r
        -U eeprom:r:hello_eep.bin:r
```

First three options are same as earlier. The **-U** options specifies that flash and EEPROM must be read from and result of the operation must be made available in RAW binary format in **hello_flash.bin** and **hello_eep.bin** respectively.

Exercise

[A] Pick up the correct alternative for each of the following questions:

[1] Which of the following statement is correct about the compiler option?

```
-Wa,-ahlms=obj/hello.lst -mmcu=atmega32
```

(i) It passes options to the assembler and product assembly language listing in obj/hello.lst.
(ii) It compiles the file, generates information suitable for use by debugger and optimizes the generated code to conserve space.

(a) Only (i) is correct.
(b) Only (ii) is correct.
(c) Both (i) and (ii) are correct.
(d) Both (i) and (ii) are incorrect.

[2] Which of the following statement is correct about the compiler option

-fshort-enums -Wall -Wstrict-prototypes

(i) It indicates that enum types should be assigned just enough space for number of values in it.
(ii) It passes options to the assembler and product assembly language listing in Wstrict-prototypes.

(a) Only (i) is correct.
(b) Only (ii) is correct.
(c) Both (i) and (ii) are correct.
(d) Both (i) and (ii) are incorrect.

[3] Which of the following statement is correct about the compiler option

-DAVRGCC_VERSION=345 DF_CPU=8000000?

(i) It defines the version of AVR GCC compiler used in the build process.
(ii) It defines the frequency of operation of ATmega32 MC.

(a) Only (i) is correct.
(b) Only (ii) is correct.
(c) Both (i) and (ii) are correct.
(d) Both (i) and (ii) are incorrect.

[4] Which of the following is the object file that is input to the linker in the command given below?

```
avr-gcc obj/hello.o -Wl,-Map=obj/hello.map -Wl,--cref
        -mmcu=atmega32 -o obj/hello.elf
```

(i) obj/hello.o
(ii) obj/hello.elf

(a) Only (i)
(b) Only (ii)
(c) Both (i) and (ii)
(d) Neither (i) nor (ii)

[5] Which of the following statement is correct about the compiler option

-Wl,-Map=obj/hello.map -Wl,--cref?

(i) It writes the linker map which includes the addresses of all the sections in the executable file obj/hello.elf, symbols in it along-with addresses and other useful information.

(ii) It appends the cross reference table containing a list of object files and symbols imported from them at the end of the map file.

(a) Only (i) is correct.
(b) Only (ii) is correct.
(c) Both (i) and (ii) are correct.
(d) Both (i) and (ii) are incorrect.

[6] Which of the following compiler option indicates that the MCU is ATmega32 and the output executable file is obj/hello.elf?

(i) -mmcu=atmega32 -o obj/hello.elf
(ii) -Wl,-Map=obj/hello.map -Wl,--cref –mcu

(a) Only (i)
Only (ii)
Both (i) and (ii)
Both (i) and (ii)

[7] Which of the following statements are correct?

(i) When DLLs are used the library gets loaded in system only once even if more than one program is using it.

(ii) Static libraries decrease the size of their executable file.

(a) Only (i) is correct.
(b) Only (ii) is correct.
(c) Both (i) and (ii) are correct.
(d) Both (i) and (ii) are incorrect.

[8] Which of the following statements are correct?

(i) libc.a is an archive file that contains object files like memccpy.o, memcpy.o, memcmp.o, fclose.o, fprintf.o, fread.o, etc.

(ii) The executable file that is created after linking uses a format called Executable Linking Format.

(a) Only (i) is correct.
(b) Only (ii) is correct.
(c) Both (i) and (ii) are correct.
(d) Both (i) and (ii) are incorrect.

[9] In which of the following sections the ELF divides an executable file?

(i) Code section
(ii) Data section
(iii) Debug section
(iv) Strings section

(a) Only (i) and (ii)
(b) Only (i), (ii) and (iii)
(c) Only (i), (ii) and (iv)
(d) (i), (ii), (iii) and (iv)

[10] Which of the following statements are correct?

(i) avrdude allows to read the current contents of flash and EEPROM memories.

(ii) By default the .hex file contains EEPROM data in the section named .eeprom.

(a) Only (i) is correct.
Only (ii) is correct.
Both (i) and (ii) are correct.
Both (i) and (ii) are incorrect.

17 Working With Make Files

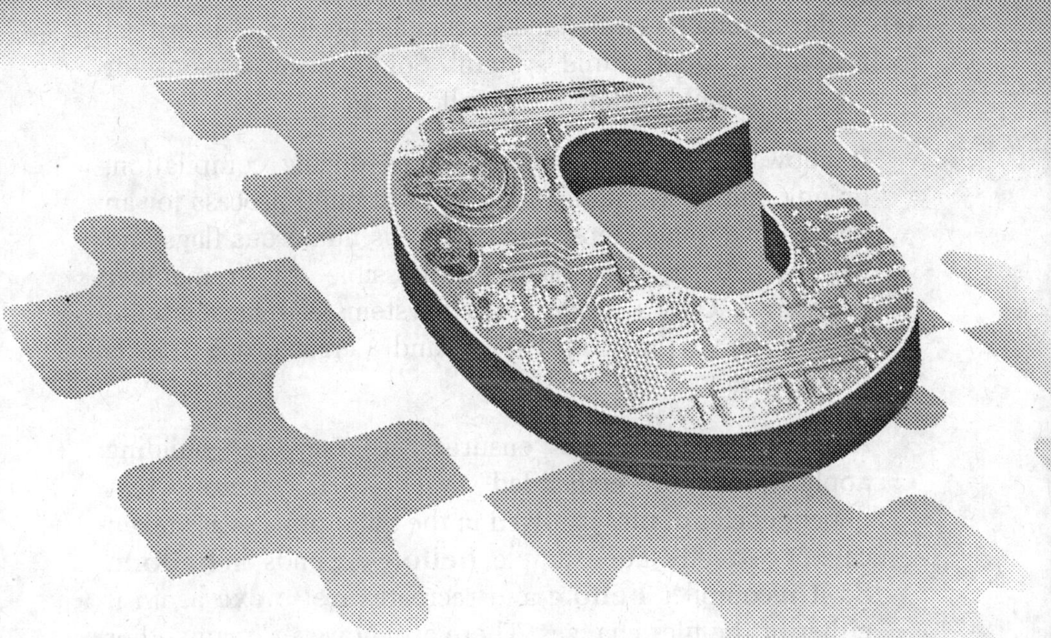

From the stage of compiling the source code for an ES to transferring it to the flash memory involves a series of steps. One has a choice of doing these steps manually over and over again for different ES programs or automating the entire process. Naturally, the second option is more sensible. This chapter focuses on creating a build system for automating the repetitive tasks involved in creating an ES.

Why A Build System?

While developing an embedded system application, it is critical to have a very good 'build system'. Some of the reasons for having a good build system are as follows:

- It allows automating complex steps during compilation, linking and post-linking steps. Typical build process for an ES has five to six steps. Each step has numerous flags and options. It is practically impossible to remember everything. Only solution in such systems is to have a build system do the repetitive and error-prone tasks mechanically.

- A build system also ensures accuracy in building applications for embedded systems. It ensures that dependencies of files involved in the build process are taken care of correctly. For example, **hello.c** depends on **hello.h**. So it recompiles **hello.c** and recreates **hello.exe** again if either of the files changes. There are, however, many other dependencies that are not so obvious. For example, **hello.h** in turn may include many other header files. As a result, dependency analysis has to be done recursively. A good build system does this for us without we being required to waste our energy for it.

- Small mistakes during the build process have big consequences. A good build system minimizes this risk, thereby ensuring success.
- For larger embedded systems projects with hundreds of files that may be part of same application, a smart build process is necessary. Only those files that have changed should be built again for subsequent builds.

We have chosen **makefiles** as a build system because they have been used for more than 30 years now on various platforms–from small to large. They are time-tested and proven. Large operating systems like Linux, FreeBSD and Solaris use makefiles to build thousands of files in a single project. **GNU make** is the tool have we have used in this book. To access it, just type **make** at **cygwin** command prompt. It reads the build instructions from a file called **makefile** which must be present in the same directory where you execute **make**.

What Are makefiles?

A file named **makefile** is created in a directory where you want to start the build process. It contains simple set of rules to build programs by doing compilation, assembly and linking. These rules can be changed and tuned if required. It is quite easy to understand the syntax of a **makefile**. A makefile has simple to understand instructions. These instructions can be quite powerful, if required. We will see examples of these instructions later in this chapter. A **makefile** can include other **makefile**s from other directories. This is similar to a header file being included in another header file. So let's now get started and create our very first makefile.

Your First makefile

Let us create a simple makefile based project. First create a directory **hello** and create two files in it 'hello.c' and 'makefile'.

Here is the file 'hello.c' :

```
#include <stdio.h>
int main ( int argc , char *argv [ ] )
{
    fprintf ( stdout, "Hello World\n" ) ;
    return 0 ;
}
```

And here is the makefile...

```
TARGET = hello
OBJS = $(TARGET).o

$(TARGET) : $(OBJS)
    $(CC) $^ -o $@

%.o : %.c
    $(CC) -c $< -o $@

clean :
    $(RM) $(OBJS) $(TARGET).exe
```

A makefile contains one or more variables. **TARGET** and **OBJS** are two such variables. Each variable is a string variable. On the right-hand side of a variable there is an expression that can be assigned to it. The value stored in a variable can be accessed by preceding the variable with a '$'.

In our makefile the **TARGET** variable is assigned the name of the program to build. i.e. **hello**. The **OBJS** variable is assigned the list of object files (separated by spaces) on which the target depends. OBJS is assigned the value **$(TARGET).o**. This results in 'hello.o' getting assigned to **OBJS**. This may be confusing because in C language to use the value stored in a variable, we just use the variable by its name. However, in makefiles we must use the $ notation to refer to values of variables.

Fourth line is a **rule** in a makefile. A rule uses following syntax:

```
Target : Dependencies
  Commands...
```

On left of the : we specify the name of the target. On its right is the list of other targets that it depends on. So in our case, **hello** depends on **hello.o**. Once **hello.o** is available, command **$(CC) $^ -o $@** is used to create the target **hello** of this rule. This command requires some explanation.

- **CC** – Is a pre-defined variable defined in a master makefile. This master makefile is automatically included in our file by the make program. It is assigned to a string **CC**.

- **$^** - Is a special variable. It will be automatically replaced with the names of all the dependencies specified on right of : sign, i.e. **hello.o**.

- **$@** - Is also a special variable. It will be replaced with the name of the target file i.e. **hello**.

So after expanding the values of these variables, the command is:

```
cc hello.o –o hello
```

Now we must specify the rule for creating **hello.o**. Rather than specifying the rule to build each **.o** file, makefile allows us to create a generalized rule:

```
%.o : %.c
    $(CC) -c $< -o $@
```

% character will be replaced by name of the **.c** file. After substitution, the rule appears as:

```
hello.o : hello.c
    $(CC) -c $< -o $@
```

The command for creating **hello.o** uses another special variable **$<**. This variable expands to the name of first dependency of the target i.e. **hello.c** in this case. Final command is:

```
cc -c hello.c -o hello.o
```

Note that **$@** is expanded to the name of *this* target–**hello.o**.

When the user types **make** in this directory, it scans **makefile** to understand the target dependencies and rules. First target in the makefile **hello** is created. For that **hello.o** on which it depends is created first and then it is linked to create **hello.exe**. We can watch this happen by typing make at the command prompt as shown below:

```
$ make
```

```
cc –c hello.c –o hello.o
cc hello.o –o hello
$ ./hello.exe
Hello World
$
```

Having covered the basics, let us now explore some of the advanced features of working with makefiles. Please note that **makefiles** can be used to build any programs–not just embedded systems programs. In the above example we saw how they can be used to create a PC-based application. We have used similar techniques to create embedded systems applications for KSET Embedded System Development Board.

More About Variables In A makefile

Variable is name defined in makefile. Each variable holds a string. Since other datatypes like arrays etc. are not supported, space-separated strings are used to represent a collection or list of items. Each variable is expanded when **makefile** is read by **make.exe**. These variables are used to store:

(a) List of filenames, for example **OBJS** = hello.o world.o
(b) Options to compiler, for example **CFLAGS** = -g -Os
(c) Program to use, for example **CC** = gcc

To obtain the value of any variable there are two possible ways:

(a) $(VAR)
(b) ${VAR}

We will use the first syntax as it is more universally accepted.

Two Types Of Variables

There are two types of variables supported by GNU make program. These are:

(a) Recursively expanded variables – created by using "=" for assignment.
(b) Simply expanded – created by using ":=" for assignment.

As the name suggests, the recursively expanded variables are expanded recursively and are prone to infinitely loop in doing so as shown in following example:

```
CFLAGS = -g -Wall
CFLAGS = $(CFLAGS) –Os
```

Second assignment causes the infinite loop as CFLAGS value is substituted endlessly.

Simply expanded variables are expanded only once as shown below:

```
CFLAGS := -g -Wall
CFLAGS := $(CFLAGS) –Os
```

As expected, CFLAGS will have a value of –g –Wall –Os after second assignment statement.

Advanced Use Of Variables

Variables in a makefile can be used in much more powerful manner than we have explored so far. Variable substitution can be used as follows:

```
SOURCES = hello.c
OBJS = $(SOURCES:.c=.o)
```

This will replace extension .c with .o for all source files and **hello.o** will be assigned to variable **OBJS**.

We can also append a value to a variable as follows:

```
CFLAGS = -g -Wall
CFLAGS += -Os
```

All the variables need not be 'makefile variables'. **make** program also uses 'enviromment variables'. What are environment variables? All program in your system run in the environment created by Windows operating system. Special variables are passed to every program executed under Windows. These are the environment variables. **make** also uses these variables in addition to those created inside the **makefile**. If environment variable is also present in the makefile by same name, its value from the environment will be used instead of the value specified inside the makefile. This allows variables inside makefile to be changed without editing the makefile. To find what environment variables are passed to **make** program, just type **set** in cygwin shell and hit **ENTER** key. A complete list of environment variables along with their values would be displayed on the screen.

More About Rules In makefiles

Every makefile has one or more rules. Name of target in each rule can be passed as argument to **make** program. It will force the **make** program to build that rule instead of 1st rule in the makefile. There are three types of rules commonly used in makefiles:

(a) Single target in a rule – hello.o : hello.c
(b) Multiple targets in a rule – hello.o world.o : hello.h. This rule indicates that both the object files depend on same header file hello.h.
(c) More than one rules for a target –

```
hello.o :  hello.h
hello.o : hello.c
```

These two rules are combined by the **make** program to create a single rule as follows:

```
hello.o : hello.h hello.c
```

All these rules are commonly used by **makefile** developers.

When **make** program evaluates rules in a **makefile**, it searches current directory for files e.g. hello.c, hello.h etc. In most large embedded systems applications, not all the files are present in the directory where **makefile** lives. A special variable called **VPATH** is used to specify the list of directories for searching 'pre-requisite' files specified in the dependencies. We have followed this approach when we created a build environment for KSET Embedded System Development Board.

Conditonals In A makefile

If you have reached so far in this book, you must have understood the power of pre-processor directives in C programming and conditional compilation that is possible using **#ifdef** - **#else** - **#endif** directives. Same power for conditional builds is available with **GNU make**. This allows us to create a single makefile that can be used to build in variety of cases. To understand how it works, consider the following example:

```
ifndef SOURCES
    SOURCES = $(wildcard *.c)
endif
```

In this example, we check if **SOURCES** variable is already defined. If it is not defined, we use special makefile function **wildcard** to get all files in current directory with **.c** extension and assign the value to **SOURCES** variable. Some other common conditional statements are as follows:

(a) **ifeq (A, B)** – Checks if two arguments A and B are equal.
(b) **ifndef VARIABLE** – Executes conditionally if VARIABLE is not defined.
(c) **ifneq (A, B)** – Checks if two arguments A and B are not equal.

Final makefile created using some of the techniques that we have learnt is as follows:

```
TARGET    := hello
SOURCES := hello.c
OBJS      := $(SOURCES:.c=.o)
CC        := gcc
CFLAGS   := -g
CFLAGS   += -O2

$(TARGET) : $(OBJS)
    $(CC) $^ -o $@

%.o : %.c
    $(CC) $(CFLAGS) -c $< -o $@
```

```
clean :
    $(RM) $(OBJS) $(TARGET).exe
```

This **makefile** uses simply expanded variables. **CC** has been assigned **gcc**. **CFLAGS** defines additional options passed during compilation of all **.c** files. Rules for generating target (hello.exe) and object files are identical to our earlier **makefile**. Only change is the addition of **clean** rule which has no dependencies. It executes command **$(RM) $(OBJS) $(TARGET).exe** which removes all object files and target executable from current folder. To execute this rule, just type **make clean** at cygwin command prompt.

Exercise

[A] Pick up the correct alternative for each of the following questions:

[1] Which of the following statements are correct?

(i) The statement **ifeq (A, B)** checks if two arguments A and B are equal.

(ii) The statement **ifndef VARIABLE** executes conditionally if **VARIABLE** is not defined.

(a) Only (i) is correct.
(b) Only (ii) is correct.
(c) Both (i) and (ii) are correct.
(d) Both (i) and (ii) are incorrect.

[2] Which of the following statements are correct?

(i) A makefile cannot include other makefiles from other directories.

(ii) A makefile contains one or more variables.

(a) Only (i) is correct.
(b) Only (ii) is correct.
(c) Both (i) and (ii) are correct.
(d) Both (i) and (ii) are incorrect.

[3] Which of the following statements are correct?

(i) Each variable in a makefile holds a string.

(ii) Space-separated strings in a makefile are used to represent a collection or list of items.

(a) Only (i) is correct.
(b) Only (ii) is correct.
(c) Both (i) and (ii) are correct.
(d) Both (i) and (ii) are incorrect.

[4] Which of the following statements are correct?

(i) The statement **ifneq (A, B)** checks if two arguments **A** and **B** are not equal.

(ii) make program does not use environment variables.

(a) Only (i) is correct.
(b) Only (ii) is correct.
(c) Both (i) and (ii) are correct.
(d) Both (i) and (ii) are incorrect.

[5] For which of the following purposes the variables in a makefile are used?

(i) To store list of filenames

(ii) To store options to compiler

(iii) To store program to use

(a) Only (i) and (ii)
(b) Only (i) and (iii)
(c) Only (ii) and (iii)
(d) (i), (ii) and (iii)

[6] Which of the following ways are used to obtain the value of any variable?

```
$(VAR)
${VAR}
```

(a) Only (i)
(b) Only (ii)
(c) Both (i) and (ii)
(d) Neither (i) nor (ii)

[7] Which of the following types of variables supported by GNU make program?

(i) Recursively expanded variables

(ii) Simply expanded variables

(a) Only (i)
(b) Only (ii)
(c) Both (i) and (ii)
(d) Neither (i) nor (ii)

[8] The example given below is intended in which of the following variables?

```
CFLAGS = -g -Wall
CFLAGS = $(CFLAGS) –Os
```

(i) Recursively expanded variables

(ii) Simply expanded variables

(a) Only (i)
(b) Only (ii)
(c) Both (i) and (ii)
(d) Neither (i) nor (ii)

[9] Which of the following statement is correct about the example given below?

```
SOURCES = hello.c
OBJS = $(SOURCES:.c=.o)
```

(i) It replaces extension **.c** with **.o** for all source files and **hello.o** will be assigned to variable **OBJS**.

(ii) It replaces extension **.o** with **.c** for all source files and **hello.o** will be assigned to variable **OBJS**.

(a) Only (i) is correct.
(b) Only (ii) is correct.
(c) Both (i) and (ii) are correct.
(d) Both (i) and (ii) are incorrect.

[10] Which of the following types of rules used in makefiles?

(i) Single target in a rule

(ii) Multiple targets in a rule

(iii) More than one rules for a target

(a) Only (i) and (ii)
(b) Only (i) and (iii)
(c) Only (ii) and (iii)
(d) (i), (ii) and (iii)

A C Primer

General

- Execution of a program always begins from **main( )**.
- Truth in C is non-zero value and falsity is 0.
- The default scope of **if**, **else**, **for**, **while**, is only the next statement.
- To include more then one statement within the **if**, **else**, **for** or **while** enclose them within a pair of braces as shown below:

```
int i = 1 ;
while ( i++ > 3 )
{
    printf ( "Prepare prayerfully, Pursue persistently " ) ;
    printf ( "Play down I." ) ;
}
```

- Conditional operators can sometimes be used in place of **if-else**. For example, the statements:

```
if ( i > 10 )
    j = k ;
else
    j = l ;
```

can be written more elegantly as,

```
i > 10 ? ( j = k ) : ( j = l ) ;
```

- **break** is used to terminate a loop or a switch.
- **continue** is used to do the next iteration of the loop bypassing the rest of the statements within the loop.
- A function can return only one value at a time.
- A function prototype declaration includes the return type of the function, name of the function and list of parameter types that it receives. For example,

```
double fun ( long value, int sum ) ;
```

Arrays

- Array is a collection of similar elements stored in adjacent memory locations.
- It is necessary to mention the dimension (size) of the array at the time of defining it (if we are not initializing the array at the same place).
- The dimension of the array must be a constant value. Variables are not allowed as dimension.
- It is not possible to increase or decrease the size of the array during program execution.
- Array elements are always counted from 0 onwards.
- Bound checking of an array is programmer's responsibility.
- Mentioning the name of the 1-D array gives its base address. For example,

```
int arr[ 5 ] ;
int *p = arr ;
```

- A 2-dimensional array is a collection of 1-D arrays.

Strings

- String is an array of characters ending with a '\o'.

- We cannot copy one string to another using the assignment operator. This can be done using the function **strcpy( )**, as shown below:

```
char s1[ ] = "Hello" ;
char s2[ 10 ] ;
strcpy ( s2, s1 ) ;
```

- There are several library functions available for working with strings. For example:

strcpy (s1, s2)	Copies **s1** to **s2**
Strcat (s1, s2)	Appends **s2** at the end of **s1**
strcmp (s1, s2)	Compares **s1** and **s2**. Returns, 0, if strings are same, non-zero otherwise
Strlen (s)	Returns the length of the string **s** excluding '\o'.

Structures

- A structure is usually a collection of dissimilar elements.

- Given below is an example of a structure.

```
struct emp
{
    char name[15] ;
    int age ;
    float salary ;
};
```

This is a structure declaration. No memory space is allocated when we declare a structure.

- In the above example, **emp** is the structure name and **name**, **age** and **salary** are structure elements.
- Structure variable is defined in the following manner:

```
struct emp e ;
```

Now the memory gets allocated for **e**.

- Size of a structure variable is the sum of the sizes of the structure elements. So, size of **e** turns out to be **21 (15 + 2 + 4)** bytes.
- Elements of a structure are always stored in contiguous memory locations.
- One structure element **e2** can be copied to another structure element **e1** in the following manner:

```
e1 = e2 ;
```

- When the structure elements are accessed using the structure variable, the dot operator is used. For example,

```
e.age = 23 ;
e.salary = 7000.00 ;
```

- Similarly, when the structure elements are accessed using the pointer to the structure, the arrow operator is used. For example,

```
struct emp *p ;
p = &e ;
p -> age = 25 ;
p -> salary = 5000.00 ;
```

Here, **p** is a pointer to the structure **emp**.

- An array of structures looks like this,

```
stuct emp e1[10] = {
                    "Abha", 24, 7000.00,
                    "Satya", 25, 10000.00,
                  };
```

Typedef

- The **typedef** keyword can be used to give a new name to an already existing type. For example,

```
typedef unsigned int UINT ;
typedef struct employee
{
    // structure elements
} EMP, *PEMP ;
EMP e ; // structure variable
PEMP ptr ; // pointer to structure
```

Typecast

- Data element of one type can be cast to another type. For example,

```
int a = 22, b = 7 ;
float c ;
```

```
c = ( float ) a / b ;
```

Here, **a** is treated as a **float** for the division operation. So **3.14** gets stored in **c** rather than **3**.

- One more example of typecasting:

```
char *p ;
void *q ;
p = ( char * ) q ;
```

Pointers

- A pointer is a variable that holds address of another variable or function. For example,

```
int i = 10 ;
int *ptr ;
ptr = &i ;
```

Here, **ptr** is a pointer pointing to the variable **i**.

- The type of the pointer **ptr** is **int** * as **ptr** is pointing to the variable of the type **int**.

- The operator **&** is called the "address of" operator and the operator * is called the "value at address" operator.

- Only following operations can be performed on pointers:

```
pointer + integer
pointer – integer
pointer – pointer
```

- On incrementing a pointer it points to the next location of its type. For example on incrementing an integer pointer it starts pointing to the next integer. Similarly on incrementing a float pointer it starts pointing to the next float.

- When a huge structure is to be passed to a function, pass the pointer to the structure rather then passing the bulky structure variable. It saves the memory space as no copying of the structure elements takes place. This operation is also fast as compared to passing the structure variables by value.

Call By Value & Call By Reference

- There are two types of function calls, as shown below:

```
# include <stdio.h>
void swapv ( int, int ) ;
void swapr ( int *, int * ) ;
int main( )
{
    int a = 10, b = 20 ;
    swapv ( a, b ) ;    // call by value
    printf ( "%d %d", a, b ) ;
    swapr ( &a, &b ) ; // call by reference
    printf ( "\n%d %d", a, b ) ;
    return 0 ;
}
void swapv ( int x, int y )
{
    int t ;
    t = a ; a = b ; b = t ;
}
void swapr ( int *x, int *y )
{
    int t ;
    t = *x ; *x = *y ; *y = t ;
}
```

The output would be:

```
10 20
20 10
```

In call by value, used in **swapv( )** function, the values of **a** and **b** get copied into variables **x** and **y**. Any change in **x** and **y** have no effect on **a** and **b**.

In call by reference, used in **swapr( )** function, the addresses of variables **a** and **b** are stored in pointers **x** and **y**. Using these pointers the values of **a** and **b** can be changed.

- Usually the parameters are passed by reference when we want to return more than one value from a function. This is explained with the help of following code:

```
void mulsum ( int, int, int *, int * ) ;
int main( )
{
    int a = 10, b = 20, sum, mul ;
    void mulsum ( int, int, int *, int * ) ;
    mulsum ( a, b, &sum, &mul ) ;
    return 0 ;
}
void mulsum ( int a1, int b1, int *psum, int *pmul )
{
    *psum = a1 + b1 ;
    *pmul = a1 * b1 ;
}
```

Data Types

- Following is the list of intrinsic data types.

Integer - short signed, short unsigned, long singed, long unsigned

Real - float, double, long double

Character - signed char, unsigned char

Storage Classes

- A storage class signifies:

  - Where the variable gets stored
  - What is its default initial value
  - What is the scope of the variable (where it is available)
  - What is its life (how long is the variable available)

There are four storage classes. Their features are listed below:

Auto Storage Class:

Storage	- Memory
Default value	- An unpredictable value, which is often called a garbage value
Scope	- Local to the block in which the variable is defined
Life	- Till control remains within the block in which the variable is defined

Register Storage Class:

Storage	- CPU registers
Default value	- Garbage value

Scope	- Local to the block in which the variable is defined
Life	- Till control remains within the block in which the variable is defined

Static Storage Class:

Storage	- Memory
Default value	- Zero
Scope	- Local to the block in which the variable is defined
Life	- Value of the variable persists between different function calls

External Storage Class:

Storage	- Memory
Default value	- Zero
Scope	- Global
Life	- As long as the program's execution doesn't come to an end

- Following example shows usage of all the storage classes.

```
# include <stdio.h>
void fun ( int ) ;
```

```
int main( )
{
      fun( ) ;
      fun( ) ;
      return 0 ;
}
void fun ( int x )
{
      auto int  i ;
      register int  j ;
      static int  k ;
      extern int  m ;  // declaration of m
      i++ ; j++ ; k++ ; m++ ;
      printf ( "\n%d %d %d %d", i, j, k, m ) ;
}
int m = 10 ;  // definition of j
```

The output would be:

```
833 827 1 11
833 827 2 12
```

Preprocessor Directives

- The preprocessor is a program that processes the source program before it is passed to the compiler.

- The file inclusion directive causes contents of one file to be included in another. For example,

  `# include "filename"`

  causes the entire contents of filename to get inserted into the source code at the point where this directive is used.

- There exists two ways to write **#include** statement. These are:

```
# include "filename"
# include<filename>
```

- The first directive searches for the file filename in the current directory as well as the specified list of directories as mentioned in the include search path that might have been set up. The second directive searches for filename in the specified list of directories only.

B Installing Tools

Before you start programming for Embedded Systems, you must install the necessary tools. The CDROM included with this book contains all the necessary tools to create and build such programs. You must install the tools on Windows 2000 SP4 or Windows XP SP2 system. The installation is divided in three steps:

(a) Install Cygwin
(b) Install WinAVR tools
(c) Setup Build Environment

Once you insert the CD in your PC's CDROM drive, an HTML file called DEFAULT.HTM will get launched in your browser. This file will show three links for carrying out the steps mentioned above. You need to click these links one after the other to carry out the three steps of installation. Make sure that you do not click the second link unless installation of cygwin (Step 1) is finished, and you do not click the third link unless installation of WinAVR tools (Step 2) is finished. The details of each of these three steps are discussed below.

Step 1: Install cygwin

Carry out the following steps:

- Click on *"Install Cygwin"* link. Following window will appear:

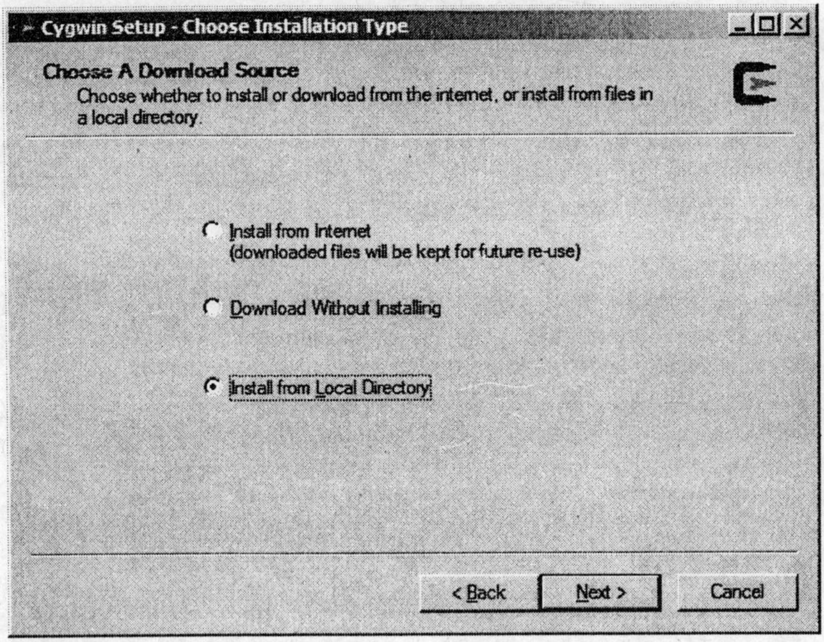

Figure B.1

- Select "Install from Local Directory" as Installation Type. Click *Next*. Window shown in Figure B.2 will appear.

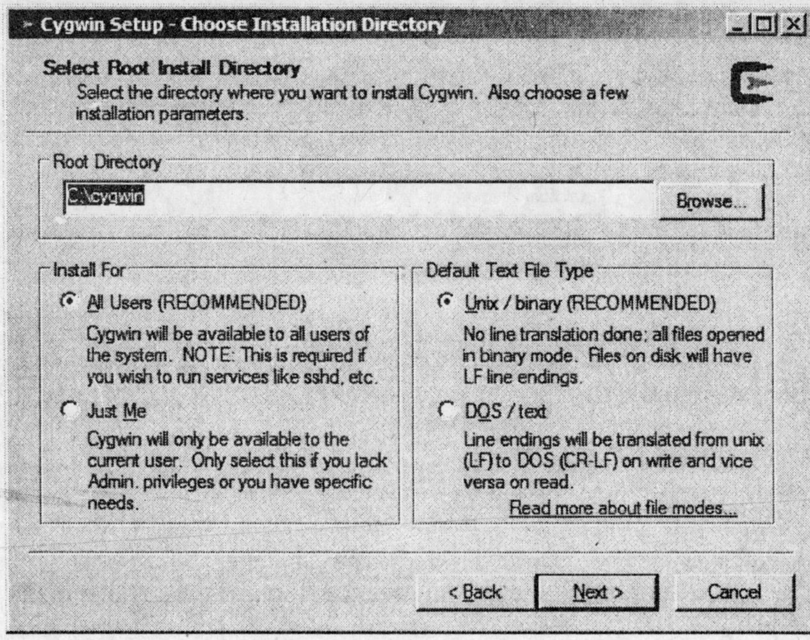

Figure B.2

- Do not make any changes in this dialog. Click *Next*. Following window will appear:

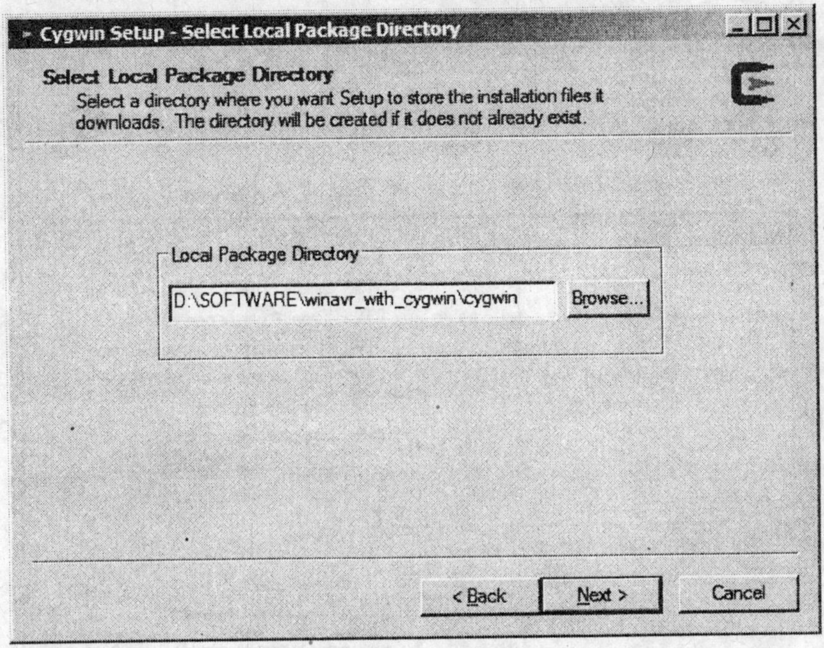

Figure B.3

- Select Local Package Directory dialog shows the folder from which cygwin will be installed. Type *D:\SOFTWARE\winavr_with_cygwin\cygwin* in *Local Package Directory* textbox. *D:* is the letter for CDROM drive from which installation is started. If your CDROM drive letter is different, for example - E:, change D: to E:. Click *Next*. Following window will appear:

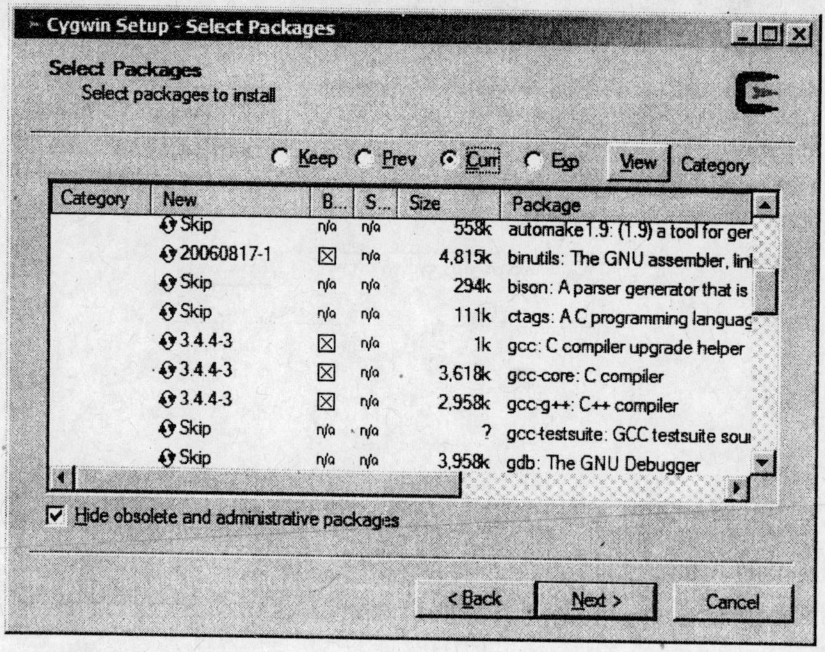

Figure B.4

- In this step, you must select packages to be installed. With your mouse, click on "Devel" Category and expand it. Search for package *gcc*. Select it for installation by clicking on the "Skip" label in its row. Go down and also select the package *make* by clicking on "Skip" label in its row. Following screen shows how the selection will appear. Click *Next* to continue installation.

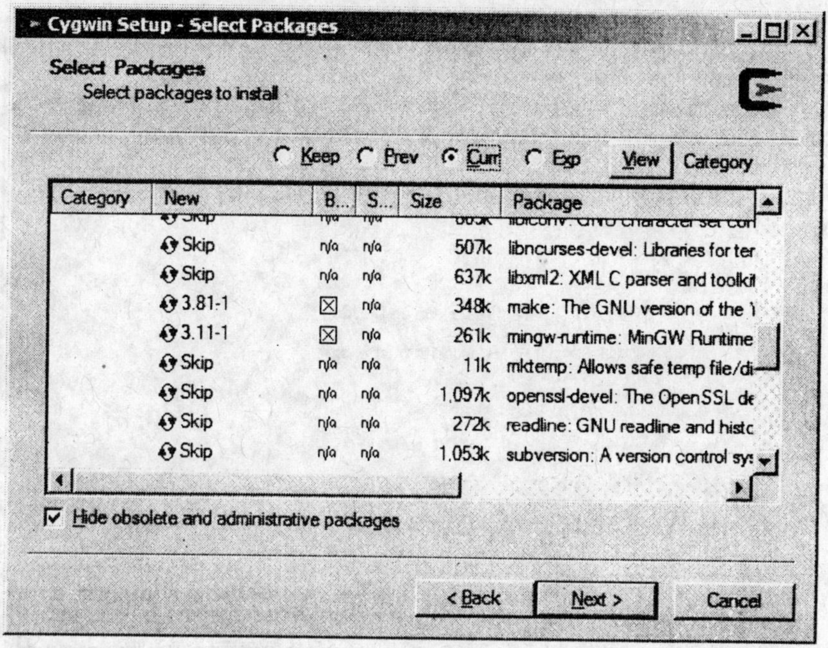

Figure B.5

- A window will show progress during the installation of cygwin packages. Wait until following window appear:

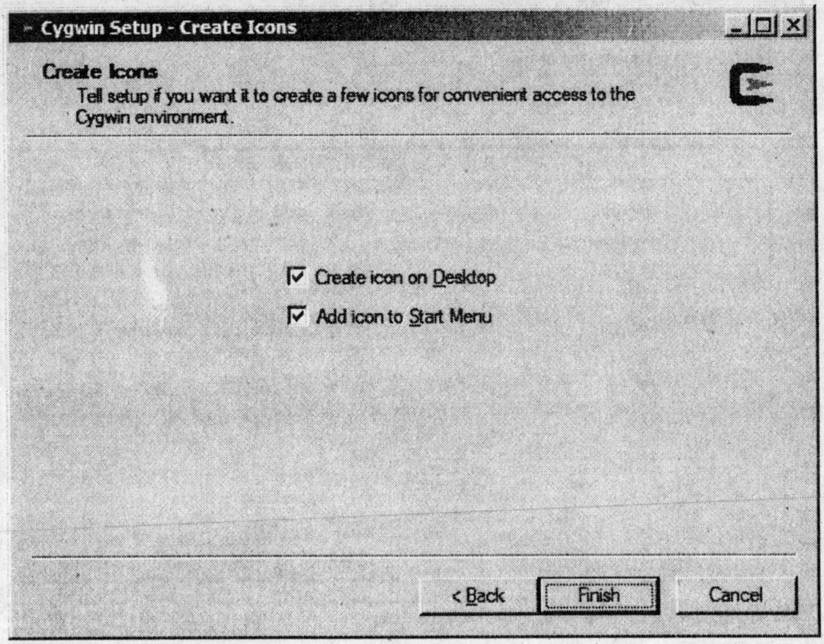

Figure B.6

- Click on *Finish* to complete the installation.

Step 2: Install WinAVR Tools

Carry out the following steps:

- Click on "Install WinAVR tools" link. Following window will appear:

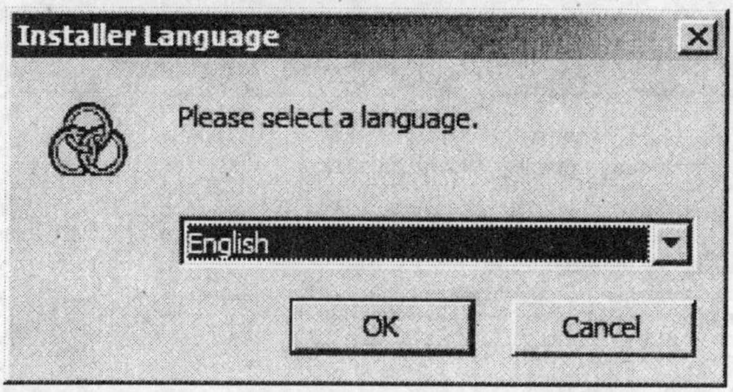

Figure B.7

- Click OK to continue. Following window will appear:

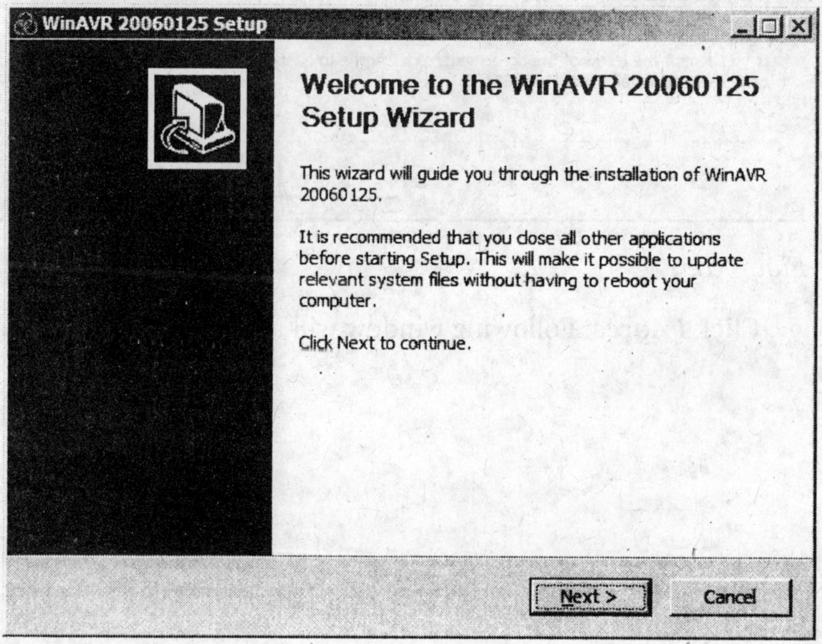

Figure B.8

- Click *Next*. Following window will appear:

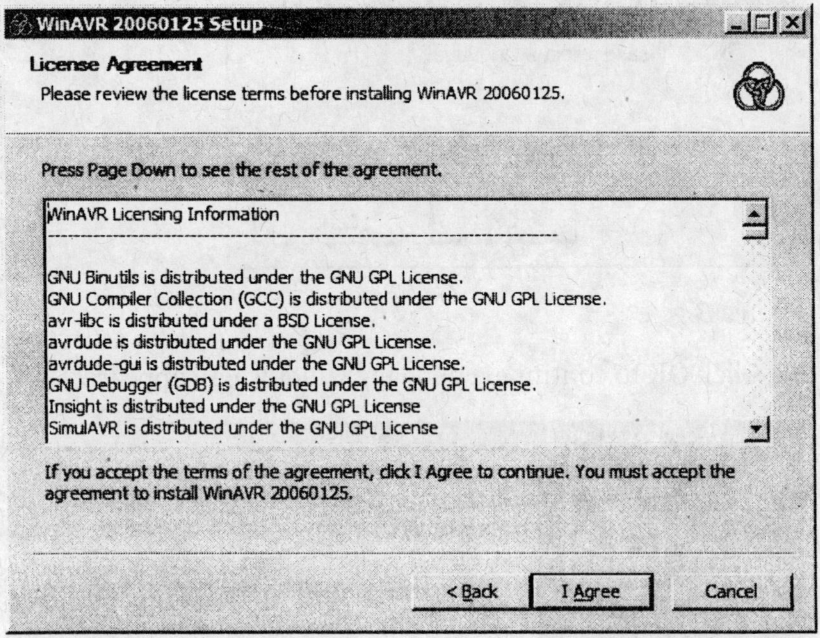

Figure B.9

- Click *I Agree*. Following window will appear:

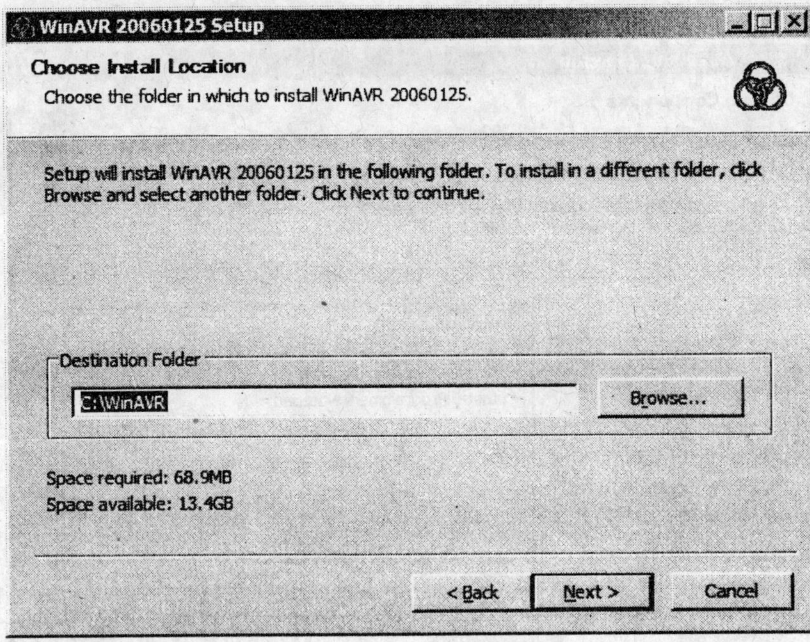

Figure B.10

- Click *Next* to continue installation. Following window will appear:

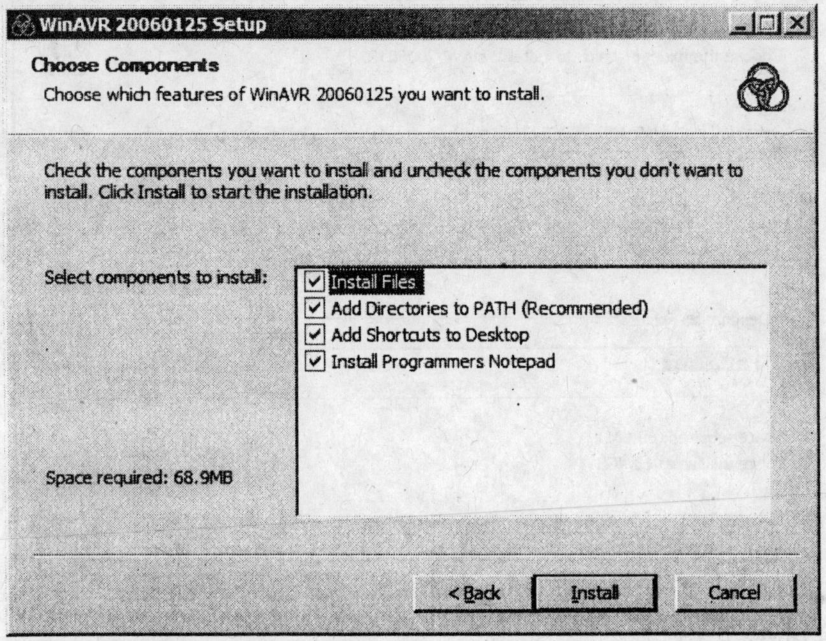

Figure B.11

- Click *Install* to begin installation process. Installation may take a few minutes. Finally following window will appear:

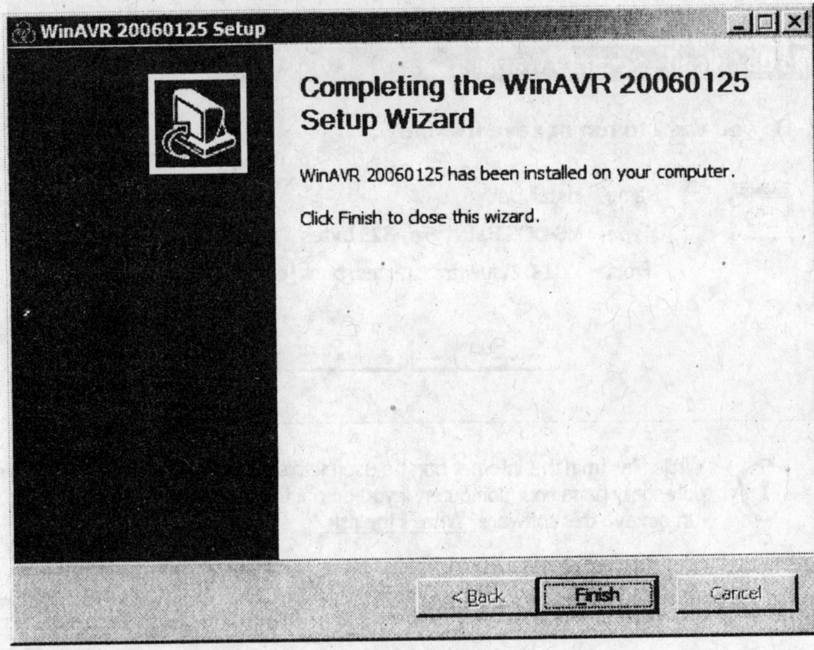

Figure B.12

- Click on *Finish* to complete the installation. An Internet Explorer window will be launched. Close that window.

Step 3: Setup Build Environment

Carry out the following steps:

- Click on "Setup Build Environment" link. Following window will appear:

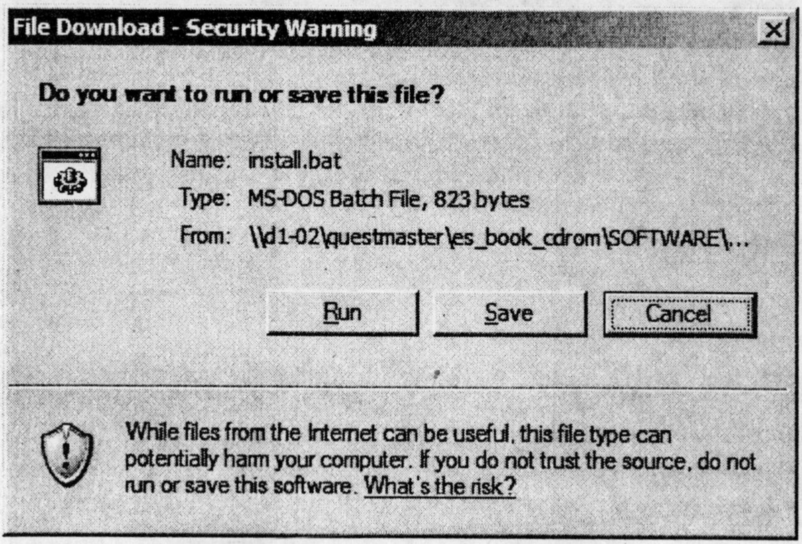

Figure B.13

- Click on *Run* button. A black console window will appear. Wait for it to close. Build environment is now successfully setup.

Index

A

B

C

D

E

F

G

H

I

K

F

G

H

I

K

O

P

R

S

T

U

V

W

KSET Embedded System Development Board Order Form

I / We want to place an order for KSET Embedded System Development Board.

My / our particulars are as follows (Please type in Capital letters)

Name ____

Address ____

____

____

City ________________ State ______________ PIN __________

Telephone number ______________ Mobile number ___________

Email ____

☐ Ordering Method I

Visit http://quest.ksetindia.com/ to order online by paying through either Credit Card or Online Banking

☐ Ordering Method II

1. Please fill in your contact details in this order form
2. Prepare a DD of Rs. 3000 in the name of KSET Pvt. Ltd. payable at Nagpur
3. Send the order form and DD to KSET Pvt. Ltd., 44-A, Hill Road, Gokulpeth, Nagpur – 440010

☐ Ordering Method III

1. Please fill in your contact details in this order form
2. Prepare a cheque of Rs. 3000 in the name of KSET Pvt. Ltd. payable at Nagpur
3. Go to the nearest HDFC bank and deposit the cheque with following account information:
   Bank – HDFC Bank, Dharampeth Extension, Nagpur, India
   Account Name – Kanetkar School of Embedded Tech. Pvt. Ltd.
   Account number – 1022 02000 1089
4. Send this order form to KSET Pvt. Ltd., 44-A, Hill Road, Gokulpeth, Nagpur – 440010, or Fax it to +91 – 712 - 2540870

For any difficulty contact KSET Pvt. Ltd. at +91-712-2531046, 2545322 or quest@ksetindia.com